Digital Project Practice for Green Finance and ESG Innovation

Environmental, social, and governance (ESG) principles are now integral to business and investment decision-making. As environmental concerns intensify and societal expectations evolve, the adoption of Green Finance and ESG strategies has become essential for sustainable growth. *Digital Project Practice for Green Finance and ESG Innovation* explores the foundations of ESG and Green Finance, their increasing relevance, and their integration into corporate strategies that drive sustainable investments and manage climate-related risks.

Managing ESG data is complex because of evolving regulatory frameworks and fragmented standards. As technological advancements are reshaping the landscape, creating both challenges and opportunities for established corporations and innovative startups alike, the book focuses on the latest technological developments in the financial sector and their implications for ESG practices. It is rooted in both practical experience and rigorous academic research, offering insights into how organizations can adapt to the changing ESG landscape. Presenting practical guidance for professionals navigating these transformations, this book provides a comprehensive overview of the evolving trends in ESG and Green Innovation.

Tobias Endress is an Assistant Professor at the Asian Institute of Technology (AIT) – School of Management. He has over 20 years of professional experience in the digital project business and innovation management. His former (non-academic) roles include project manager, product owner, and business analyst.

He has completed professional training in banking and graduated in Computer Science and Business Administration at VWA Frankfurt/Main and in Business Economics at Avans+ in Breda (NL). He obtained a Master's Degree in Leadership in Digital Communication at Berlin University of the Arts (UdK Berlin) and a Doctorate in Business Administration at the University of Gloucestershire in Cheltenham (UK). He is a fellow of the EuroMed Academy of Business and director of the Startup Grind chapter in Bangkok.

Digital Project Practice for Green Finance and ESG Innovation

Edited by
Tobias Endress

CRC Press
Taylor & Francis Group
Boca Raton London New York

CRC Press is an imprint of the
Taylor & Francis Group, an **informa** business
AN AUERBACH BOOK

Designed cover image: Olena Shkavron

First edition published 2026
by CRC Press
2385 NW Executive Center Drive, Suite 320, Boca Raton FL 33431

and by CRC Press
4 Park Square, Milton Park, Abingdon, Oxon, OX14 4RN

CRC Press is an imprint of Taylor & Francis Group, LLC

ISBN: 978-1-032-86353-5
ISBN: 978-1-032-86741-0
ISBN: 978-1-003-52895-1

DOI: 10.1201/9781003528951

Typeset in Garamond
by KnowledgeWorks Global Ltd.

Contents

Preface

Dear Reader,

Environmental, social, and governance (ESG) principles are now integral to business and investment decision-making. As environmental concerns intensify and societal expectations evolve, the adoption of Green Finance and ESG strategies has become essential for sustainable growth. This book explores the foundations of ESG and Green Finance, their increasing relevance, and their integration into corporate strategies to drive sustainable investments and manage climate-related risks.

Managing ESG data is complex, with evolving regulatory frameworks and fragmented standards. Technological advancements are reshaping the landscape, creating both challenges and opportunities for established corporations and innovative startups alike. This book is the fourth volume in the Digital Project Practice series, following *Digital Project Practice: Managing Innovation & Change*, *Digital Project Practice for New Work and Industry 4.0*, and *Digital Project Practice for Banking and FinTech*. These prior editions have been well received by both practitioners and academics, inspiring us to continue exploring the intersections of digital transformation and business practice.

This volume focuses on the latest technological developments in the financial sector and their implications for ESG practices. The chapters are rooted in both practical experience and rigorous academic research, offering insights into how organizations can adapt to the changing ESG landscape. Through this book, we aim to provide a comprehensive overview of the evolving trends in ESG and Green Innovation, presenting practical guidance for professionals navigating these transformations.

Chapter 1: The ESG Compass: Frameworks, Benchmarks, and Best Practices

ESG frameworks provide guidance, yet businesses often struggle with fragmented standards. This chapter demystifies key ESG benchmarks and best practices, helping organizations align with global sustainability expectations.

Chapter 2: Evolution of Enterprise-Level Decision-Making Models for Sustainable Development and Finance

Sustainability-driven decisions require evolving models incorporating risk, long-term value, and stakeholder expectations. Here, we explore how enterprises reshape financial decision-making in light of ESG imperatives.

Chapter 3: Corporate Model of Digital Transformation and ESG Governance

Digital transformation can enhance ESG governance but also introduces challenges in data transparency and accountability. This chapter examines how digital tools can be leveraged to strengthen corporate ESG strategies.

Chapter 4: From Reporting to Ratings: Understanding the ESG Data Value Chain

ESG reporting is evolving from voluntary disclosures to regulated frameworks. This chapter analyzes how ESG data is collected, processed, and rated, influencing investment and corporate strategies.

Chapter 5: Utilizing the Data Mesh Paradigm to Address ESG Data Management Challenges

Data fragmentation poses a significant hurdle in ESG implementation. In this chapter, we analyze the Data Mesh approach as a solution to improve data accessibility, accuracy, and integration.

Chapter 6: Digital Transformation in the Automotive Industry and Its ESG Implications

As the automotive industry undergoes digitalization, ESG considerations are reshaping production, supply chains, and emissions control. This chapter explores the implications of these transformations.

Chapter 7: Pragmatic Approaches to Lending Decisions in the Context of Climate and ESG Risks and Their Technical Perspectives

Financial institutions face mounting ESG-related risks in lending. This chapter provides practical strategies for integrating climate risk assessments into lending decisions.

Chapter 8: Exploring Climate Blended Finance for Climate Mitigation Projects: A World View Versus National Perspective

Blended finance is emerging as a key tool for scaling renewable energy investments. This chapter explores financing structures that balance risk while promoting sustainability.

Chapter 9: Future Climate Protection and Sustainability Obligations in the Financial Sector: Opportunities, Risks, Ideas

The EU is a leader in ESG regulations, influencing global markets. This chapter unpacks key regulatory developments and their practical implications for businesses and investors.

Chapter 10: The Sustainable VC Playbook: A Practical Guide for Small Fund Managers

Venture capital plays a critical role in fostering sustainable innovation. This chapter presents a roadmap for small fund managers looking to integrate ESG into their investment strategies.

The Digital Project Practice series introduces relevant methodologies, examines practical applications, and critically assesses existing approaches. It highlights the intersection of technology and human factors, fostering a dialogue among professionals and academics alike.

At its core, this book is about real-world applications in ESG, banking, and finance, providing diverse perspectives from industry leaders and researchers. We hope it inspires reflection and meaningful discussions within your organization.

With best regards,
Dr. Tobias Endress
Bangkok/Thailand, March 16, 2025

Writing Disclosure

This book includes chapters where AI tools have been used to enhance language and clarity. However, AI has been applied strictly as an assistive tool, focusing on improving readability and coherence without altering the authors' ideas or arguments. Each chapter has been thoroughly reviewed, revised, and approved by its respective author(s), who retain full responsibility for the accuracy, interpretation, and integrity of the content.

Acknowledgment

Illustrations: Olena Shkavron (cover image)

Contributors

Jacob Binder is a Master's student in Information Systems at Reutlingen University. His academic pursuits are centered on the intersection of sustainability and IT. Throughout his studies, Jacob has gained practical experience as an intern and working student at a Big Four consultancy firm, where he focused on ESG IT Architectures, ESG Data Management, Emission Baselining and Green IT Projects.

Tracy Dathe is a Professor of Business Management at Macromedia University, Berlin, Germany, and an experienced finance professional. As CFO of a multinational mid-sized automotive supplier, she oversaw commercial management at the German headquarters and subsidiaries in China, France, Italy, Sweden, the Czech Republic, Turkey, and the United States. Today, she also advises mid-sized companies as a management consultant.

Tobias Endress is an Assistant Professor and the Program Director for Business Analytics and Digital Transformation at the Asian Institute of Technology (AIT) – School of Management. He has over 20 years of professional experience in digital project management and innovation. In his previous (non-academic) roles, he has worked as a project manager, product owner, and business analyst for leading financial services companies in Europe and the United States.

He completed professional training in banking and earned degrees in Computer Science and Business Administration from VWA Frankfurt/Main, as well as in Business Economics from Avans+ in Breda (Netherlands). He holds a Master's degree in Leadership in Digital Communication from the Berlin University of the Arts (UdK Berlin) and a Doctorate in Business Administration from the University of Gloucestershire in Cheltenham (UK). Additionally, he serves as the director of the Startup Grind Chapter in Bangkok.

David Feierabend is a Professor of Innovation and Sustainability at the School of Informatics at Reutlingen University, Germany. His research interests include IT management, digital transformation, and sustainable innovation. David earned his PhD from RWTH Aachen University, Germany. He has held diverse positions in the field of innovation, digitalization, and strategy, such as Head of People & Transformation with a technology consulting firm or Head of CEO Office & M&A with Switzerland's leading digital health provider.

David Galipeau, Canadian, 35-year veteran of a hybrid career in finance, publishing, and tech as a corporate exec, dot-com entrepreneur, and social business innovator. After two successful "dot-com" start-up exits in the EU, David joined the UN in Geneva in 2005. In 2010, he was invited to the Asia-Pacific by UNDP and founded the UN Social Innovation and Entrepreneurship programs, the UN Social Impact Fund (UNSIF), and the UN Frontier Technology initiative.

David left the UN in 2019 and co-founded an impact investment fund, SDGx Singapore, and currently lectures at the UN Staff College and the Asian Institute of Technology.

Wesley L. Harris, PhD, NAE, is the Charles Stark Draper Professor of Aeronautics and Astronautics at the Department of Aeronautics and Astronautics, Massachusetts Institute of Technology.

Tareq Mahbub is an Associate Professor at the Business Department at Sakarya University, Serdivan, Turkey. He completed his PhD in management from the Asian Institute of Technology (AIT) and MBA in international business from Carleton University. His areas of interest are foreign direct investment (FDI), FDI and intellectual property rights, international market entry modes, and FDI and renewable energy. He has over 10-year experience in the pharmaceutical sector, having served as a Business Development Manager (International Marketing) for a leading U.S. FDA- and UK MHRA–certified international pharmaceutical company. His expertise spans new market development, contract manufacturing, under-licensing, and strategic alliances across both regulated and moderately regulated markets.

Marc Nathmann is Senior Legal Counsel and Attorney at Law at ING in Amsterdam. There, he advises on banking supervisory and capital markets law in the areas of payment transactions and securities. His research interests include FinTech and AI. He regularly lectures on banking, capital markets, and commercial law. He has published articles on topics dealing with the legal classification of innovations and new technologies. After his studies at the University of Münster and the German University of Administrative Sciences in Speyer, he stayed abroad at a major international law firm in Shanghai, China, worked at KPMG, a securities bank, and a FinTech consulting firm. He completed his doctorate on the subject of FinTech at the Technical University of Chemnitz.

Benjamin Tobias Peylo is Professor of Business Administration and Finance at Kempten University of Applied Sciences. His research and teaching focus on sustainable finance, and here especially on ESG risk management. He designs tools in this context and implements them in international projects together with banks and central banks.

He is also a lecturer in sustainable finance at the University of Lüneburg.

After studying finance and banking, he completed his MBA in sustainability management at the University of Lüneburg, where he also completed his doctorate. Dr. Peylo initially worked in several management consultancies with a focus on risk management and regulation. As an ESG-specialist at the Savings Banks Association of Baden-Württemberg, he dedicated ten years to strategy development and the anchoring and implementation of sustainability in savings banks.

Aphichai Pholkosol is a Doctoral Researcher at the Asian Institute of Technology (AIT) School of Management. With nearly 30 years of professional experience, he has worked extensively in investment banking, corporate finance, and financial management across multinational and local companies. He has played a vital role in financial strategy and corporate decision-making, driving growth and stability in various organizations. He holds a Master of Business Administration (MBA) from Washington State University and a Bachelor's degree in Economics from Chulalongkorn University.

Bilal (Bill) H. Rahill is a Partner at Sustainability Frameworks LLP, an Advisory Services firm he co-founded in 2017. Prior to that he was Director for Environment and Natural Resources at the World Bank and Senior Manager for Environment, Social and Governance at the International Finance Corporation. Bill started his career in the private sector in manufacturing and consulting before joining the World Bank Group. Bill advises extensively with development finance institutions and private sector finance institutions. His current areas of practice include environmental and social policies and standard, independent evaluations, impact evaluation, and natural capital and valuation policies. Bill holds an undergraduate degree in engineering and graduate degrees in management, finance and public policy.

Dennis Schlegel is a Professor of Information Systems at Reutlingen University, Germany. His research interests encompass digital transformation, the business implications of emerging technologies, and project management. After earning his PhD from Leeds Beckett University, UK, Dennis gained extensive practical experience at a Big Four consultancy firm, where he most recently served as a Senior Manager.

Elizabeth M. White is an Independent Global Expert and Executive Advisor specializing in sustainability, sustainable and conservation finance, impact investing, and impact evaluation. From 1998 to 2025, she held progressively senior roles at the World Bank Group across its public and private sector arms, culminating as Global Head for Sustainability and Impact at the International Finance Corporation. She served as a core team member and lead technical expert on several internationally adopted innovations, including the Natural Capital Protocol, the Operating Principles for Impact Management, and results-based country strategy and evaluation systems. She holds a BS in

Economics and an International MBA (IMBA) with a concentration in global economics and strategy from a top-ranked program, and completed college-level engineering studies.

Jarunee Wonglimpiyarat, PhD., ACA, FCCA, CPA, CIA, CFE, CGAP, CFSA, CRMA, FCMA, CGMA, CISA, CISM, CLP, RTTP, is a Research Scientist at the Department of Aeronautics and Astronautics, Massachusetts Institute of Technology.

Chapter 1

The ESG Compass: Frameworks, Benchmarks, and Best Practices

Aphichai Pholkosol and Tobias Endress

1.1 Mapping the ESG Landscape: Frameworks, Standards, and Initiatives

Environmental, social, and governance management is of enormous interest in business and academia. The development of theoretical models and knowledge transfer to business practice is an ongoing process. It requires various skills and resources to master this domain and establish practical approaches, especially in an increasingly complex and digital work environment (Endress & Badir, 2023; Galipeau & Endress, 2025). There is a seeming abundance of various frameworks, standards, and initiatives in the context of environmental, social, and governance (ESG). In fact, many companies, especially globally active organizations, might be affected by various of them in most of their business endeavors. While academia is working on improved understanding and integrated theories, the overall development, especially in business, is challenging in this fluid landscape with shifting paradigms. Implementing an ESG strategy is a necessary step toward financial success and a sustainable future for all stakeholders (Khalid et al., 2021). The following text provides an overview, guidance, and introduction to some of the key structures with a particular focus on managerial implications and practical implementation in organizations. In recent years, the understanding has advanced in the materiality of ESG issues. A key insight is that this materiality is likely dynamic, meaning that

DOI: 10.1201/9781003528951-1

static classifications—such as those by the Sustainability Accounting Standards Board (SASB)—may not effectively capture the evolving relationship between ESG metrics and financial performance (Freiberg et al., 2020; Kuh et al., 2020). ESG reporting fundamentally aims to incorporate (negative) externalities—traditionally absent from corporate financial statements such as profit and loss, balance sheets, or cash flow statements—into standardized corporate disclosures, ensuring a more comprehensive assessment of a company's performance, including impact and sustainability. In essence, the impact of various ESG issues on financial performance is expected to change over time. For investors, the question is how to balance ESG profiles in portfolios and make informed decisions based on risk-adjusted returns (Barber et al., 2022).

1.2 Global ESG Initiatives: Who's Setting the Rules? Understanding Standards, Ratings, and Regulations

The increased focus on corporate social responsibility (CSR) in the 2000s was reflected in the expansion of the CSR consultancy sector, growing investments in community initiatives, the establishment of dedicated CSR teams within firms, an increase in social reporting practices, the integration of CSR into corporate systems through codes and standards, and the development of partnerships between businesses and governmental or non-governmental organizations (Chakraborty, 2015). CSR in many firms is moving toward full integration with strategic management and corporate governance, including the development of mechanisms for reporting and controlling socially conscious policies and practices, and is embedded in business operations, supply chains, and decision-making processes (Carroll, 2009; Endress, 2025).

CSR gained significant momentum in both academic research and professional practice, driven by globalization, financial and environmental crises, and rapid changes in market conditions due to information and communication technologies, leading to its strategic integration into business management and governance (Mosca & Civera, 2017). The emphasis on theoretical contributions to CSR shifted to empirical research, with interests diverging into related topics like stakeholder theory, business ethics, sustainability, and corporate citizenship (Carroll, 2009). Despite this shift, the CSR concept continued to develop.

In 2001, the European Commission (EC) considered CSR as the voluntary integration of social and environmental concerns into business operations (Chakraborty, 2015) and promoted it as a European strategy in the European Commission's 2001 Green Paper (Latapí Agudelo et al., 2019). CSR was defined as "a concept whereby companies integrate social and environmental concerns in their business operations and in their interaction with their stakeholders on a voluntary basis" (European Commission, 2001). In 2011, the EC redefined CSR as "the responsibility of enterprises for their impact on society." To fully meet their CSR obligations, firms should have in place a process to integrate social, environmental, ethical human rights, and consumer concerns into their business operations and core strategy in close cooperation with their stakeholders. The goal is to maximize the creation of shared value for both owners/shareholders and other stakeholders while also identifying, preventing, and mitigating any potential adverse impacts on society at large (European Commission, 2001). Table 1.1 outlines the development of CSR concepts from the 1950s to the 21st century (Abe & Ruanglikhitkul, 2013).

Table 1.1 Development of CSR Concepts

Period	*Name of Concept*	*Description*	*Literature*
1950s	Social responsibility of businessmen	Businessmen have an obligation to pursue policies, make decisions, and take actions that align with society's objectives and values.	Bowen (1953)
		Some socially responsible business decisions can be justified by the long-term economic gains they bring to the company, effectively rewarding its commitment to social responsibility.	Davis (1960)
		Private contributions to society's economic and human resources, along with a business's willingness to ensure those resources are used for broader social purposes.	Frederick (1960)

(Continued)

Table 1.1 ***(Continued)*** **Development of CSR Concepts**

Period	*Name of Concept*	*Description*	*Literature*
1960s–1970s	Stakeholder approach	A responsible company prioritizes the interests of employees, suppliers, dealers, local communities, and the nation, not just maximizing returns for shareholders.	Johnson (1971)
	Three-dimensional model	The concept includes corporate responsibilities (economic, legal, ethical, and philanthropic), social issues in business (like labor standards, human rights, environmental protection, and anti-corruption), and corporate actions (reactive, defensive, accommodative, and proactive).	Carroll (1979)
1970s–1980s	Three-dimensional model of principles, policies, and processes	Integrating corporate responsibility principles, social issue management policies, and action processes into a dynamic, evolving system.	Wartick and Cochran (1985)

(Continued)

Table 1.1 *(Continued)* **Development of CSR Concepts**

Period	*Name of Concept*	*Description*	*Literature*
	Institutional framework and extended corporate actions	Four types of corporate responsibilities (economic, legal, ethical, and philanthropic) are connected to three institutional levels (legal, organizational, and individual), with corporate actions including assessment, stakeholder management, and implementation management.	Wood (1991)
21st century	Three-domains approach	Three domains of corporate responsibilities: economic, legal, and ethical.	Schwartz and Carroll (2003)
	New concept	A process to integrate social, environmental, ethical, human rights, and consumer concerns into business operations and core strategy, in close collaboration with stakeholders.	European Commission (2011)

From a business perspective, interest in CSR "best practices" took center stage, driven by the persistent demand for a solid business case for CSR (Carroll, 2009). Kotler and Lee (2011) categorized examples of CSR best practices into six key social initiatives: cause promotion, cause-related marketing, corporate social marketing, corporate philanthropy, community volunteering, and socially responsible business practices that may assist firms with their CSR programs. According to Carroll (2015), the business case for CSR involves rational justifications from a financial perspective, asserting that the market will reward CSR-oriented firms in economic and financial terms. Despite the complexity and varying results, many studies have shown a generally positive relationship between CSR and firm profitability. However, executives prefer practical, well-reasoned arguments that can be applied in business, focusing on enhancing legitimacy and reputation, reducing costs and risks, building competitive advantage, and creating synergistic value (Carroll, 2015).

Business for social responsibility (BSR) is a global non-profit that helps businesses integrate CSR into their operations through information, tools, training, and advisory services, with research showing that such integration leads to increased sales and market share, stronger brand positioning, enhanced corporate image, improved employee attraction and retention, reduced operating costs, and greater investor appeal (Kotler & Lee, 2011). Strategic CSR enhances shared value by investing in social aspects that strengthen firm competitiveness, creating a mutually beneficial relationship where both the firm and the community benefit (Porter & Kramer, 2006). BSR views CSR as a broad set of policies, practices, and programs that are integrated into the firm's operations, supply chains, and decision-making processes. It also notes that various terms are frequently used interchangeably with CSR, including business ethics, corporate citizenship, corporate accountability, and sustainability (Carroll, 2015).

1.2.1 Formalization of ESG

The focus on CSR has shifted from charitable and ethical reasons to a "business case" approach, leading to a greater emphasis on sustainability and ESG practices and risks (Pollman, 2021). The term ESG was officially introduced in 2004 with the publication of the "Who Cares Wins" report by the United Nations Global Compact in collaboration with major financial institutions, highlighting the importance of integrating ESG into firms' operations (Krantz, 2024). The "Who Cares Wins" report (United Nations Global Compact, 2004) highlighted it as a collaborative effort by financial institutions to develop guidelines for integrating environmental, social, and governance issues into financial practices (Pollman, 2022). Including environmental, social, and corporate governance factors in investment decisions will ultimately contribute to more stable and predictable markets, which should be in the interest of all market actors (United Nations Global Compact, 2004).

The term "ESG" is widely used by institutional investors and professionals to refer not only to sustainability measures or specific environmental, social, or governance practices but to all non-financial factors affecting a firm's financial performance, including corporate governance, labor standards, HR management, and environmental practices (Ho, 2015). ESG has already become a commonly used term and trend among corporations and investors in the capital market. ESG data is the most effective way to quantify a firm's impact on society (Kaźmierczak, 2022).

Bergman et al. (2020) provided the following criteria for ESG, as shown in Table 1.2.

Table 1.2 ESG Criteria

Pillar	*Criteria*
Environmental (E)	The "E" captures energy efficiencies, carbon footprints, greenhouse gas emissions, deforestation, biodiversity, climate change and pollution mitigation, waste management, and water usage.
Social (S)	The "S" covers labor standards, wages and benefits, workplace and board diversity, racial justice, pay equity, human rights, talent management, community relations, privacy and data protection, health and safety, supply-chain management, and other human capital and social justice issues.
Governance (G)	The "G" covers the governance of the "E" and "S" categories, corporate board composition and structure, strategic sustainability oversight and compliance, executive compensation, political contributions and lobbying, and bribery and corruption.

In 2015, the Paris Agreement (United Nations Framework Convention on Climate Change, 2015) and the adoption of the 17 Sustainable Development Goals (SDGs) (United Nations, 2015) established a new social contract that positioned corporations as key players in global sustainability, leading CSR literature to focus on SDG implementation and impact while continuing to emphasize the creation of shared value (Latapí Agudelo et al., 2019). The UN's SDGs represent a global effort to address poverty, environmental protection, and prosperity, prompting businesses to contribute as global citizens, thus evolving CSR as a strategic approach (Mosca & Civera, 2017).

However, there has been a segment of stakeholders and groups strongly opposing ESG by questioning the principles and effectiveness of incorporating ESG criteria in investment decisions. This so-called anti-ESG movement includes a diverse range of viewpoints that oppose the emphasis on ESG factors, advocating for business and investment practices that prioritize financial returns over ESG considerations (ESGVoices, 2024; Padfield, 2023; Zhang, 2024). Some critics reject sustainability altogether, while others support it but remain highly skeptical of corporate claims, particularly from banks, regarding ESG investing (Winston, 2023). Various groups have been vocal in their opposition to ESG. Free-market thinktanks were among the first to criticize ESG for politicizing investment decisions. Industry advocacy groups, particularly from the fossil fuel sector, oppose ESG's focus on sustainability, viewing it as a threat to traditional energy sources. Additionally, conservative and libertarian political leaders globally argue that ESG undermines economic interests and have called for legislative action to limit its influence on business practices (ESGVoices, 2024).

The rise of anti-ESG sentiment has driven the creation of investment strategies and financial products that reject or oppose ESG criteria, leading to the development of "anti-ESG" funds prioritizing sectors like fossil fuels, defense, and tobacco, appealing to investors who question the financial or ideological basis of ESG. The anti-ESG movement has triggered a debate about corporate responsibility, prompting some firms to reconsider their ESG involvement while pushing others to focus on the authenticity of their sustainability efforts, ultimately leading to greater scrutiny of corporate sustainability strategies. In response to the anti-ESG movement, several jurisdictions have introduced laws restricting the use of ESG criteria in investments, including bans on ESG considerations for state pension funds and measures to protect industries like coal and oil. This reflects a broader push for economic freedom and market-driven decision-making over ESG principles (ESGVoices, 2024).

In some political discussions, ESG is often associated with "woke capitalism" (Downes, 2024), a term coined by Ross Douthat when writing a piece for the New York Times, who defined it as "how companies signal their support for progressive causes in order to maintain their influence in society" (Douthat, 2018). In the United States, Republican lawmakers have criticized ESG as a form of "woke capitalism" that prioritizes liberal agendas over maximizing investment returns. In contrast, Democratic lawmakers have pushed back, framing the criticism of ethically responsible business practices as "an attempt to manufacture a culture war and protect corporate special interests" (Meredith, 2024). Across the United States, politicians have introduced or passed legislation restricting states from doing business with firms that implement ESG practices, claiming that ESG is a means for corporations to push political agendas, undermine shareholder value, and unfairly disadvantage certain industries (Hilson, 2024; ProMarket, 2023; Sætra, 2024).

The pushback against the ESG movement has prompted states like West Virginia to block ESG considerations in investments, preventing banks such as HSBC, Citi, Goldman Sachs, JPMorgan Chase, Morgan Stanley, and Wells Fargo from offering services to the state due to their alleged boycott of fossil fuels. Similarly, Florida has enacted laws restricting ESG-focused investments (Downes, 2024). The pushback against climate policies extends beyond the United States, with signs of a "greenlash" emerging in Europe as businesses and citizens begin to feel the financial impacts of the energy transition (Meredith, 2024). For example, a key concern regarding the cost of climate action in Europe is its impact on agriculture, which covers 40% of the land. Farmers in Europe are concerned that climate action, particularly reducing emissions, will negatively impact their profits. In response, farmers worldwide, including in the United States, wrote an open letter protesting the new EU's anti-greenwashing law, which bans unverified environmental claims and restricts sustainability labels not based on certified standards (Stine, 2024).

1.3 CSR Definitions

There is no single, universally accepted definition of CSR (Dahlsrud, 2008; Kaźmierczak, 2022). CSR is often defined in various ways, but all consistently refer to five core dimensions: environmental, social, economic, stakeholder, and voluntariness. CSR has various definitions for three main reasons. First, it is a multidimensional concept. Second, there is disagreement on what social responsibility includes. Third, social responsibilities are dynamic, evolving based on societal needs, public expectations, and business opportunities (Chen et al., 2020). The analysis shows that CSR definitions are mostly aligned, indicating that the confusion is more about how CSR is understood in different situations than the actual definition itself. CSR definitions describe the concept but often lack practical guidance for managing its complexities. The real challenge for businesses is understanding how CSR is perceived in their specific context and incorporating this understanding into their strategies to guide business decisions (Dahlsrud, 2008). Table 1.3 outlines the development of CSR definitions from the 1950s to the 2020s.

The 2011 redefined EC definition (European Commission, 2011) aligns with internationally recognized CSR principles and guidelines, including the OECD Guidelines for Multinational Enterprises, the ISO 26000 Guidance Standard on Social Responsibility—highlighted by its seven core subjects shown in Table 1.4—and the United Nations Guiding Principles on Business and Human Rights

Table 1.3 Development of CSR Definitions

Definition Source	*Definition*
Bowen (1953)	It refers to the obligations of businessmen to pursue those policies, to make those decisions, or to follow those lines of action that are desirable in terms of the objectives and values of our society.
Davis (1960)	Businessmen's decisions and actions are taken for reasons at least partially beyond the firm's direct economic or technical interest.
Frederick (1960)	Businessmen should oversee the operation of an economic system that fulfills the public's expectations.
McGuire (1963)	The idea of social responsibility supposes that the corporation has not only economic and legal obligations but also certain responsibilities to society that extend beyond these obligations.
Johnson (1971)	A socially responsible firm has a managerial staff that balances multiple interests. Instead of striving only for more significant profits for its stockholders, a responsible enterprise also considers employees, suppliers, dealers, local communities, and the nation.

(Continued)

Table 1.3 *(Continued)* Development of CSR Definitions

Definition Source	*Definition*
Carroll (1979)	The social responsibility of business encompasses the economic, legal, ethical, and discretionary expectations that society has of organizations at a given point in time.
Jones (1980)	The notion that corporations have an obligation to constituent groups in society other than stockholders, and beyond that prescribed by law or union contract.
Frederick et al. (1992)	A principle stating that corporations should be accountable for the effects of any of their actions on their community and environment.
Hopkins (1999)	CSR is concerned with treating the stakeholders of the firm ethically or in a socially responsible manner. Stakeholders exist both within a firm and outside. Consequently, behaving socially responsibly will increase the human development of stakeholders both within and outside the corporation.
Elkington (1997, 2000)	The Triple Bottom Line (TBL) concept argues that businesses should measure success beyond just financial profit by also considering their social (people) and environmental (planet) impacts. He emphasizes that long-term business sustainability depends on balancing these three dimensions—Profit, People, and Planet—to create value for both shareholders and society.
European Commission (2001)	A concept whereby companies integrate social and environmental concerns in their business operations and in their interaction with their stakeholders on a voluntary basis.
Hopkins (2003)	CSR is concerned with treating the stakeholders of the firm ethically or in a responsible manner. "Ethically or responsible" means treating stakeholders in a manner deemed acceptable in civilized societies. Social includes economic responsibility. Stakeholders exist both within a firm and outside. The wider aim of social responsibility is to create higher and higher standards of living, while preserving the profitability of the corporation, for people both within and outside the corporation.

(*Continued*)

Table 1.3 *(Continued)* Development of CSR Definitions

Definition Source	*Definition*
van Marrewijk (2003)	In general, corporate sustainability and CSR refer to company activities—voluntary by definition—demonstrating the inclusion of social and environmental concerns in business operations and in interactions with stakeholders.
European Commission (2011)	The responsibility of enterprises for their impacts on society.
United Nations Industrial Development Organization (UNIDO) (n.d.)	A management concept whereby companies integrate social and environmental concerns in their business operations and interactions with their stakeholders. CSR is generally understood as being the way through which a company achieves a balance of economic, environmental, and social imperatives ("Triple-Bottom-Line-Approach"), while at the same time addressing the expectations of shareholders and stakeholders.

Table 1.4 Differences Between CSR and ESG

Aspect	*CSR*	*ESG*
Measurability	CSR is an internal framework that can be difficult or impossible for external observers to measure objectively. It leans toward quality.	ESG is highly measurable and quantifiable, providing fact-based evidence that is crucial for investors and stakeholders. It leans toward quantity.
Usefulness	Firms use CSR to achieve internal goals, such as greater social responsibility and developing sustainable workplace cultures.	Outside entities, like investors, use ESG to obtain measurable proof regarding the effectiveness of a firm's efforts.
Communication	CSR helps a firm communicate its values to employees and stakeholders, fostering a better work environment and potential for community outreach.	ESG helps a firm demonstrate to current and potential investors that its social, environmental, and governance efforts are effective.

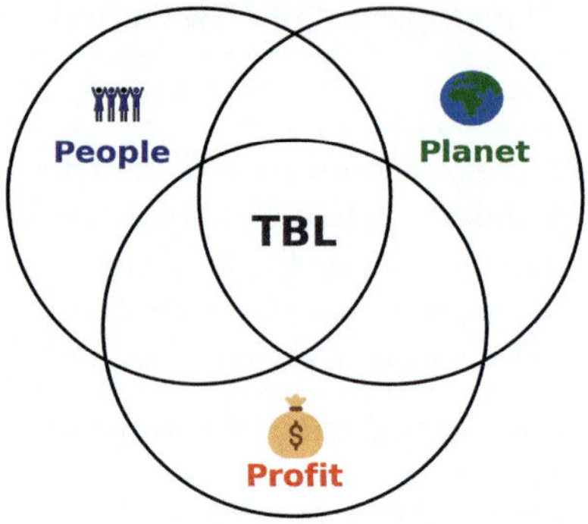

Figure 1.1 The interconnection of the elements of the Triple Bottom Line concept (TBL)—people, planet, and profit.

(European Commission, 2011). According to UNIDO (n.d.), the "Triple Bottom Line" approach (see Figure 1.1) provides a framework for assessing corporate performance across economic, social, and environmental dimensions.

This approach aims to align businesses with sustainable global development by broadening their objectives beyond profit to include financial stability, environmental responsibility, and social conformity. The definitions of CSR in the 21st century reflected the idea that corporations needed to adapt to a new role in society, respond to social expectations, and make strategic decisions to achieve sustainability (Latapí Agudelo et al., 2019).

1.4 Decoding CSR and ESG: A Guide to Frameworks and Global Initiatives

CSR and ESG are two sides of a firm's "pro-social" approach. CSR guides components of the ESG strategy, while ESG measures the effectiveness and scope of the CSR goals. CSR aims to align a firm's business values and mission with its environmental and social activities and policies, while ESG builds on this by establishing measurable goals. For example, a CSR initiative may declare a commitment to carbon neutrality, and the ESG strategy will define the specific steps to reduce the carbon footprint by a quantifiable amount (Biles, 2021). CSR practices are self-regulated and qualitative, leading to variation and challenges in definition across firms, while ESG offers investors measurable criteria for evaluating opportunities. When used together, CSR creates an internal framework for employee communication and driving awareness of initiatives, while ESG sets measurable goals and provides solid metrics for evaluation (O'Neill, 2024).

Firms adopting ESG must disclose extensive quantitative and qualitative information. Global frameworks, standards, questionnaires, and ratings provide uniformity in assessing ESG performance, while CSR outcomes rely primarily on each firm's individual efforts (KnowESG, 2023). In many regions, ESG reporting is now mandatory and regulated, requiring firms to track and disclose ESG information, while CSR remains largely voluntary at the firm's discretion (Novisto, 2024). CSR is an internal framework focusing on qualitative goals for social responsibility and sustainable workplace cultures, while ESG provides measurable, quantifiable data crucial for investors and stakeholders seeking fact-based evidence of a company's efforts. When comparing CSR and ESG, both contribute significantly to a business's social responsibility efforts, but they have distinct differences, particularly in the benefits they offer (Kaźmierczak, 2022).

The consulting company TRC (2022) identified the three main differences between CSR and ESG in terms of measurability, usefulness, and communication (see Table 1.4).

In essence, CSR represents a firm's framework for sustainability and responsible cultural influence primarily utilized by firms, whereas ESG provides a measurable assessment of a company's overall sustainability performance favored by investors (Kaźmierczak, 2022). Despite the difference between CSR and ESG, both should be integral to a business's efforts to enhance responsibility for employee well-being, environmental sustainability, and community welfare. CSR is a firm's initial step to demonstrate its commitment to the important issues of buyers, shareholders, and employees, displaying efforts toward greater transparency in social responsibility. Then, the firm can integrate ESG into its business model to obtain quantitative data on the lasting impact of its efforts (TRC, 2022).

Many organizations use CSR and ESG interchangeably, though each has distinct characteristics. Literature and practitioners often state that CSR leads to ESG or that ESG is an advanced form of CSR, both important for sustainable business development. They aim to guide businesses in integrating social interests, environmental protection, and stakeholder relations into their business strategies to implement policies and practices that benefit local communities and society (Kaźmierczak, 2022).

1.5 ESG Investing

ESG investing has its origins in socially responsible investing (SRI), which can be traced back to the 1960s and 1970s when it was significantly influenced by civil rights, anti-war, and environmental movements (Townsend, 2020). Others describe SRI as an investment process that integrates both positive and negative non-financial factors, such as social, environmental, and governance, into investment decision-making (Renneboog et al., 2008). Puaschunder (2016) asserts that SRI is an investment approach that seeks to maximize profits while promoting social initiatives by integrating social, environmental, and financial factors to achieve both economic and social value.

Responsible investors typically avoid investing in so-called "sin stocks" like alcohol, gambling, tobacco, and weapons while preferring firms that follow best practices in environmental sustainability, labor conditions, and community relations, and they are likely to support shareholder engagement (Capelle-Blancard & Monjon, 2012). Since the 1960s, a series of social campaigns, such as the emergence of the anti-war movement and the maturity of movements on racial equality, women's rights, consumer protection, and the environment, have heightened investor awareness of the social consequences of their investments (Renneboog et al., 2008; Townsend, 2020).

This resulted in the establishment of the first mutual funds reflecting faith-based values, civil-rights-era sensibilities, and environmental concerns in the early 1970s (Townsend, 2020). Established in 1971 in the United States, the Pax World Fund was the first modern SRI mutual fund to avoid investments in weapon contractors for those opposed to the Vietnam War and militarism (Renneboog et al., 2008). By the 1980s, SRI in North America had standardized around creating portfolios that mirrored the broad market while excluding investments in alcohol, tobacco, weapons, gambling, pornography, and nuclear energy, forming the backbone of the traditional SRI process (Townsend, 2020). SRI rapidly expanded in the United States and Great Britain during the 1980s, but it only started to gain significant traction in continental Europe in the 1990s (Olmedo et al., 2010).

Some argue that SRI integrates ESG criteria into investment decisions to generate long-term competitive financial returns and positive societal impact (Social Investment Forum, 2009). Common (Renneboog et al., 2007). Today, SRI is known as sustainable, responsible, and impact investing, and it plays a key role in capital markets and financial services. In liquid markets like stocks and bonds, modern SRI includes two approaches: values-based investing, which aligns with traditional SRI, and ESG analysis, which uses nontraditional data to find firms that can succeed despite resource scarcity, increasing regulations, population growth, and climate change. ESG analytics allows institutional investors to identify long-term risk factors and investment opportunities, focusing on risks that traditional Wall Street analysis often overlooks (Townsend, 2020).

The United Nations has significantly advanced ESG investing through initiatives like the UN Global Compact and the Principles for Responsible Investment (PRI). Established in 2000, the UN Global Compact promotes ten principles focused on human rights, labor, anti-corruption, and the environment, and has been adopted by nearly 10,000 firms in 168 countries. The PRI, launched in 2005 by then-Secretary-General Kofi Annan, further supports responsible investment practices (Townsend, 2020). Three key factors driving large investors to analyze ESG issues are evolving discussions on incorporating sustainability into fiduciary duty, heightened awareness of climate change risks, and significant corporate governance failures (Townsend, 2020). This growth in ESG investing has driven increased investor demand for precise ESG data to inform investment decisions and influence corporate behavior, resulting in the emergence of sustainability indices and ESG agencies (Olmedo et al., 2010).

Due to the rise of the anti-ESG movement, anti-ESG investing has gained traction (Hartill, 2024) (Hartill, 2024), and anti-ESG funds have been created (ESGVoices, 2024). Proponents of anti-ESG investing prioritize maximizing profits, disregarding governance or societal impact, and believe firms should be evaluated solely on financial performance. Critics also challenge the validity of ESG metrics, accusing firms of "greenwashing" through misleading environmental claims. Additionally, some oppose ESG practices due to ideological concerns, viewing issues like climate change and diversity, equality, and inclusion initiatives as politically charged (Hartill, 2024). Anti-ESG funds have existed since the early 2000s but recently gained more attention as some investors argue that ESG investing conflicts with shareholder interests, leading to the creation of anti-ESG funds that exclude firms meeting specific ESG criteria (Thune, 2023).

A mid-2023 Morningstar report identified 27 anti-ESG funds, grouped into five categories: Anti-ESG funds, which invest in firms penalized by ESG ratings; political funds, aligned with conservative agendas; renouncer funds, which remove ESG references from their materials; vice funds, focusing on sin stocks like tobacco and alcohol; and voter funds, passively managed funds that vote against environmentally and socially driven shareholder proposals. As of March 2023, the funds held $2.1 billion in assets, and although this may seem small, the report notes that these assets grew sevenfold in the past year (Hartill, 2024).

1.6 From GRI to TCFD: Understanding the ESG Alphabet Soup

Initially, firm-initiated disclosures of sustainability information were often reactive, typically issued in press releases or posted on company websites following high-profile scandals. However, interest in ESG practices and reporting has significantly increased in recent years, with investors and businesses increasingly focusing on these issues (Rouen et al., 2022). Sustainability reporting began in the 1990s and is relatively recent compared to the mandatory financial reporting established during the Great Depression (Global Reporting Initiative, n.d.). However, it is increasingly becoming a legal requirement and less of a voluntary practice, with governments, stock exchanges, market regulators, investors, civil society, and other stakeholders demanding more detailed information on organizations' sustainability impacts (Global Reporting Initiative, n.d.). Back in the early 1990s, fewer than 20 publicly traded firms worldwide included ESG data in their reports, showing how much its importance has grown today. In response to the increasing demand for ESG information from investors, stakeholders, and regulators, firms began centralizing their ESG disclosures into a single document known as the ESG report (Rouen et al., 2022).

ESG is a non-financial metric that measures a firm's sustainability practices in the areas of environmental, social, and governance reporting. ESG reporting has become increasingly popular as stakeholders and fund managers believe that firms with comprehensive ESG disclosures achieve better operating performance, higher returns, and reduced idiosyncratic risk. The Financial Times Lexicon defines ESG as a term used in capital markets by investors to evaluate corporate behavior and predict future financial performance, with analysts and investors frequently consulting ESG scores for this purpose (Shaikh, 2022). Driven by stakeholder pressure and global standards, increased ESG disclosure by firms has significantly enhanced market transparency and investor information, proving that measurable data leads to improvement, especially in understanding climate change impacts on investment markets (Townsend, 2020). As crucial non-financial information, ESG disclosures improve understanding of a firm's business, support the achievement of strategic environmental goals, and address stakeholder concerns about managers' integration of ESG considerations (Albitar et al., 2023). While CSR focuses on qualitative approaches and aligns with societal values, ESG reporting introduces a quantitative aspect by providing specific, measurable criteria (Kandpal et al., 2024).

Many firms emphasize sustainability and release extensive ESG data, but the relevance of these efforts for firm value is often questioned, as much of the information may be immaterial from an investment perspective. Leading organizations like the Global Reporting Initiative (GRI), the International Integrated Reporting Council (IIRC), and the SASB work to identify key industry-specific issues to improve corporate disclosures and guide investment decisions (Khan et al., 2015). They all rely on the "Triple Bottom Line" framework (see Figure 1.1) as a fundamental tool for integrating non-financial performance metrics into the evaluation of corporate activities (Bose, 2020).

The GRI is the most widely used framework for corporate reporting based on the "Triple Bottom Line" and the most widely adopted standard for sustainability reporting (Bose, 2020). It is a multi-stakeholder process for sustainability reporting. The GRI was established in Boston, USA, in 1997 in response to the Exxon Valdez oil spill. It originated from the non-profit organizations CERES and the Tellus Institute, supported by the UN Environment Programme. Initially focused on ensuring corporate accountability for responsible environmental practices, GRI's scope later expanded to cover social, economic, and governance issues. Table 1.5 presents the GRI standards, which represent global best practices for publicly sustainable reporting on a range of economic, environmental, and social impacts, providing information about an organization's positive or negative contributions to sustainable development (Global Reporting Initiative, 2021).

The IIRC was established through the collaboration of two leading sustainability accounting organizations, the Prince's Accounting for Sustainability Project (A4S) and the GRI, following a December 2009 speech by the Prince of Wales (Charles, 2009) and was formally incorporated in August 2010. The IIRC's goal is to establish a globally accepted framework for sustainability accounting aimed

Table 1.5 GRI Standards

Category	*Standard*
Universal	GRI 1: Foundation 2021 GRI 2: General Disclosures 2021 GRI 3: Material Topics2021
Sector	GRI 11: Oil and Gas Sector 2021 GRI 12: Coal Sector 2021 GRI 13: Agriculture, Aquaculture, and Fishing Sectors 2022 GRI 14: Mining Sector 2024
Topic	GRI 101: Biodiversity 2024 GRI 201: Economic Performance 2016 GRI 202: Market Presence 2016 GRI 203: Indirect Economic Impacts 2016 GRI 204: Procurement Practices 2016 GRI 205: Anti-corruption 2016 GRI 206: Anti-competitive Behavior 2016 GRI 207: Tax 2019 GRI 301: Materials 2016 GRI 302: Energy 2016 GRI 303: Water and Effluents 2018 GRI 304: Biodiversity 2016 GRI 305: Emissions 2016 GRI 306: Waste 2020 GRI 306: Effluents and Waste 2016 GRI 308: Supplier Environmental Assessment 2016 GRI 401: Employment 2016 GRI 402: Labor/Management Relations 2016 GRI 403: Occupational Health and Safety 2018 GRI 404: Training and Education 2016 GRI 405: Diversity and Equal Opportunity 2016 GRI 406: Non-discrimination 2016 GRI 407: Freedom of Association and Collective Bargaining 2016 GRI 408: Child Labor 2016 GRI 409: Forced or Compulsory Labor 2016 GRI 410: Security Practices 2016 GRI 411: Rights of Indigenous Peoples 2016 GRI 413: Local Communities 2016 GRI 414: Supplier Social Assessment 2016 GRI 415: Public Policy 2016 GRI 416: Customer Health and Safety 2016 GRI 417: Marketing and Labeling 2016 GRI 418: Customer Privacy 2016

at developing comprehensive and clear information about an organization's overall performance, both future and past, to support a more sustainable global economy (Flower, 2015). The IIRC framework is much harder to implement than the GRI guidelines. Consequently, the adoption of the IIRC framework has lagged far behind the GRI, with only about 15% of organizations using the GRI framework for sustainability reporting also using the IIRC framework (Bose, 2020).

Unlike the GRI, but similar to the IIRC, the SASB focuses on investors as its primary audience (Bose, 2020). Founded in 2011 as a non-profit organization, SASB aimed to establish a common language for businesses and investors regarding the financial impacts of sustainability. The increasing complexity of the corporate sustainability disclosure landscape led to calls for simplification. In response, the IIRC and SASB merged in June 2021 to form the Value Reporting Foundation, marking significant progress toward simplifying the disclosure landscape. The Value Reporting Foundation offers a comprehensive set of resources, including the Integrated Thinking Principles, Integrated Reporting Framework, and SASB standards, to help businesses and investors build a shared understanding of enterprise value (Sustainability Accounting Standards Board (SASB), 2018, 2023).

In 2018, SASB released standards detailing the minimum sustainability reporting requirements for 77 industries in 11 sectors (Bose, 2020). Table 1.6 presents

Table 1.6 SASB Standards and Industry Categories

Sector	*Industry*
Consumer Goods	Apparel, Accessories & Footwear; Appliances; Building Products & Furnishings; E-Commerce; Household & Personal Products; Multiline and Specialty Retailers & Distributors; Toys and Sporting Goods
Extractives & Minerals Processing	Coal Operations; Construction Materials; Iron & Steel Producers; Metals & Mining; Oil & Gas-Exploration & Production; Oil & Gas-Midstream; Oil & Gas-Refining & Marketing; Oil & Gas-Services
Financials	Asset Management & Custody Activities; Commercial Banks; Consumer Finance; Insurance; Investment Banking & Brokerage; Mortgage Finance; Security & Commodiy Exchanges
Food & Beverage	Agricultural Products; Alcoholic Beverages; Food Retailers & Distributors; Meat, Poultry & Dairy; Non-alcoholic Beverages; Processed Foods; Restaurants; Tobacco
Health Care	Biotechnology & Pharmaceuticals; Drug Retailers; Health Care Delivery; Health Care Distributors; Health Care Equipment & Supplies; Managed Care

(*Continued*)

Table 1.6 *(Continued)* SASB Standards and Industry Categories

Sector	*Industry*
Infrastructure	Electric Utilities & Power Generators; Engineering & Construction Services; Gas Utilities & Distributors; Home Builders; Real Estate; Real Estate Services; Waste Management; Water Utilities & Services
Renewable Resources & Alternative Energy	Biofuels; Forestry Management; Fuel Cells & Industrial Batteries; Pulp & Paper Products; Solar Technology & Project Developers; Wind Technology & Project Developers
Resource Transformation	Aerospace & Defense; Chemicals; Containers & Packaging; Electrical & Electronic Equipment; Industrial Machinery & Goods
Services	Adversting & Marketing; Casinos & Gaming; Education; Hotels & Lodging; Leisure Facilities; Media & Entertainment; Professional & Commercial Services
Techonology & Communications	Electronic Manufacturing Services & Original Design Manufacturing; Hardware; Internet Media & Services; Semiconductors; Software & IT Services; Telecommunications
Transportation	Air Freight & Logistics; Airlines; Auto Parts; Automobiles; Car Rentals & Leasing; Cruise Lines; Marine Transportation; Rail Transportation; Road Transportation

SASB Standards, which are designed to identify and standardize disclosure for the sustainability issues most relevant to investor decision-making (Sustainability Accounting Standards Board (SASB), 2018, 2023).

In May 2019, Nasdaq introduced a new global ESG reporting guide for public and private firms. The guide includes 30 ESG metrics, focusing on the most impactful ones. It provides clear insights on measurement, disclosure, and connections to frameworks to enhance ESG reporting for Nasdaq-listed firms (Harvey, 2019), as shown in Table 1.7.

There are several frameworks for climate-related indicators, including the Climate Disclosure Standards Board (CDSB) (IFRS Foundation, n.d.), the Carbon Disclosure Project (CDP, n.d.), and the Financial Stability Board's Task Force on Climate-related Financial Disclosures (TCFD). The CDP measures the environmental impact of corporate activities, while the TCFD evaluates how environmental changes affect corporate financial performance and balance sheets (Bose, 2020).

Table 1.7 Nasdaq's ESG Metrics

Environmental (E)	*Social (S)*	*Governance (G)*
E1. GHG Emissions E2. Emissions Intensity E3. Energy usage E4. Energy Intensity E5. Energy Mix E6. Water Usage E7. Environmental Operations E8. Climate Oversight/ Board E9. Climate Oversight/ Management E10. Climate Risk Mitigation	S1. CEO Pay Ratio S2. Gender Pay Ratio S3. Employee Turnover S4. Gender Diversity S5. Temporary Worker Ratio S6. Non-Discrimination S7. Injury Rate S8. Global Health & Safety S9. Child & Forced Labor S10. Human Rights	G1. Board Diversity G2. Board Independence G3. Incentivized Pay G4. Collective Bargaining G5. Supplier Code of Conduct G6. Ethics & Anti-Corruption G7. Data Privacy G8. ESG Reporting G9. Disclosure Practices G10. External Assurance

Consolidation and harmonization efforts in this field are ongoing. In 2023, the TCFD announced that it had fulfilled its mandate and would be disbanded. The Financial Stability Board (FSB) requested that the IFRS Foundation take over the monitoring of companies' climate-related disclosures (IFRS Foundation, 2023; TCFD, 2023).

CDP, originally known as the Carbon Disclosure Project, rebranded as CDP to reflect its expanded focus beyond carbon emissions, now covering broader environmental issues such as water security and deforestation (CDP, n.d.).

1.7 Navigating ESG Frameworks: From Principles to Practice

The relationship between ESG and firm performance can be unexpected in many respects. According to Serafeim and Yoon (2022), this is because most ESG factors are not inherently financially material to a company. As a result, aggregating scores across a broad range of ESG issues tends to produce statistics with low signal-to-noise ratios from a business performance standpoint. While standardized frameworks like those provided by SASB can help identify potentially material issues, they may also introduce significant measurement errors (Serafeim & Yoon, 2022).

Research has shown that businesses, particularly family firms, face challenges in adopting ESG practices, often due to a lack of awareness about ESG parameters and their long-term impact on business sustainability. At the same time, studies indicate that company size alone does not significantly influence ESG performance (Bang & Ramachandran, 2025). Still, many people might agree that now, ESG has become a necessity, not an option. Building a viable ESG program is often challenging for companies, primarily due to the significant upfront investment needed to establish a baseline for assessing material issues. However, this initial capital investment is essential, as it lays the groundwork for aligning future operations and performance with ESG guidelines (Khalid et al., 2021).

This baseline can be used to introduce specific benchmarks both within the organization and for external stakeholders like investors. It is also necessary to adapt and enhance industry-specific sectors and suitable frameworks. Still, materiality can vary within the same industry, not just across different subindustries but also among individual companies. For example, while labor standards in the supply chain are important for apparel companies, the level of risk they face can be very different. A company that sources most of its materials from a high-risk area for human rights issues, like Bangladesh, is likely to face greater challenges than one with a supply chain based in a low-risk country, such as Canada (Serafeim et al., 2022).

1.8 Discussion and Recommendations

As CSR has evolved and become more defined, businesses increasingly recognize that their success is closely linked to societal well-being. This growing awareness has led firms to integrate CSR more strategically into their operations, which results in significant changes in how they operate and interact with the community. CSR-focused firms attract responsible investors who integrate both positive and negative non-financial factors, such as social, environmental, and governance, into investment decision-making. These investors require firms to provide comprehensive ESG metrics and data. Therefore, ESG reporting frameworks and ratings have emerged as tools to include extensive quantitative and qualitative information for investors and stakeholders to assess a firm's long-term viability and the unmanaged ESG risks of firms, ideally reducing information asymmetry for its stakeholders.

However, fragmented standards and limited data availability remain challenges in navigating the ESG landscape. The following chapters of this book will provide real-world examples and best practices for data collection and management. Long-term efforts and a clear strategy seem particularly important in this context. Not all ESG-relevant aspects and criteria are easily quantifiable, and ESG may not always directly lead to increased earnings growth, cost savings, or business performance.

ESG trends vary widely across regions and regulatory landscapes. While some emphasize the need for more accurate and timely data, others see regulatory requirements as a competitive burden—leading to calls for strict anti-ESG measures. The debate is often intense, influenced by ideology and public perception, making it challenging for organizations to navigate these shifting dynamics.

A solid approach remains: maintaining a modern data architecture aligned with leading standards to stay prepared for future changes. Further consolidation is likely, and for managers, staying informed on the latest developments is essential.

References

Abe, M., & Ruanglikhitkul, W. (2013). Developments in the Concept of Corporate Social Responsibility (CSR). In *From Corporate Social Responsibility to Corporate Sustainability* (pp. 9–26). UN. https://doi.org/10.18356/1c39e4c3-en

Albitar, K., Abdoush, T., & Hussainey, K. (2023). Do Corporate Governance Mechanisms and ESG Disclosure Drive CSR Narrative Tones? *International Journal of Finance and Economics, 28*(4), 3876–3890. https://doi.org/10.1002/ijfe.2625

Bang, N. P., & Ramachandran, K. (2025). Inaction Is Not an Option: ESG and Family Firms. *Vikalpa: The Journal for Decision Makers*, 02560909241309521. https://doi.org/10.1177/02560909241309521

Barber, D., Kopp, A., Cottet, R., & Susinno, G. (2022). *How to Improve the ESG Profile of Portfolios While Keeping a Similar Risk-Adjusted Return* (SSRN Scholarly Paper No. 4076841). Social Science Research Network. https://papers.ssrn.com/abstract=4076841

Bergman, M. S., Deckelbaum, A. J., & Karp, B. S. (2020). Introduction to ESG. Harvard Law School Forum on Corporate Governance. https://corpgov.law.harvard.edu/2020/08/01/introduction-to-esg/

Biles, B. (2021, October 6). *Two Sides of the Same Coin: Why Companies Need CSR and ESG.* https://www.americanvetsgroup.com/two-sides-of-the-same-coin-why-companies-need-csr-and-esg

Bose, S. (2020). Evolution of ESG Reporting Frameworks. In D. C. Esty & T. Cort (Eds.), *Values at Work* (pp. 13–33). Springer International Publishing. https://doi.org/10.1007/978-3-030-55613-6_2

Bowen, H. R. (1953). *Social Responsibilities of the Businessman.* Harper. https://doi.org/10.2307/j.ctt20q1w8f

Capelle-Blancard, G., & Monjon, S. (2012). Trends in the Literature on Socially Responsible Investment: Looking for the Keys Under the Lamppost. *Business Ethics: A European Review, 21*(3), 239–250. https://doi.org/10.1111/j.1467-8608.2012.01658.x

Carroll, A. B. (1979). A Three-Dimensional Conceptual Model of Corporate Performance. *The Academy of Management Review, 4*(4), 497. https://doi.org/10.2307/257850

Carroll, A. B. (2009). A History of Corporate Social Responsibility: Concepts and Practices. In A. Crane, D. Matten, A. McWilliams, J. Moon, & D. S. Siegel (Eds.), *The Oxford Handbook of Corporate Social Responsibility* (1st ed., pp. 19–46). Oxford University Press. https://doi.org/10.1093/oxfordhb/9780199211593.003.0002

Carroll, A. B. (2015). Corporate Social Responsibility. *Organizational Dynamics, 44*(2), 87–96. https://doi.org/10.1016/j.orgdyn.2015.02.002

CDP. (n.d.). *CDP's Alignment with Disclosure Frameworks and Standards.* Retrieved March 15, 2025, from https://www.cdp.net/en/about/framework-alignment

Chakraborty, U. K. (2015). *Developments in the Concept of Corporate Social Responsibility (CSR).* 23–45.

Charles, P. (2009, December 17). *A speech by HRH The Prince of Wales at the Accounting for Sustainability project seminar, St James's Palace*. https://www.royal.uk/clarencehouse/speech/speech-hrh-prince-wales-accounting-sustainability-project-seminar-st-jamess-palace

Chen, Y.-R. R., Hung-Baesecke, C.-J. F., Bowen, S. A., Zerfass, A., Stacks, D. W., & Boyd, B. (2020). The Role of Leadership in Shared Value Creation from the Public's Perspective: A Multi-Continental Study. *Public Relations Review, 46*(1), 101749. https://doi.org/10.1016/j.pubrev.2018.12.006

Dahlsrud, A. (2008). How Corporate Social Responsibility Is Defined: An Analysis of 37 Definitions. *Corporate Social Responsibility and Environmental Management, 15*(1), 1–13. https://doi.org/10.1002/csr.132

Davis, K. (1960). Can Business Afford to Ignore Social Responsibilities? *California Management Review, 2*(3), 70–76. https://doi.org/10.2307/41166246

Douthat, R. (2018, February 28). Opinion | The Rise of Woke Capital. *The New York Times*. https://www.nytimes.com/2018/02/28/opinion/corporate-america-activism.html

Downes, S. (2024, April 30). *How Is 'Woke Capitalism' Row Impacting ESG at Major Firms?* https://sustainabilitymag.com/articles/how-is-woke-capitalism-row-impacting-esg-at-major-firms

Elkington, J. (1997). *Cannibals with Forks: The Triple Bottom Line of 21st Century Business*. Capstone.

Elkington, J. (2000). Cannibals with Forks: The Triple Bottom Line of 21st Century Business. *Journal of Business Ethics, 23*(2), 229–231. https://doi.org/10.1023/A:1006129603978

Endress, T. (2025). Digital Procurement and Sustainability along the Value Chain. In D. Galipeau & T. Endress (Eds.), *A Practical Approach to Digital Technologies for Sustainability*. Taylor & Francis.

Endress, T., & Badir, Y. F. (Eds.). (2023). *Business and Management in Asia: Digital Innovation and Sustainability*. Springer Nature. https://doi.org/10.1007/978-981-19-6418-3

ESGVoices. (2024, February 13). *Anti-ESG Movement: Voices Challenging ESG Investing*. ESG Voices. https://www.esgvoices.com/post/anti-esg-movement-voices-challenging-esg-investing

European Commission. (2001). *Promoting a European Framework for Corporate Social Responsibility* [Green Paper]. https://ec.europa.eu/commission/presscorner/api/files/document/print/en/doc_01_9/DOC_01_9_EN.pdf

European Commission. (2011). *A Renewed EU Strategy 2011-14 for Corporate Social Responsibility*. https://eur-lex.europa.eu/legal-content/EN/TXT/?uri=CELEX:52011DC0681

Flower, J. (2015). The International Integrated Reporting Council: A Story of Failure. *Critical Perspectives on Accounting, 27*, 1–17. https://doi.org/10.1016/j.cpa.2014.07.002

Frederick, W. C. (1960). The Growing Concern Over Business Responsibility. *California Management Review, 2*(4), 54–61. https://doi.org/10.2307/41165405

Frederick, W. C., Davis, K., & Post, J. E. (1992). *Business and Society: Corporate Strategy, Public Policy, Ethics* (7th ed.). McGraw-Hill.

Freiberg, D., Rogers, J., & Serafeim, G. (2020). *How ESG Issues Become Financially Material to Corporations and Their Investors*. Harvard Business School Working Paper, No. 20-056, https://www.hbs.edu/faculty/Pages/item.aspx?num=57161

Galipeau, D., & Endress, T. (Eds.). (2025). *A Practical Approach to Digital Technologies for Sustainability*. Taylor & Francis.

Global Reporting Initiative. (n.d.). *The GRI Standards: A Guide for Policymakers*. https://www.globalreporting.org/media/nmmnwfsm/gri-policymakers-guide.pdf

Global Reporting Initiative. (2021). *GRI Standards English Language*. https://www.globalreporting.org/how-to-use-the-gri-standards/gri-standards-english-language/

Hartill, R. (2024, April 22). *What Is Anti-ESG Investing?* The Motley Fool. https://www.fool.com/terms/a/anti-esg-investing/

Harvey, I. (2019). *ESG Reporting Guide 2.0: A Support Resource for Companies*. Nasdaq. https://www.nasdaq.com/docs/2019/11/26/2019-ESG-Reporting-Guide.pdf

Hilson, C. (2024). Climate Change and the Politicization of ESG in the US. *Frontiers in Political Science, 6*, 1332399. https://doi.org/10.3389/fpos.2024.1332399

Ho, V. H. (2015). Risk-related activism: The business case for monitoring nonfinancial risk. *Journal of Corporation Law, 41*(4), 647–704. http://dx.doi.org/10.2139/ssrn.2478121

Hopkins, M. (1999). *The Planetary Bargain: Corporate Social Responsibility Comes of Age* (1st ed.). Palgrave Macmillan UK. https://doi.org/10.1007/978-1-349-27066-8

Hopkins, M. (2003). *The Planetary Bargain: Corporate Social Responsibility Matters*. Earthscan Publications.

IFRS Foundation. (n.d.). *Climate Disclosure Standards Board (CDSB)*. Retrieved March 15, 2025, from https://www.ifrs.org/sustainability/climate-disclosure-standards-board/

IFRS Foundation. (2023, July). *IFRS - ISSB and TCFD*. https://www.ifrs.org/sustainability/tcfd/

Johnson, H. L. (1971). *Business in Contemporary Society: Framework and Issues*. Wadsworth Pub. Co.

Jones, T. M. (1980). Corporate Social Responsibility Revisited, Redefined. *California Management Review, 22*(3), 59–67. https://doi.org/10.2307/41164877

Kandpal, V., Jaswal, A., Santibanez Gonzalez, E. D. R., & Agarwal, N. (2024). Corporate Social Responsibility (C.S.R.) and E.S.G. Reporting: Redefining Business in the Twenty-First Century. In V. Kandpal, A. Jaswal, E. D. R. Santibanez Gonzalez, & N. Agarwal (Eds.), *Sustainable Energy Transition* (pp. 239–272). Springer Nature Switzerland. https://doi.org/10.1007/978-3-031-52943-6_8

Kaźmierczak, M. (2022). A Literature Review on the Difference between CSR and ESG. *Scientific Papers of Silesian University of Technology. Organization and Management Series, 2022*(162), 275–289. https://doi.org/10.29119/1641-3466.2022.162.16

Khalid, S., Hung, K., & Wiley, J. (2021). The ESG Value Opportunity: A Decision Point for Utilities. *Climate and Energy, 38*(5), 10–17. https://doi.org/10.1002/gas.22261

Khan, M., Serafeim, G., & Yoon, A. (2015). *Corporate Sustainability: First Evidence on Materiality*. https://dash.harvard.edu/entities/publication/73120379-2467-6bd4-e053-0100007fdf3b

Kotler, P., & Lee, N. R. (2011). *Corporate Social Responsibility* (1st ed.).

Krantz, T. (2024, July 17). *The History of Environmental, Social and Governance (ESG) | IBM*. https://www.ibm.com/think/topics/environmental-social-and-governance-history

Kuh, T., Shepley, A., Bala, G., & Flowers, M. (2020, January 17). *Dynamic materiality: Measuring what matters*. SSRN. https://doi.org/10.2139/ssrn.3521035

Latapí Agudelo, M. A., Jóhannsdóttir, L., & Davídsdóttir, B. (2019). A Literature Review of the History and Evolution of Corporate Social Responsibility. *International Journal of Corporate Social Responsibility, 4*(1), 1. https://doi.org/10.1186/s40991-018-0039-y

McGuire, J. W. (1963). *Business and Society*. McGraw-Hill.

Meredith, S. (2024, February 27). *Bank CEO Shrugs Off U.S. War on "woke" Capital, Says ESG Investing Is Good for Business*. CNBC. https://www.cnbc.com/2024/02/27/war-on-woke-capitalism-stanchart-ceo-says-esg-is-good-for-business.html

Mosca, F., & Civera, C. (2017). The Evolution of CSR: An Integrated Approach. *Symphonya. Emerging Issues in Management*, *1*, 16–35. https://doi.org/10.4468/2017.1.03mosca.civera

Novisto. (2022). What is the difference between CSR and ESG? Novisto. https://novisto.com/whats-the-difference-between-csr-and-esg/

O'Neill, S. (2024, August 19). *What Is the Difference between CSR and ESG?* The Corporate Governance Institute. https://www.thecorporategovernanceinstitute.com/insights/lexicon/what-is-the-difference-between-csr-and-esg/

Olmedo, E. E., Torres, M. J. M., & Izquierdo, M. A. F. (2010). Socially Responsible Investing: Sustainability Indices, ESG Rating and Information Provider Agencies. *International Journal of Sustainable Economy*, *2*(4), 442. https://doi.org/10.1504/IJSE.2010.035490

Padfield, S. (2023). An Introduction to Anti-ESG Legislation. *Transactions: The Tennessee Journal of Business Law*, *24*(2). https://ir.law.utk.edu/transactions/vol24/iss2/6/

Pollman, E. (2021). Corporate Social Responsibility, ESG, and Compliance. In B. Van Rooij & D. D. Sokol (Eds.), *The Cambridge Handbook of Compliance* (1st ed., pp. 662–672). Cambridge University Press. https://doi.org/10.1017/9781108759458.045

Pollman, E. (2022). *The Making and Meaning of ESG* (SSRN Scholarly Paper No. 4219857). Social Science Research Network. https://papers.ssrn.com/abstract=4219857

Porter, M. E., & Kramer, M. R. (2006). Strategy and Society: The Link Between Competitive Advantage and Corporate Social Responsibility. *Harvard Business Review*. https://hbr.org/2006/12/strategy-and-society-the-link-between-competitive-advantage-and-corporate-social-responsibility

ProMarket. (2023, July 1). Event Notes: Is Corporate ESG "Woke" Capitalism? *ProMarket*. https://www.promarket.org/2023/07/01/event-notes-is-corporate-esg-woke-capitalism/

Puaschunder, J. M. (2016). On the Emergence, Current State, and Future Perspectives of Socially Responsible Investment (SRI). *Consilience*, *16*, 38–63.

Renneboog, L., ter Horst, J., & Zhang, C. (2007). *Socially Responsible Investments: Methodology, Risk Exposure and Performance* (SSRN Scholarly Paper No. 985267). Social Science Research Network. https://doi.org/10.2139/ssrn.985267

Renneboog, L., Ter Horst, J., & Zhang, C. (2008). Socially Responsible Investments: Institutional Aspects, Performance, and Investor Behavior. *Journal of Banking & Finance*, *32*(9), 1723–1742. https://doi.org/10.1016/j.jbankfin.2007.12.039

Rouen, E., Sachdeva, K., & Yoon, A. (2022). The Evolution of ESG Reports and the Role of Voluntary Standards. *SSRN Electronic Journal*. https://doi.org/10.2139/ssrn.4227934

Sætra, H. S. (2024). The ESG Backlash: Politics, Ideology, and the Future of Sustainable Business. *SSRN Electronic Journal*. https://doi.org/10.2139/ssrn.4782018

Schwartz, M. S., & Carroll, A. B. (2003). Corporate Social Responsibility: A Three-Domain Approach. *Business Ethics Quarterly*, *13*(4), 503–530. https://doi.org/10.5840/beq200313435

Serafeim, G., & Yoon, A. S. (2022). Understanding the Business Relevance of ESG Issues. *Journal of Financial Reporting*, *7*(2), 207–212. https://doi.org/10.2308/JFR-2022-010

Shaikh, I. (2022). Environmental, Social, and Governance (ESG) Practice and Firm Performance: An International Evidence. *Journal of Business Economics and Management*, *23*(1), 218–237. https://doi.org/10.3846/jbem.2022.16202

Social Investment Forum. (2009). *Social Investment Forum 2009 Annual Report*. Social Investment Forum.

Stine, A. (2024, July 3). *What is 'Greenlash' and How Is It a Danger to Climate Action?* Non Profit News|Nonprofit Quarterly. https://nonprofitquarterly.org/what-is-greenlash-and-how-is-it-a-danger-to-climate-action/

Sustainability Accounting Standards Board (SASB). (2018). *SASB Standards. IFRS Foundation.* IFRS Foundation. https://sasb.ifrs.org/standards/download/

Sustainability Accounting Standards Board (SASB). (2023). *SASB Standards Amendments for International Applicability.* IFRS Foundation. https://sasb.ifrs.org/standards/download/

TCFD. (2023, October 12). About | Task Force on Climate-Related Financial Disclosures (TCFD). *Task Force on Climate-Related Financial Disclosures.* https://www.fsb-tcfd.org/about/

Thune, K. (2023). *What Is an Anti-ESG ETF? Inside the Conservative Investment Movement.* Etf.Com. http://www.etf.com/sections/etf-basics/what-anti-esg-etf-inside-conservative-investment-movement

Townsend, B. (2020). From SRI to ESG: The Origins of Socially Responsible and Sustainable Investing. *The Journal of Impact and ESG Investing, 1*(1), 10–25.

TRC. (2022, June 19). *ESG vs. CSR | Differences, Definitions & Implementation.* TRC Companies. https://www.trccompanies.com/insights/esg-vs-csr-how-environmental-social-governance-differs-from-corporate-social-responsibility/

United Nations. (2015). *Transforming Our World: The 2030 Agenda for Sustainable Development (A/RES/70/1).* https://sdgs.un.org/2030agenda

United Nations Framework Convention on Climate Change. (2015). *Paris Agreement.* https://unfccc.int/sites/default/files/english_paris_agreement.pdf

United Nations Global Compact. (2004). *Who Cares Wins: Connecting Financial Markets to a Changing World.* https://documents1.worldbank.org/curated/en/280911488968799581/pdf/113237-WP-WhoCaresWins-2004.pdf

United Nations Industrial Development Organization. (n.d.). *What is CSR?* UNIDO. Retrieved March 15, 2025, from https://www.unido.org/our-focus-advancing-economic-competitiveness-competitive-trade-capacities-and-corporate-responsibility-corporate-social-responsibility-market-integration/what-csr

Van Marrewijk, M. (2003). Concepts and Definitions of CSR and Corporate Sustainability: Between Agency and Communion. *Journal of Business Ethics, 44*(2), 95–105. https://doi.org/10.1023/A:1023331212247

Wartick, S. L., & Cochran, P. L. (1985). The Evolution of the Corporate Social Performance Model. *The Academy of Management Review, 10*(4), 758. https://doi.org/10.2307/258044

Winston, A. (2023). ESG Is Under Attack. How Should Your Company Respond? *Harvard Business Review.* https://hbr.org/2023/12/esg-is-under-attack-how-should-your-company-respond

Wood, D. J. (1991). Corporate Social Performance Revisited. *The Academy of Management Review, 16*(4), 691. https://doi.org/10.2307/258977

Zhang, D. (2024). *How Anti-ESG Pressure Affects Investment: Evidence from Retirement Savings.* SSRN. https://doi.org/10.2139/ssrn.4898300

Chapter 2

Evolution of Enterprise-Level Decision-Making Models for Sustainable Development and Finance

Bilal (Bill) H. Rahill and Elizabeth M. White

2.1 Introduction

Sustainable development discourse has been ubiquitous since the concept was introduced some forty years ago.[1] Material progress in achieving sustainable environmental and social development outcomes remains a challenge for much of society and the industries and businesses that the world depends upon. While the intentions of many businesses are increasingly aligned with the objectives of sustainable development, often anchored in the Sustainable Development Goals (SDGs) (United Nations, 2015), conceptual approaches that can be operationalized and integrated into enterprise-level decision-making processes have only recently evolved in a manner that allows enterprises to fully appreciate the environmental and social risks and opportunities associated with their operations beyond the traditional environmental and social considerations that are often captured in regulatory frameworks. These regulatory frameworks are often narrow and impose constraints on operations without recognizing the increasingly significant risks associated with supply chains and system-wide risks and impacts on nature and the services provided by nature. Traditional approaches are also almost exclusively

DOI: 10.1201/9781003528951-2

focused on risk identification and mitigation and don't develop an understanding of key dependencies upstream of operations and potential co-benefits and outcomes downstream of operations that would yield a more holistic view of the business activity within its broader social and environmental ecosystem.

Furthermore, even in the face of the increasingly evident and accelerating impacts of a changing climate, enterprises often remain on the sidelines of action, awaiting government directives and regulations that they may perceive as constraints to the profitability and financial sustainability of their operations. Considering the extensive transition that is required on the energy front as well as on the sustainability front more generally,[2] more holistic decision-making frameworks have evolved to more effectively capture the underlying conceptual constructs that integrate sustainable development concepts and thinking and operationalize them in systems-based approaches that are increasingly accessible to businesses, large and small. A holistic approach, for instance, integrates climate, biodiversity, and pollution considerations of enterprises in terms of their dependencies as well as on their impacts beyond their operational footprint or of a single system (United Nations Environment Programme, 2021).

This chapter explores the integration of environmental and social dimensions into enterprise-level strategies and operations through innovative decision-making models, contextualized within the evolving framework for natural capital valuation[3] in business and the rapidly expanding practice of impact investing. The decision-making models discussed in this chapter represent a significant evolution over a 10-year period from a conceptual framework that expands the consideration of an enterprise-level opportunity for affecting change beyond financial performance to a framework for assessing the development opportunities and outcomes of impact investing.

Three pioneering frameworks reshaping sustainable development decision-making and sustainable finance are presented, briefly illustrated with real-world examples and referenced for ease of follow-up for further exploration and application. Requirements for successful adoption and implementation of these approaches and their implications for impact investing are discussed, emphasizing the critical themes of sustainability, scale, and durability for wider adoption by a broad range of enterprises across industries. Approaches for data integration into decision-making models and application of artificial intelligence are also briefly explored and discussed with a view on the near future.

2.2 Initial Evolution—The Five Capitals Model

Originating from sustainable development literature, the Five Capitals Model (FCM) (Forum for the Future, 2015),[4] illustrated in Figure 2.1, categorizes an organization's use of resources and potential contributions to development outcomes into natural, human, social, manufactured, and financial capital, as defined in

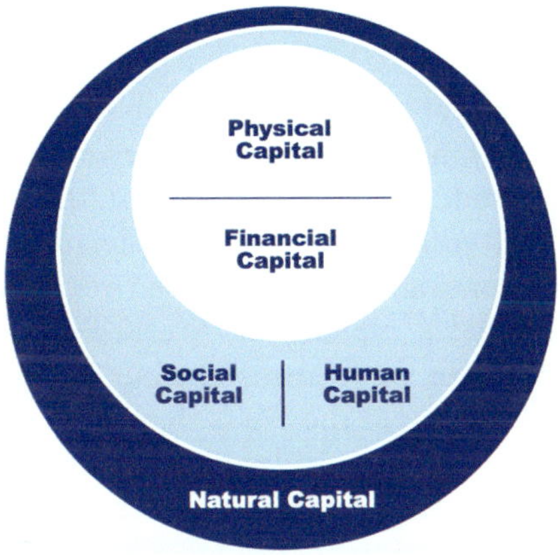

Figure 2.1 Five Capitals Model.

Table 2.1. The FCM represents an important evolution over the people, planet, and profit (PPP) model of sustainable development that gained traction more than a generation ago. The PPP model expanded the scope of corporate objectives beyond narrow financial returns and encouraged enterprises to recognize opportunities for environmental stewardship and social development and equity. The FCM recognizes that wealth and welfare cannot be measured solely based on traditional measures of financial and physical capitals, with the latter mostly recorded as financial capital in financial statements. Traditional wealth models based on financial and physical capital are incomplete and inadequate to account for the complexity of

Table 2.1 Five Capitals Definitions

Natural capital is any stock or flow of energy and material that produces goods and services. It includes: resources—renewable and nonrenewable materials; sinks—that absorb, neutralize, or recycle wastes; processes—such as climate regulation. Natural capital is the basis not only of production but of life itself.
Social capital represents the network of relationships of various societal groups, indigenous communities, schools, businesses, trade unions, voluntary organizations, public services, and its value in supporting the functioning of society.
Human capital consists of people's health and well-being, knowledge, and skills that are necessary for the creation of physical and financial capitals as the basis for livelihoods and a productive economy.
Financial capital is a traditional economic measure of value, which is intrinsically linked to natural, social, human, and physical capital.
Physical capital comprises material goods (e.g., tools, machines, equipment) or fixed assets (e.g., dams, buildings, highways) that contribute to production processes and economic activity rather than being the output itself.

today's world and the need to more effectively integrate sustainable development objectives and outcomes.

FCM has found useful application in the public sector as a way of measuring a country's wealth and long-term prosperity beyond the traditional measurement of gross domestic product. The World Bank (2021) has adopted a capitals approach in assessing the wealth of countries to demonstrate that development is achieved through the management of a broad portfolio of assets including natural, human, and produced capital. The World Bank also found that material well-being is under threat from unsustainable exploitation of nature, from mismanagement and mispricing of the assets that make up national wealth, and from a lack of collective action at local, national, and regional levels. There is a central role for private sector enterprises in supporting adjustments and a transition to more sustainable development through a more effective management of all capital assets.

The FCM can also be considered as an educational tool, helping enterprises understand the interplay between different forms of capital and the importance of maintaining or further developing specific aspects through targeted investments and operational decisions at the enterprise level. FCM represents an opportunity for enterprises to begin the process of developing an understanding of the full risks, impacts, and opportunities associated with their operations, using the FCM as an expanded balance sheet covering all relevant assets to support commercial and economic activities. Application of the FCM has traditionally been qualitative in nature although public sector applications have increasingly integrated valuation aspects,[5] particularly aspects related to natural capital and ecosystem services. The FCM has nonetheless limitations as a decision-making tool for private sector enterprises, as it may require the application of advanced valuation techniques, which may lead to capital account valuations with no market benchmarks or references, hence with limited materiality other than relative changes in capital accounts over time as an indication of progress.

Notwithstanding its potential complexity in a private sector setting, the perceived utility of the FCM motivated the membership of the Capitals Coalition to develop an approach that might be more accessible to companies wishing to explore the benefits of a capitals approach (Capitals Coalition, 2021). The principles developed under the integrated capitals approach recognize the undeniable interconnectedness of nature, climate, and the social dimensions of resource dependencies and use, representing an opportunity for companies to apply an integrated approach in the assessment of their dependencies, impacts, and potential benefits of ongoing operations or proposed investment projects. An integrated capitals assessment typically adopts a system-based approach at a landscape level, in accordance with the scope and footprint of actual or proposed operations. A core component of the approach is the consideration of surrounding systems and their interconnectedness, which may represent a different level of complexity compared to a single capital assessment but yields a more holistic view of risks, dependencies, and opportunities.

Perhaps the most lasting impact of the FCM for private sector enterprises is the spotlight it has shone on the importance of natural capital as fundamental for all economic activities (World Economic Forum, 2020) and the importance of a system-based approach to effectively managing risks of externalities associated with a transition to a more sustainable development path. The World Economic Forum (2020) found that "*$44 trillion of economic value generation – over half the world's total GDP – is moderately or highly dependent on nature and its services and, as a result, exposed to risks from nature loss*".

Both these aspects are fundamental to the emergence of the Natural Capital Protocol and the broader efforts on the capitals front of the last ten years (Capitals Coalition, 2021), as discussed in the next section. This development has also further focused efforts on valuation approaches and the integration of different sources of data to support more quantitative decision-making through a variety of valuation models.

2.3 Intermediate Evolution—Natural Capital and the Natural Capital Protocol

Integrating natural capital[6] into business strategy and operations is not just about environmental stewardship and risk management; it is also about unlocking tangible business benefits and societal value. By valuing natural resources as capital, companies can identify areas where they can manage resources more strategically, improve resource use efficiency, develop new products and services that meet the growing demand for sustainable solutions, and contribute positively to local social and environmental development and sustainability.

For instance, a company that understands its reliance on clean water as an ecosystem service can implement more effective watershed management practices, reducing the risk of supply disruptions, and build future scenarios and strategies to address climate change risk on water availability and water quality, further strengthening its resilience. Other companies may develop new technologies that decrease industry reliance on water in production processes—providing a business opportunity while limiting industry drawdown of water—which may be particularly important in water-stressed areas. Other water users also benefit while the efforts contribute to the SDGs, such as water availability for human use and agricultural activities.

Yet, while most enterprises depend on natural resources such as water, clean air, minerals, and biodiversity in some way, these natural inputs are frequently undervalued, if valued at all, and have not been effectively incorporated into business decisions unless they already represent a scarce resource. Natural Capital valuation has helped fill this gap. This proactive approach can enhance competitiveness and help open new markets, while contributing to the long-term success of the business, its shareholders, and society. In addition, while the environment is the focus of a natural capital approach, society is a significant beneficiary, and capturing the social value of nature is an important dimension of the approach given its potential as a significant co-benefit.

The Natural Capital Protocol, first launched in 2016, has been at the forefront of efforts to increase consideration of the value of nature as an essential part of corporate and financial institution decision-making. It addressed the gap of undervaluing nature by offering a clear, systematic method for identifying, measuring, and integrating impacts and dependencies on nature into business strategies and practices. It provides a standardized framework designed to help generate trusted, credible, and actionable information for business managers to inform decisions based on four stages: "Why", "What", "How", and "What Next", and nine steps (Natural Capital Coalition, 2016; Figure 2.2).

These stages contain specific questions to be answered when integrating natural capital into business processes. Although set out linearly, the Natural Capital Protocol is iterative and allows users to adjust and adapt their approach as they progress through the framework. It also provides flexibility in valuation—using qualitative, quantitative, or monetized options depending on business needs, resources, and required sophistication. Over time, the Natural Capital Protocol has been augmented with additional sector guidelines, innovative digital solutions to support uptake, collaborative approaches to help provide open-source data and valuation factors, business and industry-specific case studies, and important reporting and disclosure initiatives to help ensure mainstreaming. For instance, the European Union introduced ecosystem accounts into its natural capital accounting practices (European Commission, 2020), and the Value Balancing Alliance built on the natural capital protocol to develop a methodology for internal management information systems so that data is combined for business decisions (Value Balancing Alliance, 2021). While there are no requirements currently for businesses to disclose natural capital values, businesses can use the natural capital protocol and accounting methodologies to support various disclosure frameworks. Unilever utilized the Natural Capital Protocol to understand the value of ecosystem services in their supply chains, leading to more sustainable sourcing decisions and improved risk management (Natural Capital Coalition, 2016; Unilever, 2020).

Recent innovations have successfully integrated more sophisticated data platforms into natural capital valuation and decision-support systems. These platforms enhance the ability of businesses to accurately assess and monitor their natural resource dependencies and impacts and to value them. For example, data platforms such as GIST Impact (GIST Impact, 2024) track water usage or carbon emissions enabling businesses to identify areas where they can reduce their environmental footprint and go further in valuing the broader impacts of resource use (Redgrave, 2024), including through monetization. Patagonia (2024) and Walmart (2024) developed the HIGG index in the apparel industry to assess the environmental sustainability of their supply chains and identify areas of improvement. Insights from the Higg Index and natural capital valuation via environmental profit and

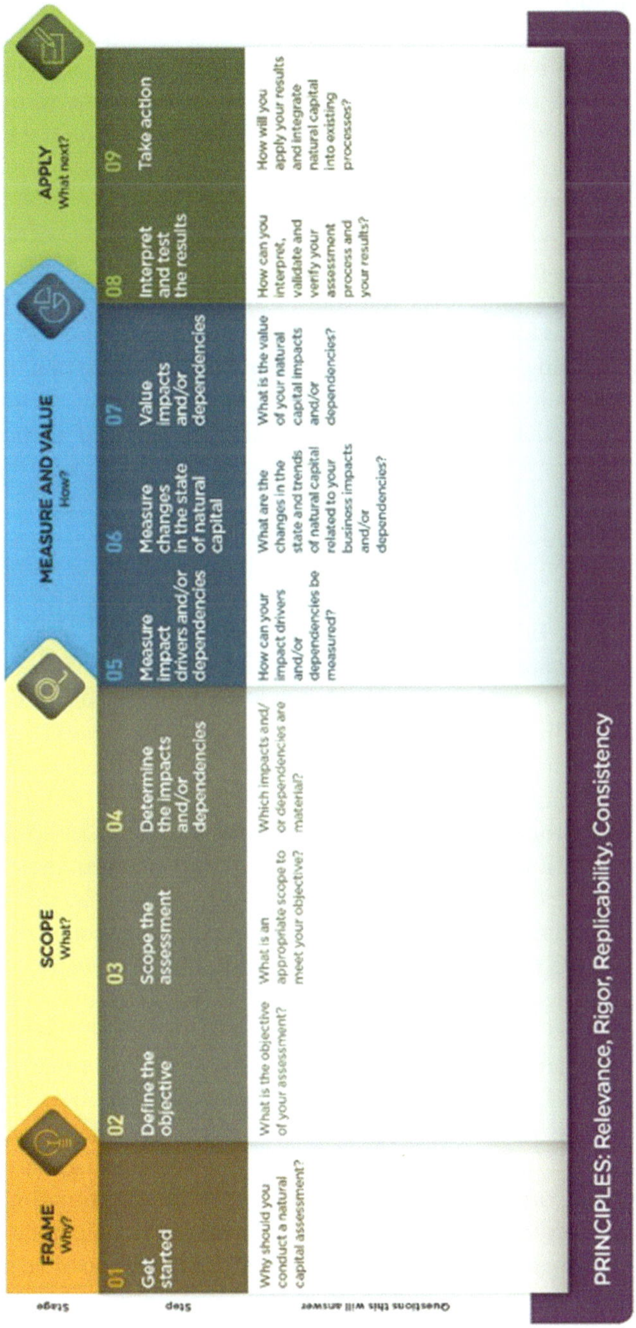

Figure 2.2 **The Natural Capital Protocol—Four key assessment steps.**

Source: Capitals Coalition.

loss accounts help Patagonia design products that are more sustainable, meeting consumer demand for eco-friendly goods and opening new market opportunities (Patagonia, 2024). This index is leveraged by other platforms that add on advanced analytics, reporting, and performance tracking (Patagonia, 2024; Walmart, 2024). Going forward, the use of Blockchain may help address criticism and expand the credibility of these types of platforms. While the examples of leaders are large multinationals, these tools and others under development are available for medium-sized and smaller enterprises. Data platforms such as GIST Impact are designed to be adaptable and scalable, enabling businesses of all sizes to assess and reduce their environmental footprint effectively (GIST Impact, 2024). Additionally, various emerging tools and frameworks under development aim to provide tailored solutions for smaller enterprises, offering scalable and cost-effective approaches to integrating sustainability into business practices and decision-making. This should help ensure that companies of all sizes can participate in and benefit from advancements in natural capital strategies and management, thereby fostering broader adoption of sustainable practices throughout the industry (UNEP Finance Initiative, 2023).

These approaches and tools can help measure impacts at a landscape level—for instance, pulling data on the environmental state from satellites or using drones and artificial intelligence to compare differences in the environmental state over time. Drones equipped with cameras and sensors can take high-resolution images of farmland, showing exactly where the soil is healthy or where it needs attention. When captured over time and at scale, businesses can better quantify their contributions to sustainability goals and report on their progress beyond inputs and outputs more transparently. This type of information can help value agricultural investments more holistically.

For example, a partnership between development finance institutions, environmental economists, and geospatial imaging providers showed the power of automated natural capital valuation models to identify the impacts of different agricultural activities on nature and local communities, and the monetized returns which can be integrated into economic spillover models or, eventually, compared to industry averages. The models were built on results chains from types of investments to landscape-level impacts on nature, geospatial data, and relevant monetary values from use cases in the literature. These were then automated to help the user select the most impactful investments. These types of innovations can be used by impact investors immediately and feed into economy-wide estimations so that they include the real cost and value of nature. The below graphic shared by the International Finance Corporation at a public consultation on estimating natural capital values in London in September 2023 was developed in collaboration with IDEEA Group and using Earth Map interface and illustrates the possible pathways from different investment themes and their linked impact drivers and potential impacts, negative and positive, on natural capital, both stock and flows of ecosystem services (Figure 2.3).

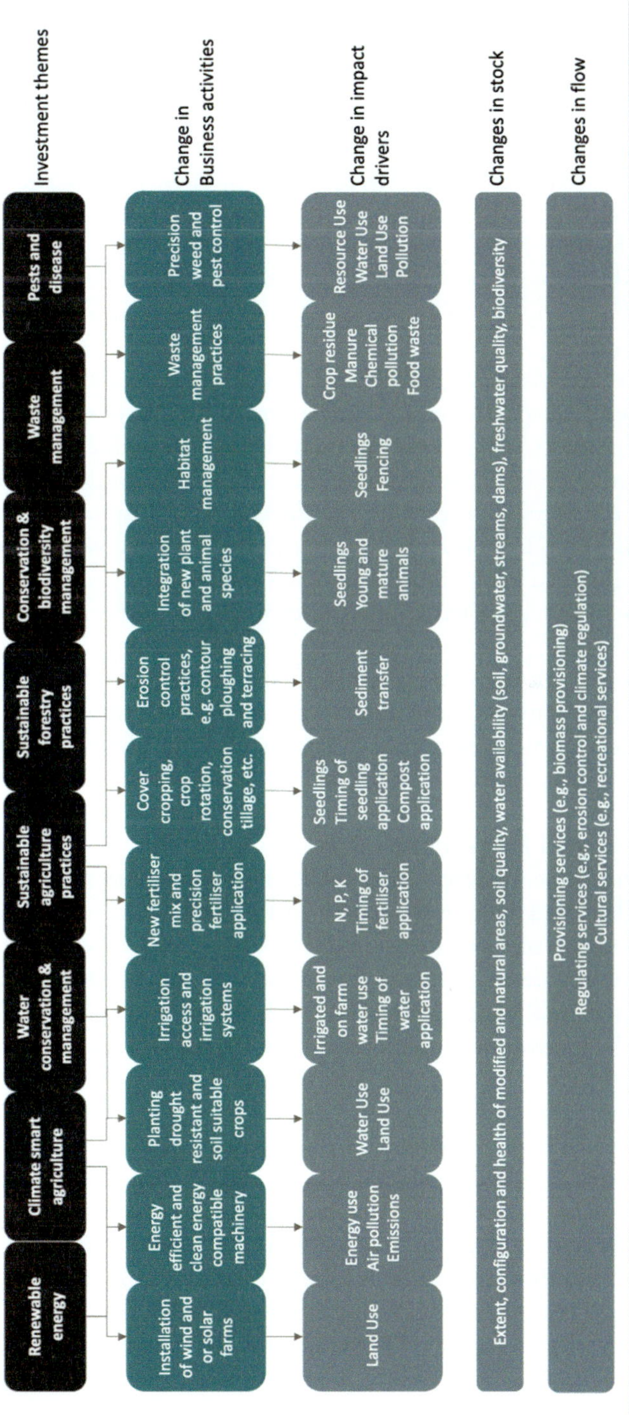

Figure 2.3 Environmental pathways and outcomes in agriculture projects.

Artificial Intelligence is likely to accelerate the integration of natural capital into enterprise decision-making. By connecting to real-time data from other platforms and embedding it in custom logic models, companies will be able to conduct just-in-time scenario planning, risk assessments, and financial resource prioritization by simulating the potential impacts of environmental changes on business operations and, consequently, on markets. These models, if connected to more centralized data exchanges, can learn across enterprises within an industry, allowing for a broader set of actors to support the transition to more sustainable markets. In addition to the agricultural example illustrated above, these advancements are also being tested at the national level, helping to jump-start natural capital accounting.

This matters as it can lead to greater business sustainability and resilience including allowing for environmental uncertainties and helping businesses adapt to evolving conditions, while valuation can help those same companies select between alternative strategies or communicate across communities and competitors to develop shared solutions to common challenges related to natural resource use (Turner & Daily, 2022). Moreover, digital advances, coupled with smart reforms, regulations, industry demonstration, capacity-building initiatives, and financial incentives, can scale nature-based enterprise decisions at the industry level and market-wide.

The Natural Capital Protocol is also reshaping the landscape of sustainable finance. Its focus on data-driven valuation and impact measurement supports the development of more accurate and comprehensive sustainability reporting (Global Reporting Initiative, 2021). This is crucial for impact investors who seek to assess the environmental performance and risk profile of their investments and for financiers to compare the value of their investments across investing opportunities. Financial institutions can also evaluate the natural capital-related risks and opportunities associated with investments. There are also opportunities to use natural capital valuation within sustainability instruments, demonstrating how financial returns are complemented by environmental and societal benefits, both direct and indirect. HSBC has incorporated the natural capital protocol into its risk assessment processes for project financing, enabling it to evaluate the natural capital risks of large-scale projects. This approach supports sustainable development while ensuring that investments are resilient to environmental changes.[7] This approach led to the rejection of several high-risk projects that failed to meet sustainability criteria, thus preventing potential environmental damage and instead financing a major reforestation project in Brazil's Atlantic Forest. The latter leveraged natural capital valuation to assess the project's ecological and carbon sequestration benefits. This initiative not only restored 10,000 hectares of forest but also generated carbon credits, enhancing both environmental and financial returns.[8]

2.4 Evolution of Sustainable Decision-Making at Landscape Level

The discussion so far points to necessary shifts in enterprise decision-making. Early applications of the Natural Capital Protocol in business decision-making have highlighted three fundamental shifts occurring when implementing a natural capital approach (International Finance Corporation and the Capitals Coalition, 2020) in decision-making. These shifts represent material developments in how businesses can strengthen their decision-making frameworks to more effectively assess nature-related risks and opportunities, building on the well-established practices related to impact assessment, management systems, application of environmental and social standards and risk management, and efforts to internalize the cost of environmental and social impacts. When companies start to embrace these three shifts, as detailed in Table 2.2, they can gain a competitive advantage through better strategic, risk, and opportunity management as they are better positioned to address the challenges associated with their dependencies on natural capital, including the effects of a rapidly changing climate.

The relevance of these shifts and their continued materiality provides an opportunity for businesses to help shape their operating environment for a more sustainable and profitable future. It is very much in companies' interest to help shift the

Table 2.2 Three Shifts Toward Sustainable Decision-Making

From Measurement to Valuation. In this shift, natural capital thinking allows businesses to recognize that the environment is something that can be valued from both a business and societal perspective. This allows businesses to inform context and trade-offs through adopting a "value-"based approach. These values can be expressed in qualitative, quantitative, or monetary terms.
From Impacts to Assets and Shared Dependencies. Natural capital thinking encourages businesses to see the environment as something they depend upon that is critical to their long-term viability, rather than something they impact upon, which needs to be mitigated or managed. Often, a natural capital asset (e.g., watershed) is a shared dependency with other stakeholders who also value and depend on the same natural resources. This sets the stage for the third shift.
From Site-Level Operations to a Broader Value Chain and Landscape Approach. A natural capital approach highlights the interconnectivity between issues, stakeholders, and initiatives within a wider geographic area, beyond direct site-level operations. The resulting landscape or seascape perspective allows. The businesses need to find options for responding to natural capital dependencies and impacts that are beyond their ability to implement alone. Perhaps even more importantly, the approach allows for the consideration of cumulative impact on resources.

market to incorporate natural capital approaches as this will support the development of a more conducive enabling environment. For first and early movers, capturing opportunities before they are mainstreamed can present a unique business opportunity leading to a competitive advantage, but this is also often accompanied by higher risk and possibly additional cost. Where natural capital is concerned, it is generally considered as a shared asset that requires shared solutions at the landscape or seascape level.

2.5 The Evolution Continues: Technical and Organizational Adaptations

Innovation in this space continues, building on the Environmental Profit and Loss, Integrated Profit and Loss Statements, and Impact Investing Frameworks[9] that provide needed frameworks for corporate decision-makers, investors, and consumers. Whatever the tool, integrating environmental and social valuation into corporate decision-making requires both technical and governance adaptations.

First, *robust and rigorous data* is essential for accurately valuing environmental and social effects in corporate decision-making, as it provides the foundation for reliable assessments and informed strategic choices. Rigorous data collection and analysis are needed to ensure that the information used for decision-making is valid and actionable. Without such data, companies risk making decisions based on incomplete or misleading information, which can undermine sustainability efforts and long-term strategic goals (Schaltegger & Burritt, 2023). In addition, standardized methodologies, such as those being developed for natural capital accounting and integrated reporting, are necessary to ensure consistency and transparency across different organizations, corporate units, and reporting periods. This helps benchmark performance, compare results, and make informed investment decisions. By employing common frameworks, companies can more effectively communicate their sustainability performance to stakeholders and align their practices with industry standards, thereby enhancing credibility and trust (Bebbington et al., 2023).

Second, *tools and technologies* are crucial to help not only ensure accuracy, but also use across the organization. The application of specialized tools for environmental and social impact assessment, such as Life Cycle Assessment (LCA) and Environmental Management Information Systems (EMIS), enhances the precision and reliability of impact valuations (Schaltegger & Burritt, 2023). Cloud-based platforms and blockchain technologies can improve data transparency and traceability, enabling real-time updates for some information and analysis and reducing the likelihood of errors or discrepancies (White, 2017). In addition, automation of models in simple formats that can be used by different staff—especially important when data moves from environmental and social specialists through to strategists and industry specialists—further enhances consistency. By leveraging methodologies such as scenario modeling, companies can better anticipate and manage environmental and social risks, optimize their sustainability strategies, and capitalize on emerging opportunities (Elkington, 2020; GRI, 2021). Enterprise-wide IT systems, such as Enterprise Resource Planning and EMIS, provide a central platform for collecting, integrating, and analyzing data across various departments and functions within an organization. Ensuring that internal systems that use information speak to each other avoids inconsistency (Kumar & Thakur, 2022).

Feedback loops enabled by high-quality monitoring and evaluation (M&E) systems help move information based on robust data to users at different levels of the organization—creating the third foundational element. M&E systems are crucial for learning and decision-making from front-line operations to senior management and executives. For instance, Yang and Zhang demonstrate that integrating real-time data from remote sensing enables organizations to adapt quickly to emerging issues and adjust strategies. On the front lines, this data might include detailed metrics on resource usage, emissions, and operational efficiency. These granular insights allow front-line staff to make immediate adjustments to improve processes and address local issues effectively (Ambasht, 2023). For middle management, M&E systems provide a more comprehensive view of performance that combines data from various operational levels with trend analysis and performance metrics. This data enables middle managers to evaluate current practices' effectiveness, identify improvement areas, and implement targeted interventions. By leveraging integrated data systems, management teams can ensure that adjustments in approaches align with strategic goals and contribute to overall natural capital success (Carvalho et al., 2023).

Finally, at the senior management and board levels, integrated valuation supported by data, tools/technologies, and well-designed monitoring and evaluating systems contribute to *strategic decision-making*. For senior executives and board members, this might involve aggregated sustainability performance data, risk assessments, long-term impact projections, or forecasts and strategic recommendations based on AI. This level of analysis supports strategic planning, resource allocation, and policy development, enabling leaders to make informed decisions that align with both immediate objectives and long-term ones (Wang et al., 2022; Wu et al., 2019; Zhou et al., 2021).

Organization-wide change is facilitated by ensuring organizational practices embed good corporate governance of environmental and social valuation. The International Finance Corporation's parameters of corporate governance (International Finance Corporation, 2021a, 2021b) provide a framework to strengthen the governance of valuation throughout the firm. This may include strengthened commitment to integrated valuation through policy, capacity building, and planning; enhanced board structure and functioning including expertise on environmental and social issues; stronger control environment that manages risk and is explicit about the economic and stakeholder benefits/costs as part of decision making; disclosure and transparency that meet regulatory requirements and provides metrics and information to the board and stakeholders including minority shareholders (International Finance Corporation, 2021a, 2021b). Through good corporate governance, there is greater clarity on where environmental and social valuation is relevant for different organizational applications.

2.6 Going Beyond the Firm: System-Level Evolution

To further solidify and scale firm-level adoption of environmental and social valuation, markets must adapt, and the enabling context mature. The added benefit of shifting business models to sustainability is stronger viability of the market itself, which depends on natural resources—fresh water, clean air, robust biodiversity, productive land—and on the well-being and stability of societies. These market-based approaches focus on driving sustainability at scale and in a durable way.

Recent work by the Natural Capital Coalition and the International Finance Corporation developed a market maturity diagnostic to identify solutions to specific industry natural capital challenges, to value them as part of collaborative discussion across industry stakeholders, and to create roadmaps to market maturity. In addition to the general industry pressures—such as consumer preferences or sector-specific climate vulnerabilities—the diagnostic delved into four drivers of industry adoption of environmental sustainability practices: firm-level practices/demonstration; regulatory and legal environment; organizational networks and capacity; and financial mechanisms that provide different incentives for robust consideration of nature and society in business decisions. (International Finance Corporation, 2020).

These include:

- **Firms:** Leading companies can influence regulatory developments and other firms in the market through demonstration, networks, and industry initiatives, thereby institutional norms and expectations (Lubin & Esty, 2010). As more businesses and investors prioritize sustainability, systemic changes in how industries grow and operate begin to materialize (Sillanpää & Ncibi, 2019). Microeconomic factors such as incentives, firm policies, and firm dynamics help to deepen practices.
- **Regulation:** As the practices of leading firms become more mainstream, regulatory bodies may adopt similar standards, driving industry-wide adherence and creating a level playing field (Lubin & Esty, 2010). In some contexts, regulations may come before firm-level changes—though often the shift is more iterative and in large part influenced by leading firms and other corporate drivers (Sillanpää & Ncibi, 2019). Public value theory (Mazzucato & Ryan-Collins, 2022) supports the role of regulations and policies that support the ability of regulators to enforce the rules of the game and to use various market-wide incentive systems to scale adoption across the industry. Regulations can also create perverse incentives, for instance, if they are too early or expensive for market-wide adoption.

- **Networks and Capacity Building:** By investing in capacity building, such as training and development, companies can enhance their ability to implement and sustain these models. This creates a ripple effect, encouraging other businesses to invest in similar capacities. In addition, supporting market participants, such as consulting firms, assurance companies, or technology providers, brings foundational elements needed by firms to integrate valuation into decision-making. This includes those mentioned in the preceding section (data, tools, technologies, and governance).
- **Financial Mechanisms:** Innovative financial mechanisms, such as impact-oriented investments, conservation grants, or sustainability-linked investments, influence the ability of firms to put in place environmental and social initiatives. While many of these currently focus on ambitious metrics related to environmental and social goals, over time these can include integrated capital valuations. This helps the companies that demonstrate the financial viability of sustainable practices attract investors, including those interested in long-term value creation, thus reshaping financial markets.

It takes a systems-based approach for firm-level environmental and social valuation practices to be durable. Firms, regulators, networks, and investors respond to environmental and social pressure from consumers,[10] social and political trends, and the viability of the environment's state. Market maturity analysis can inform a firm or industry of the likely risks and opportunities to its sustainability and identify areas of collaboration. An ongoing process of understanding how these confluences come together and building this into scenario analysis and predictive analytics provide a roadmap for markets to move to greater levels of sustainability.

2.7 Ultimate Evolution: Investing in Impact at Scale

Impact investing, once a niche strategy, is becoming more mainstream as innovations like natural capital valuation and integrated capitals reshape decision-making processes and make impact part of the core business of investors and companies. The increased attention to common principles, metrics, and methodologies; availability of use cases; and digital tools shift the conversation from a basic narrative of environmental and social compliance vs. impact, to one that understands and embraces that improved environmental and social performance often yields positive environmental and social benefits—bringing enterprise value and investment value. Environmental and social performance coupled with corporate targets and programs going beyond regulatory or industry standards crosses an "impact threshold" where firms may claim greater additionality from their investments. Thematic strategies, changes in business models, and the introduction/expansion of environmentally or socially positive products or services deepen the scope and scale of the value that firms can create from their investments. This creates many different types of opportunities for impact investing in sustainability.

In addition, valuation raised the sites of companies and investors to understand the ecosystem of industry (e.g., firms, regulators, institutions, financiers) as essential for durable solutions for impact, and expanded impact measures geographically and temporarily. For instance, in the *Blue Natural Capital* (International Finance Corporation, 2021a), the authors showed how in the case of the island of Palawan (Philippines), tourism operators, environmental regulators, and financiers could collaborate to develop sustainable tourism practices that would mitigate the damage to coral reefs caused by over-tourism and improper waste management. The first step was to understand the impact drivers, value them, and use this to influence the market on coordinated actions to safeguard the natural resources that underpin economic activities, ensuring long-term resilience and profitability for all stakeholders. The integration of blue natural capital into tourism development helped maintain the ecological health of the reefs while boosting the sector's recovery post-pandemic (International Finance Corporation, 2021b).

Leading impact investors have brought the valuation of environmental outcomes into their scoring frameworks. For instance, the International Finance Corporation's Anticipated Impact Measurement and Monitoring Framework scores its investments on project direct effects (stakeholder, economy-wide, environmental, and societal effects) and market effects (ability to create sector-wide changes to enhance competitiveness, resilience, and sustainability). In key emission-producing sectors, IFC implements carbon pricing in its project finance considerations.[11] Other development finance institutions are exploring ways to integrate environmental valuation into economy-wide models to provide a more holistic view of value. In the ecosystem of valuation, organizations like the Value Balancing Alliance are helping to bring coherence and consistency to how firms value contributions to the environment, society, and the economy—and bring this information to be comparable to financial data. These efforts, among others, are promising to hasten the evolution of the practice and to further support mainstreaming of enterprise-level informed decision-making that is supportive of positive environmental and social outcomes for a wide range of companies across different sectors of the economy.

2.8 Evolution Is Survival

A growing number of businesses wish to align their operations with the objectives of sustainable development as captured in the SDGs, either organically driven by a sense of responsibility and accountability to society, or as a response to an actual or perceived intensification of risks to their viability due to changing consumer preferences or as a supply chain participant. This development is also a response to the rapid greening of finance and the emergence of impact investing as an avenue to mobilize financing from investors and financial institutions. Meeting regulatory requirements is no longer sufficient to demonstrate responsible management, as it does not demonstrate a company's ability to deal with emerging risks or its resilience to a changing climate and establish its credentials as a sustainable enterprise cognizant of its dependencies on nature and its potential for supporting positive environmental and social outcomes.

This chapter explored the evolution of conceptual approaches that can be operationalized and integrated into enterprise-level decision-making processes in a manner that allows enterprises to more fully appreciate the environmental and social risks and opportunities associated with their operations. Three pioneering frameworks reshaping sustainable development decision-making and sustainable finance were presented, providing insights from studies, real-life examples, and academic research to show how new decision-making approaches can be put into practice to promote environmentally and socially friendly business practices.

Leading companies in this space that have integrated environmental and social dimensions into their decision-making have experienced important shifts in their approach. The FCM has elevated the notion of environmental, social, and human capital as assets that companies must manage alongside the traditional financial and physical capitals. This has supported a shift from an impact-focused approach to one recognizing shared dependencies on assets, particularly natural capital. The emergence of natural capital as an asset class has led to important innovations supporting business decision-making, including the development of the Natural Capital Protocol, which is helping many companies begin the process of integrating nature into their decision-making. With the advent of natural capital as an asset class and the further development of the methodology, including integrated capitals assessments, enterprises have a growing number of tools and methodologies to consider in their sustainability. In parallel to these developments, several data platforms and data providers have emerged to support aspects related to valuation as it is applied to different asset classes and allows for more holistic decision-making, which is made possible by several technical and organizational adaptations.

Finally, adoption or adaptation of one or more of the valuation tools and instruments can lay the groundwork for accessing green finance and attracting impact investors. By integrating these decision-making approaches, companies can be ready to adhere to regulatory changes, meet the expectations of stakeholders, and gain advantages in a market that is increasingly focused on sustainability. This examination contributes to the conversation on resource use in business emphasizing the crucial role of integrated decision-making approaches, in advancing sustainable development, impact investing, and long-term business success.

Notes

1. The contemporary definition of sustainable development is generally attributed to the Brundtland Report, World Commission on Environment and Development: Our Common Future, 1987. "*Sustainable development is development that meets the needs of the present without compromising the ability of future generations to meet their own needs*".
2. Transformation is needed for six systems: economy and finance; food and water; energy, human settlements; human health, equity and peace; and environment.

3. In environmental economics, valuation means more than just monetization. It refers to the process of estimating the relative importance, worth, or usefulness of natural capital to people. Valuation can therefore be qualitative, quantitative or monetary or a combination of these.
4. The Five Capitals Model was further developed and popularized by Forum for the Future, building on earlier work on capitals by Paul Hawken, Amory Lovins, and L. Hunter Lovins as well as Jonathan Porritt (2007). *Capitalism as if the World Matters.* Earthscan.
5. For example, the Government of the United Kingdom established the Natural Capital Committee to advise on the sustainable use of natural resources and to integrate natural capital into national accounting. The Canadian government's Environmental Valuation Reference Inventory is a database used by public agencies to assess the value of environmental goods and services within the Five Capitals framework.
6. Natural capital encompasses the essential ecosystem services provided by nature, such as pollination, water purification, climate regulation, and soil fertility. It also includes the biological diversity that is vital to sustaining these ecosystem services. Recognizing and valuing natural capital is crucial because it highlights the economic, strategic, and operational risks associated with the depletion or degradation of natural resources and can help identify opportunities to gain a competitive position.
7. https://www.hsbc.com/-/files/hsbc/our-approach/risk-and-responsibility/pdfs/221019-hsbc-statement-on-nature.pdf?download=1
8. https://www.wri.org/insights/brazils-forests-are-being-restored-now-we-can-see-where; https://carboncreditsconsulting.com/the-atlantic-forest-a-unique-biome-in-brazil/
9. Impact investing frameworks provide structured approaches for investors to integrate impact considerations into their decision-making processes, ensuring that investments contribute positively to society and the environment while achieving financial objectives
10. Consumers are included at this point in the context and represent demand around a product and may drive behavior changes in the markets depending on the use of incentives (or disincentives) to increase (or decrease) the demand of good (bad) public goods. Such incentives (or disincentives) can include corrective subsidies (or taxes) that are imperfections in the market targeting at specific consumption goods, such as alcohol or tobacco, or, particular inputs, such as, perhaps, brown coal or pesticides. Any market distortions removal based on the public policies and regulatory regimes does not necessarily result in positive consumer behavior.
11. https://www.e3g.org/bank-metrics/shadow-carbon-pricing-ifc/

Bibliography

Ambasht, A. (2023). Real-Time Data Integration and Analytics: Empowering Data-Driven Decision Making. *International Journal of Computer Trends and Technology, 71*(7), 8–14. https://doi.org/10.14445/22312803/IJCTT-V71I7P102

Bebbington, J. (2021). Foundations of Environmental Accounting. In J. Bebbington, C. Larrinaga, B. O'Dwyer, & I. Thomson (Eds.), *Routledge Handbook of Environmental Accounting* (pp. 17–28). Abingdon.

Bebbington, J., Gray, R., & Larrinaga, C. (2000). Editorial: Environmental and Social Accounting in Europe. *European Accounting Review*, *9*(1), 3–6.

Bebbington, J., Laine, M., Larrinaga, C., & Michelon, G. (2023). Environmental Accounting in the European Accounting Review: A Reflection. *European Accounting Review*, *32*, 1107–1128.

Capitals Coalition. (2021). *Principles of Integrated Capitals Assessments*. https://capitalscoalition.org/wp-content/uploads/2021/01/Principles_of_integrated_capitals_assessments_final.pdf

Carvalho, F., Treasure, L., Robinson, S. J. B., Blaydes, H., Exley, G., Hayes, R., Howell, B., Keith, A., Montag, H., Parker, G., Sharp, S. P., Witten, C., & Armstrong, A. (2023). Towards a Standardized Protocol to Assess Natural Capital and Ecosystem Services in Solar Parks. *Ecological Solutions and Evidence*, *4*(1), Article e12210. https://doi.org/10.1002/2688-8319.12210

Elkington, J. (2020). *Green Swans: The Coming Boom in Regenerative Capitalism*. Greenleaf Book Group. https://fastcompanypress.com/authors/green-swans/

European Commission. (2020). *EU Ecosystem Accounts: An Overview*. European Commission, Directorate-General for Environment.

Forum for the Future. (2015). *The Five Capitals Model – A Framework for Sustainability*. Forum for the Future.

GIST Impact. (2024). *Scalable Tools for Environmental Impact*. https://www.gistimpact.com/impact-intelligence/

Global Reporting Initiative (GRI). (2021). *GRI Standards: Framework for Sustainability Reporting*. Retrieved from https://www.globalreporting.org

International Finance Corporation. (2020). *How Natural Capital Approaches Can Support Sustainable Investments and Markets*. Elizabeth M. White, Bilal Rahill, Mark Gough, and James Spurgeon.

International Finance Corporation. (2021a). *Blue Natural Capital: Enhancing Business Outcomes and Sustainability of Coastal Tourism Markets*. Elizabeth M. White and Bilal Rahill.

International Finance Corporation. (2021b). *Corporate Governance and Environmental and Social Management*.

International Finance Corporation and the Capitals Coalition (2020). *Using Natural Capital Approaches to Manage Shared Dependencies - Delivering Sustainable Development and Enhanced Resilience*. Elizabeth White, Mark Gough, James Spurgeon, and Bilal Rahill.

Kumar, S., & Thakur, M. (2022). Integration of ERP and EMIS Systems for Enhanced Sustainability Management: A Review. *International Journal of Information Management*, *62*, 102457. https://doi.org/10.1016/j.ijinfomgt.2021.102457

Lubin, D. A., & Esty, D. C. (2010). The Sustainability Imperative. *Harvard Business Review*, *88*(5), 42–50.

Mazzucato, M. (2022). Collective Value Creation: A New Approach to Stakeholder Value. *International Review of Applied Economics*, *38*(1–2), 43–57. https://doi.org/10.1080/02692171.2022.2144149

Mazzucato, M., & Ryan-Collins, J. (2022). Putting Value Creation Back into "public Value": From Market-Fixing to Market-Shaping. *Journal of Economic Policy Reform*, *25*(4), 345–360. https://doi.org/10.1080/17487870.2022.2053537

Natural Capital Coalition. (2016). *Natural Capital Protocol*. Natural Capital Coalition.

Patagonia. (2024). *The HIGG Index and Its Impact on Supply Chain Sustainability*. https://www.patagonia.com/our-footprint/supply-chain-environmental-responsibility-program.html

Porritt, J. (2007). *Capitalism as If the World Matters*. Earthscan.
Redgrave, G. (2024). Outlook for Natural Capital in 2024: Reporting, Restoration and Implementation. *Environmental Finance*. https://www.environmental-finance.com/content/analysis/outlook-for-natural-capital-in-2024-reporting-restoration-and-implementation.html
Schaltegger, S., & Burritt, R. L. (2023). Business Models for Sustainability: A Review and Research Agenda. *Journal of Cleaner Production*, *374*, 134895.
Sillanpää, M., & Ncibi, M. C. (2019). *Circular Economy: Case Studies about the Transition from the Linear Economy*. https://www.researchgate.net/publication/333223330_The_Circular_Economy_Case_Studies_about_the_Transition_from_the_Linear_Economy
Turner, K., & Daily, G. C. (2022). Valuing Ecosystem Services and Natural Capital: Innovations and Applications in Impact Investing. *Journal of Environmental Management*, *310*, 114698. https://doi.org/10.1016/j.jenvman.2022.114698
UNEP Finance Initiative. (2023). *Greening the SMEs*. https://www.unepfi.org/publications/greening-the-smes-improving-sme-access-to-green-finance-in-mauritius/
Unilever. (2020). *Unilever's Sustainable Sourcing: Leveraging Natural Capital Insights*. https://www.googlecloudpresscorner.com/2020-09-22-Unilever-and-Google-Cloud-Team-up-to-Reimagine-the-Future-of-Sustainable-Sourcing
United Nations. (2015). *Transforming Our World: The 2030 Agenda for Sustainable Development*. https://sustainabledevelopment.un.org/content/documents/21252030%20Agenda%20for%20Sustainable%20Development%20web.pdf
United Nations Environment Programme. (2021). *Making Peace with Nature: A Scientific Blueprint to Tackle the Climate, Biodiversity and Pollution Emergencies*. Nairobi. https://www.unep.org/resources/making-peace-nature
Value Balancing Alliance. (2021). *Value Balancing Alliance: Methodology and Framework*. Methodology Impact Statement General Paper Version 0.1. https://www.value-balancing.com/_Resources/Persistent/2/6/e/6/26e6d344f3bfa26825244ccfa4a9743f8299e7cf/20210210_VBA%20Impact%20Statement_GeneralPaper.pdf
Walmart. (2024). *Sustainability in Supply Chains: The Role of the HIGG Index*. https://snaplincconsulting.com/walmart-sustainability-compliance
Wang, H. et al. (2022). Blockchain and Digital Twins in Environmental and Social Monitoring. *Journal of Cleaner Production*, *331*, 129774.
Wang, R., Zhou, S., & Wang, T. (2020). Corporate Governance, Integrated Reporting and the Use of Credibility-Enhancing Mechanisms on Integrated Reports. *European Accounting Review*, *29*(4), 631–663.
Wang, Y., Cai, G., Yang, L., Zhang, N., & Du, M. (2022). Monitoring of Urban Ecological Environment Including Air Quality Using Satellite Imagery. *PloS One*, *17*(8), e0266759. https://doi.org/10.1371/journal.pone.0266759
White, G. (2017). Future Applications of Blockchain in Business and Management: A Delphi Study. *Strategic Change*, *26*(5), 439–451. https://doi.org/10.1002/jsc.2144
World Bank. (2021). *The Changing Wealth of Nations 2021: Managing Assets for the Future*. Washington, DC.
World Economic Forum. (2020). *The New Nature Economy Report*. https://www.weforum.org/publications/new-nature-economy-report-series/
Wu, J. et al. (2019). Predictive Analytics for Environmental Management. *Journal of Environmental Informatics*, *34*(2), 101–114.
Zhou, Y. et al. (2021). AI and Big Data in Sustainability Modeling. *Sustainability Science*, *16*, 87–99.

Chapter 3

Corporate Model of Digital Transformation and ESG Governance

Wesley L. Harris and Jarunee Wonglimpiyarat

3.1 Introduction

After joining the World Trade Organization (WTO), China attempts to remodel itself from the world's factory towards an innovation-driven economy. At present, it is one of the fastest growing economies in the world (with an averaged growth rate of 10% per annum).[1] In 2023, China was placed in 21st position according to the International Institute for Management Development (IMD) world competitiveness ranking. Table 3.1 provides an overview of the economic and innovation performance of China.

Figure 3.1 depicts the progress of China towards a global competitor. Chinese President Xi Jinping has introduced 'Made in China 2025' strategy in an attempts to transform the nation to the next level on the global stage. Made in China 2025 is a state-led industrial policy to move the country from being the world's factory (low-end manufacturing with the use of cheap labour costs) towards producing high-value products and services. The policy aims to update China's manufacturing base with a focus on developing high-tech industries including the information and communications technology (ICT) sector. China plays a leading role in the global high-tech manufacturing by increasing R&D investments. China has invested more than 2% of its gross domestic product (GDP) to R&D since 2013. The R&D investments to GDP in 2022 were 2.55%.[2]

China has stepped up efforts to make breakthroughs in the ICT sector. Huawei is one of the ICT solutions providers attempting to restructure the global ICT

DOI: 10.1201/9781003528951-3

Table 3.1 Overview of Economic and Innovation Performance of China

Indicator	*Year*	*China*
Population (million)	2023	1409 million
Gross domestic product (GDP)	2023	USD 17.7 trillion
GDP growth (%)	2023	5.2
IMD world competitiveness ranking	2022 2023	17 21
% of research and development (R&D) expenditure to GDP	2022	2.55
No. of patent applications – Residents – Non-residents	 2022 2022	 1,464,605 121,734
Total researchers in full-time equivalency (FTE) (million)	2022	6.354
Number of scientific journal publications	2022	740,000

Source: The authors' design, based on the World Competitiveness Scoreboard (various years) by International Institute for Management Development (IMD), World Economic Forum (WEF) Global Competitiveness Report, World Bank, United Nations Conference on Trade and Development (UNCTAD), OECD Main Science and Technology Indicators, World Intellectual Property Organization.

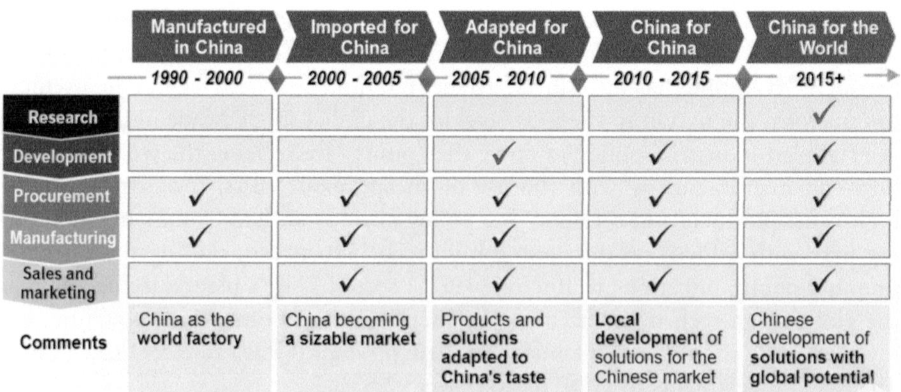

Figure 3.1 The progress of China towards a global competitor.

Source: www.weforum.org

Figure 3.2 The United Nations Sustainable Development Goals (SDGs).

Source: United Nations.

infrastructure network system. Huawei was founded in 1987 by Ren Zhengfei. The company is headquartered in Shenzhen, Guangdong, China. The vision and mission of Huawei are to bring digital to every person, home, and organisation for a fully connected, intelligent world. It is the world leader in the telecommunications industry and is ranked 96th on the Fortune Global 500 in 2022.

The United Nations (UN) had defined 17 Sustainable Development Goals (SDGs) (Figure 3.2), encouraging all the nations to improve health and education, reduce inequality, and spur economic growth. The SDGS are based on the momentum of the Millennium Development Goals (MDGs) and cover various challenges beyond MDGs such as equity, peace, innovation, economic inequality, and sustainable consumption.

This chapter analyses Huawei's model of digital transformation and ESG governance to achieve to the UN SDGs. The case study of Huawei is used in this study as the company is the leading company in the ICT industry building new digital infrastructure through 2030 vision for green development.

The chapter is organised as follows. Following the introductory section, Section 2 reviews the literature on ESG, innovation management, and the process of innovation diffusion. Section 3 presents the research methodology. Section 4 analyses the case of Huawei with regard to its commitments on the UN SDGs, ESG pillars, and business model innovation strategies towards sustainability. Section 5 concludes the study.

3.2 Theoretical Framework

3.2.1 Environmental, Social, and Governance

Environmental, social, and governance (ESG) has become a growing concern for the global economy. ESG refers to the criteria for measuring a company's impact.

ESG deals with the internal governance, which would make the company more transparent (Whelan et al., 2021). ESG can be seen as a part of stakeholder theories where the companies conduct their businesses (Ahmed & Uddin, 2018; Neu et al., 1998). Investors generally view ESG as criteria for evaluating corporate behaviour and financial performance. Many companies have reported the sustainability activities, which are non-financial performance along with their financial performance reporting (Merino-Saum et al., 2018). Table 3.2 provides the attributes of ESG.

Under the trend of green economy, the G7 economies (Canada, France, Germany, Italy, Japan, UK, USA, European Union) have highlighted the importance of sustainable development practices through ESGs. The governments have paid importance on green development as they introduce measures to stimulate economic growth (Balogh et al., 2022; Whelan et al., 2021). ESG is used as a comprehensive framework to help maximise stakeholder well-being and promote sustainable development – an important aspect to achieve the UN SDGs or Agenda 2030. According to the stakeholder theory (Freeman, 1984), the socially responsible behaviour would better satisfy the interests of non-owner stakeholders (e.g., debtors, employees, customers, and regulators) (Fatemi et al., 2018).

For investors who are interested in the companies' making impacts on the ESG dimensions, ESG has been used as a factor for investors in making investment decisions. Many companies set ESG goals to manage the impact of their

Table 3.2 ESG Attributes

ESG	*Definition*	*Attributes*
Environmental (E)	Protection of the environment	• Greenhouse gas emissions reduction • Climate policies • Water pollution management • Natural resource conservation • Deforestation
Social (S)	Consideration of society and relationships with stakeholders	• Workplace health and safety • Child labour • Human rights • Data security • Gender, equality, and diversity • Community relations • Training and education
Governance (G)	Process and structure of the business	• Corporate governance • Policies and codes of conduct • Structure of board and its diversity • Management compensation • Hiring practices • Shareholders' rights

Source: The author's design (based on mckinsey.com).

business operations on society and the environment. They have set their operational goals in line with the SDGs as a self-monitoring mechanism and self-regulation strategy. Thus, many corporations nowadays have set ESG as a part of their business strategy and made a disclosure through the Global Reporting Initiative (GRI) or ESG reporting (Nuskiya et al., 2021). Table 3.3 summarises the global standards on sustainability reporting – Triple Bottom Line Reporting, Integrated Reporting, GRI, IFRS S1 General Requirements for Disclosure of Sustainability-related Financial Information, and IFRS S2 Climate-related Disclosures.

3.3 Methodology

The study uses a case study methodology (Eisenhardt, 1989; Yin, 2013) to analyse Huawei's model of digital transformation in the smartphone, its ESG governance, and commitments to achieve the UN SDGs. The reason in selecting the case study of Huawei is because it is the leading company in the ICT sector building new digital infrastructure through 2030 vision for green development. Although the existing literature in innovation management is already voluminous, there have been few studies focusing on the linkages between innovation management, ESG, and sustainability. The research attempts to fill the gap in existing research with the aim to analyse the commitments towards the UN SDG of Huawei.

The steps of research analysis are as follows:

(1)	Analyses through training machine learning algorithms
	The annual sustainability reports of Huawei and Shell in the past 14 years (years 2010–2023) were extracted via machine learning, whereby the algorithms were trained to extract data on sustainability activities and initiatives. The selection criteria of the annual sustainability reports were that they were available online, in PDF format, and in English language. Machine learning can help identify the trends and the way both companies aimed to contribute to achieving the UN SDGs.
(2)	Evaluating the commitments towards the UN SDGs using the innovation diffusion model
	The baseline in evaluating the sustainable performance – the commitments towards SDGs – was based on the theoretical framework of innovation diffusion by Fisher and Pry (1971). According to Fisher and Pry (1971), the 5% penetration of the market would indicate the chance of successful achievement. The criteria of determining the successful contribution to SDGs in the case of Huawei were based on this 5% threshold. The use of machine learning algorithms can provide insights into Huawei's sustainability strategies. Further, the synthesis of Huawei business model innovation of provides insights into the company's ESG strategies in advancing the SDGs.

Table 3.3 Global Standards on Sustainability Reporting

	Triple Bottom Line Reporting	*Integrated Reporting*	*Global Reporting Initiatives (GRI)*	*IFRS S1 General Requirements for Disclosure of Sustainability-related Financial Information*	*IFRS S2 Climate-related Disclosures*
Timeline	Under implementation to build a more sustainable future	Released in 2013 by the International Integrated Reporting Council (IIRC)	The GRI is a mandatory global standard for sustainability reporting since 2016	IFRS1 would become effective for periods beginning on or after 1 January 2024	IFRS2 would become effective for periods beginning on or after 1 January 2024
Scope	Global: Voluntary framework for corporations	Global: Voluntary framework for financial institutions, corporations, and non-profit organisations	Global: Framework for reporting on ESG factors, which is applicable to all types of entities	Global: All types of entities	Global: All types of entities

Objectives	• Evaluate a company's performance based on financial factors as well as social and environmental factors	• Integrate financial and non-financial aspects into a single, comprehensive report that presents an interconnected view of a company's performance, strategy, governance, and prospects	• Encourage the organisations to promote sustainable development	• Provide guidelines on sustainability-related disclosures applicable to all types of entities	• Provide guidelines on climate-related disclosures including risks and opportunities for businesses and stakeholders
	• Increase awareness of social and environmental challenges	• Encourage sustainable business practice and resilience	• Enable organisations to understand and communicate the impacts of their activities on people and the environment	• Emphasise the importance of consistent and comparable reporting	• Enhance transparency on how climate-related risks and opportunities are identified, assessed, managed, and integrated into an entity's decision-making processes

(Continued)

Table 3.3 *(Continued)* Global Standards on Sustainability Reporting

	Triple Bottom Line Reporting	*Integrated Reporting*	*Global Reporting Initiatives (GRI)*	*IFRS S1 General Requirements for Disclosure of Sustainability-related Financial Information*	*IFRS S2 Climate-related Disclosures*
	• Encourage businesses to consider the broader implications of their activities		• Build capacity for sustainability reporting		
Materiality	Double materiality	Double materiality	Double materiality	Double materiality	Double materiality
Issue focus	Profit (economic), people (social), and planet (environmental)	Strategy, governance, performance, and prospects	Organisations' sustainability impacts and progress towards a more sustainable future	Sustainability-related and ESG information	Climate-related risks and opportunities impacting the organisations' financial performance

Disclosure related to	• Profit – Economic performance in terms of traditional financial measures	• Governance structure	• Economic performance	• Sustainability-related matters, including governance, strategy, risk management, targets, and performance	• Financial impact of climate-related risks and opportunities
	• People – Social performance, the company's impact on society, including aspects such as human rights, labour practices, and community engagement	• Board composition	• Environmental performance	• Governance	• Organisation's plan for managing climate-related risks and opportunities

(*Continued*)

Table 3.3 *(Continued)* **Global Standards on Sustainability Reporting**

	Triple Bottom Line Reporting	*Integrated Reporting*	*Global Reporting Initiatives (GRI)*	*IFRS S1 General Requirements for Disclosure of Sustainability-related Financial Information*	*IFRS S2 Climate-related Disclosures*
	• Planet – Environmental performance, including the ecological footprint, resource usage, and environmental impact	• Roles and responsibilities	• Social performance	• Strategy	• Metrics and targets for greenhouse gas emissions reduction
		• Ethical value	• Governance	• Risk management	
		• Business model		• Targets	
		• Human and intellectual capital		• Performance	

In-depth of information	Disclosures on the financial, social, and environmental impacts	Disclosures on social capital, nature capital, risks and opportunities, and progress towards sustainability targets	Disclosures on organisation's sustainability performance and impacts	Disclosures on management approach to sustainability-related risks and opportunities	Disclosures on governance, risks and opportunities, financial impacts, plans, and CapEx to mitigate the risks of climate change
Stakeholder focus	Investors and general public	Investors and stakeholders	Investors and stakeholders	Investors and stakeholders	Investors and stakeholders
Corporate reporting side	Disclosure on a company's social, environmental, and financial performance	Annual reports, sustainability reports, and other corporate disclosures	Annual report, sustainability report, or a separate report	Annual report, sustainability report, or a separate report	Annual report, sustainability report, or a separate report

Source: The authors' design.

3.4 Analyses of Findings

The following section analyses Huawei's competitive position, assessing its market standing, strategic advantages, and industry challenges. It also discusses Huawei's ESG strategies and sustainability goals, evaluating the company's approach to environmental responsibility, social impact, and corporate governance.

3.4.1 Huawei's Competition Position

The analyses of Huawei's competition position in the smartphone business, based on Porter Five Forces Model (Porter, 1980), are shown in Figure 3.3. In 2018, former U.S. President Donald Trump started the U.S.-China trade war and banned the communication devices of Huawei. However, the company denied the U.S. claim and kept investing heavily in R&D in order to stay ahead in the ICT sector.

Table 3.4 presents the strengths, weaknesses, opportunities, and threats (SWOT) analyses of Huawei's smartphone business.

Despite the pressure from U.S. ban, Huawei's financial performance has increasingly improved (Figure 3.4). In 2023, its revenue increased by 9.63% to CYN 704.2 billion yuan, whereas the net profit increased by 144.5% to CYN 87 billion. The ability to compete with a rebound in its smartphone business has shown a sustainable competitive advantage.

3.4.2 Huawei ESG Strategies and Sustainability Goals

Taking into account Huawei's sustainability efforts, the company has set ambitious plans to meet its sustainability goals aligning with the UN SDGs. Figure 3.5 depicts Huawei's ESG ranking compared to other companies in the same industry. The company was ranked 80% in the telecommunications industry in 2024 (csrhub.com).

Huawei has pursued four sustainability strategies as follows:

-	**Digital Inclusion**
	Huawei launched TECH4ALL initiative to drive equity in education and the healthcare system. The company also introduced TECH4Nature using artificial intelligence (AI) to conserve wildlife and biodiversity.
-	**Environmental Protection**
	Huawei prioritises digitising and decarbonating in the pursuit of green development with the aim to reduce carbon emissions. Huawei promotes the green future by using bioplastics in various products and utilising clean energy sources such as wind, hydropower to reduce the company's carbon footprint.

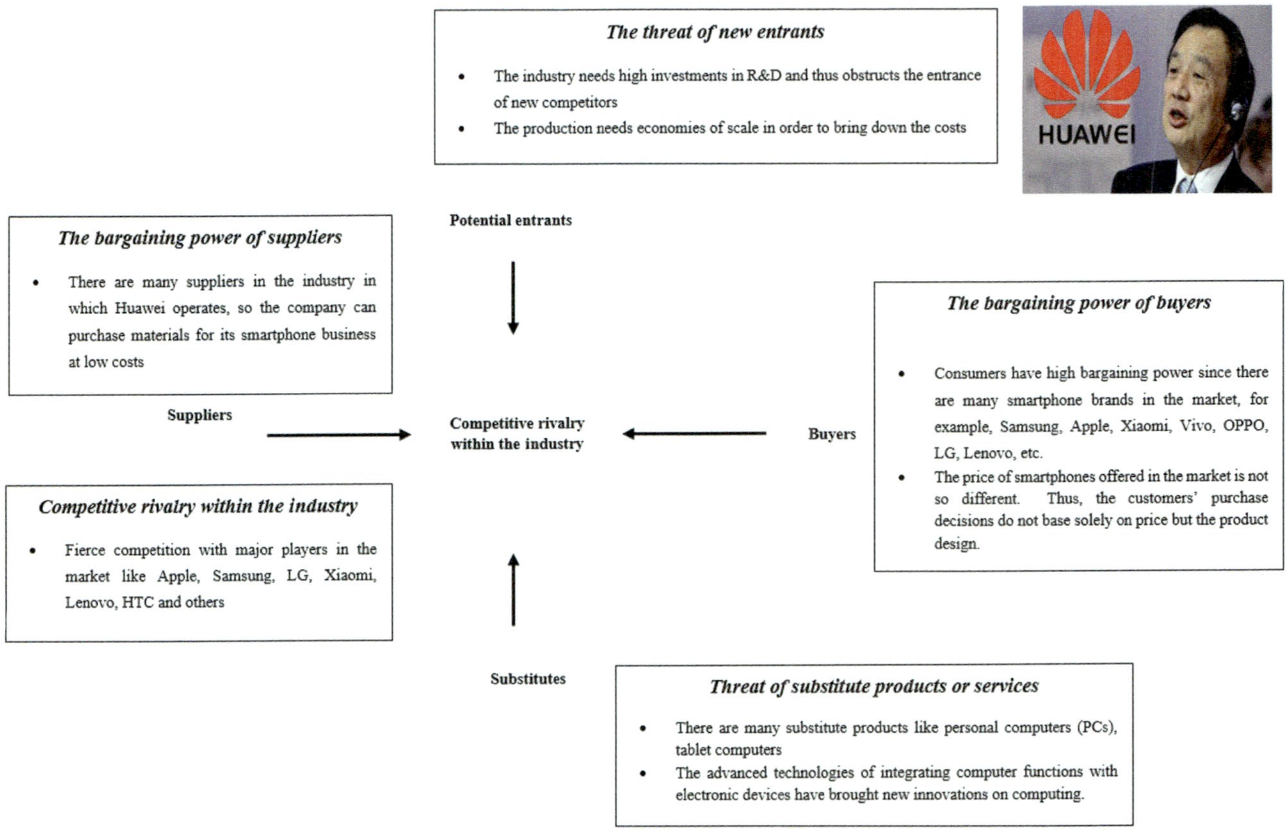

Figure 3.3 Five Forces Model – Analyses of Huawei smartphone business.

-	**Security and Trustworthiness**
	Huawei has strived towards achieving the UNSDGs such as industry, innovation, and infrastructure by developing cybersecurity and trustworthy products and services. The company uses artificial intelligence (AI) defence mechanisms to protect customer's security and privacy.
-	**Healthy and Harmonious Ecosystem**
	Huawei promotes cultural integration so that people from different backgrounds feel a part of the company culture. The company provides an integrity-based operation with zero tolerance for bribery and corruption, and launches various initiatives to improve ICT education for young individuals.

Table 3.4 SWOT Analyses of Huawei Smartphone Business

	SWOT Analyses of Huawei Smartphone Business
Strengths	• The products of Huawei are of high quality (features and performance) and less expensive than those of the U.S. smartphone brands. Its focus on the premium quality thus attracts consumers' attention. • Huawei's heavy investments in R&D have helped it advance 5G technologies (Cui & Liu, 2019). In 2021, the company's R&D investments were CNY 142.7 billion, which was approximately 22.4% of the company's annual revenue. • The pursuit of strategic partnerships to operate research and innovation centres has helped improve photography, image computing, virtual reality, and augmented reality technologies. • Huawei products have brand value as the company is ranked among the top 10 most valuable brands. • The 100% employee ownership increases employee loyalty and reduces staff turnover.
Weaknesses	• The global demand in smartphones decreases as the market approaches saturation. • Huawei is a Chinese brand whereby the consumers have a negative attitude against Chinese products. • Controversies over corporate espionage have impaired Huawei's image. • Huawei shares are not listed in the stock exchange. Thus, the company might face difficulties in raising more capital for business expansion.

(*Continued*)

Table 3.4 *(Continued)* SWOT Analyses of Huawei Smartphone Business

	SWOT Analyses of Huawei Smartphone Business
Opportunities	• The young generations (generations X, Y, and Z) are receptive to new technologies and innovations. • The trend of mobile commerce can increase the demand of using smartphones as sales channels to customers. • Huawei has its own R&D centres in many countries to support the launch of new technologies. • Increasing demand of smartphones in developing countries
Threats	• The political pressures and U.S. sanctions • There are many new competitors in the market like Xiaomi and ZTE offering similar quality and competitive pricing. • Low tariffs in China on competing products from other WTO countries have induced foreign competitors to enter the Chinese market.

Source: The authors' design.

The theoretical framework of innovation diffusion by Fisher and Pry (1971) is helpful in forecasting the trend of diffusion. According to Fisher and Pry's (1971) criteria, the 5% contribution (compared to the industry) indicates the chance of successful achievement. Of all 17 UN SDGs, Huawei surpassed 5% threshold in most SDGs. Huawei performed very well on SDG 12 (Responsible Consumption and Production). Specifically, the company had strong performance with regard to SDG 4 (Quality Education) as the company placed

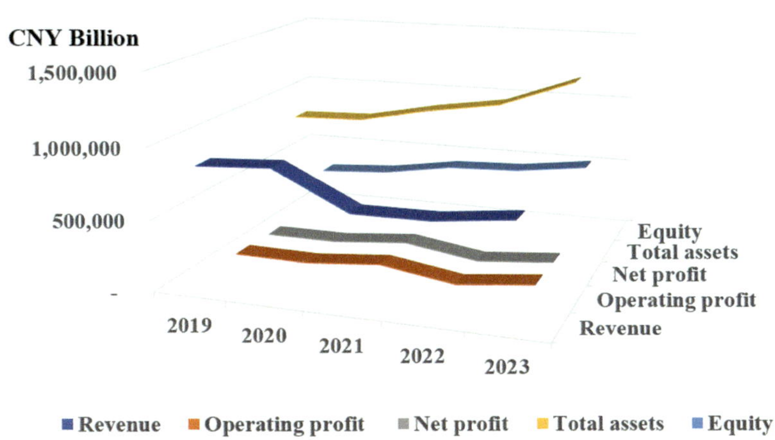

Figure 3.4 Huawei financial performance.

Source: Huawei Annual Reports.

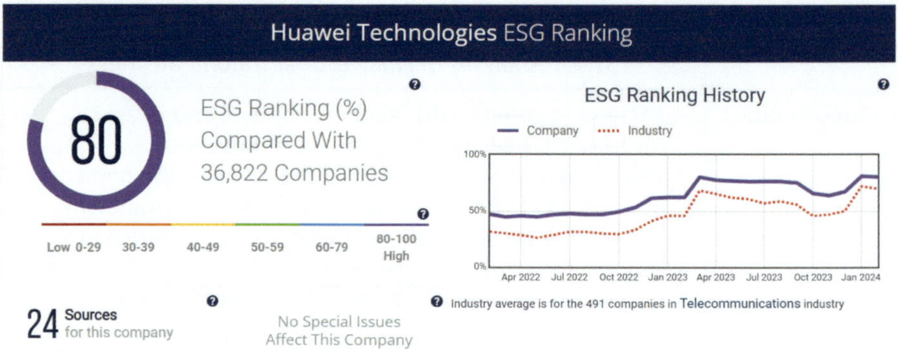

Figure 3.5 Huawei ESG ranking in 2024.

Source: Csrhub.Com.

importance on developing technological skills in ICT. Shell performed well regarding SDG 7 (Affordable and Clean Energy) as the company put emphasis on creating a more sustainable energy. However, Huawei did not perform well concerning SDG 13 (Climate Action), SDG 14 (Life Below Water) and SDG 17 (Partnerships to achieve the Goal) as the percentage of contribution was below 5%.

Figure 3.6 shows the SDG performance of Huawei in percentage contribution, categorised by 3 pillars of ESG. The analyses of Huawei have shown some intersections on ESG pillars. Based on the results from the machine learning

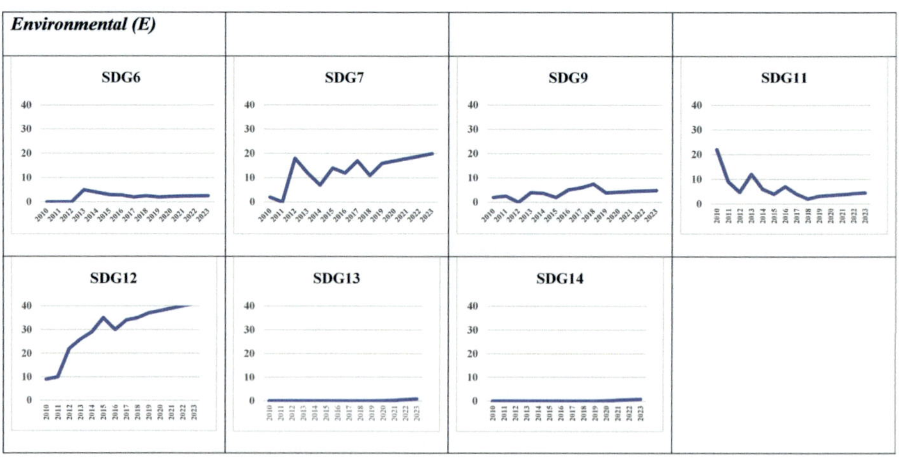

Figure 3.6 (a–c) Three pillars of ESG showing the SDG performance of Huawei (% contribution). *(Continued)*

Source: The authors' design.

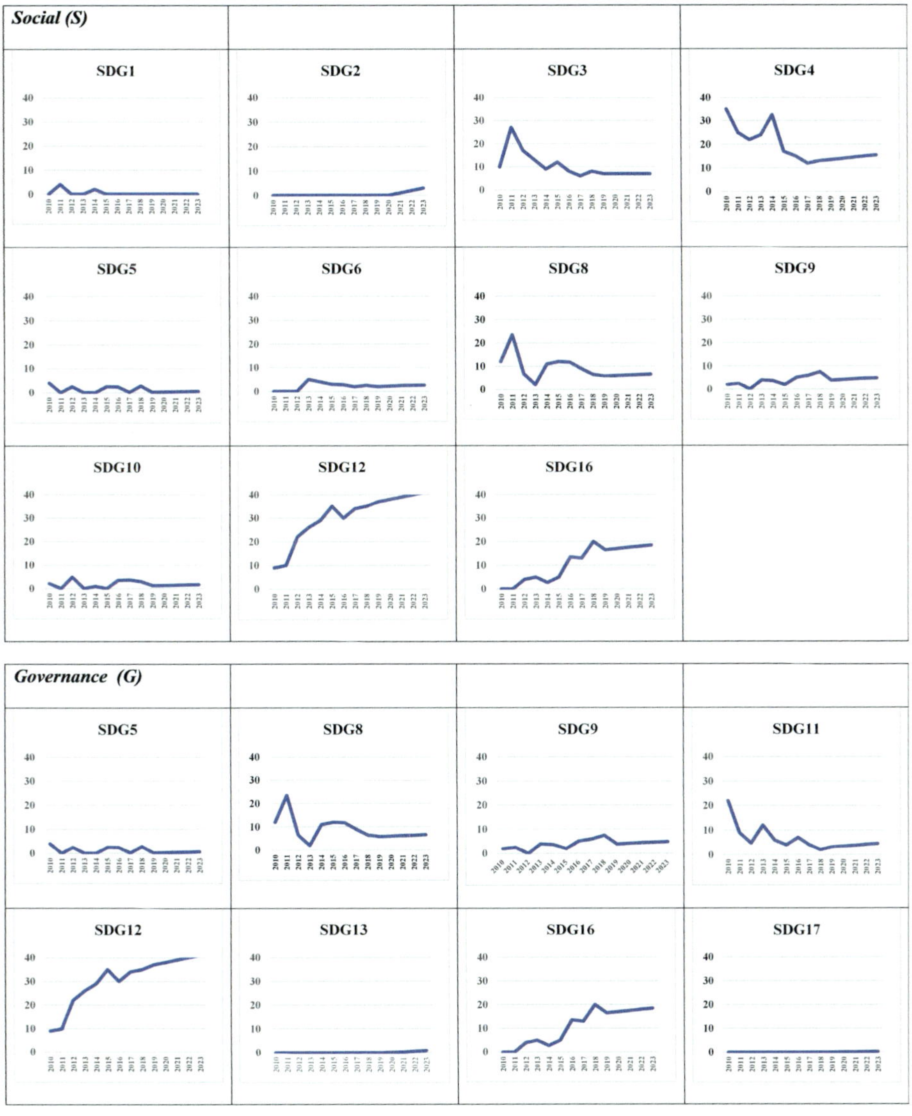

Figure 3.6 ***(Continued)***

algorithms, the performance of Huawei concerning the commitments towards the UN SDGs over the past 10 years (years 2010–2019) can be summarised in Figure 3.7. The assessment of Huawei's performance was based on Fisher and Pry (1971)'s theory of innovation diffusion. Huawei performed very well in progressing towards UN SDGs No. 3, 4, 7, 8, 11, 12, and 16 as the diffusion rate was greater than 5%.

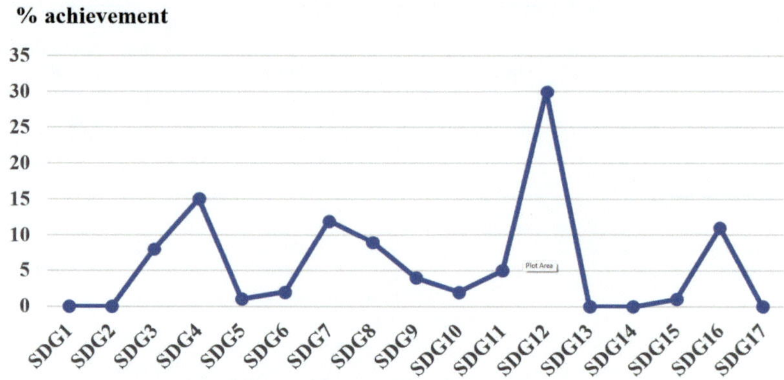

Figure 3.7 Huawei's progress towards the UN SDGs.

Source: The author's design.

The machine learning results interpreted through the lens of innovation diffusion framework (Fisher & Pry, 1971) had revealed interesting insights of the progress in achieving the UN SDGs so far. In summary, Huawei had impressive performance with regard to the following SDGs:

SDG 3	Good Health and Well-being
SDG 4	Quality Education
SDG 7	Affordable and Clean Energy
SDG 8	Decent Work and Economic Growth
SDG 11	Sustainable Cities and Communities
SDG 12	Responsible Consumption and Production
SDG 16	Peace and Justice Strong Institutions

However, Huawei did not perform well in the following SDGs:

SDG 1	No Poverty
SDG 2	Zero Hunger
SDG 5	Gender Equality
SDG 6	Clean Water and Sanitation
SDG 9	Industry, Innovation, and Infrastructure

SDG 10	Reduced Inequality
SDG 13	Climate Action
SDG 14	Life Below Water
SDG 15	Life on Land
SDG 17	Partnerships to Achieve the Goal

From Figure 3.7 portraying the percentage of achievement, it revealed interesting insights of Huawei regarding its commitment to accelerate the UN SDGs. Huawei had placed a focus on achieving SDG 12 Responsible Consumption and Production (30% achievement), SDG 7 Affordable and Clean Energy (12% achievement), and SDG 4 Quality Education (6% achievement). This has shown that the company effectively supported the UN 2030 agenda for sustainable development.

Figure 3.8 shows the synthesis of Huawei's business model innovation reflecting the ESG strategies. It also shows the value, indicators, and activities in building a sustainable future in the ICT industry. Huawei has shown its commitments on UN SDGs and evolving with ambitious goals – Huawei's

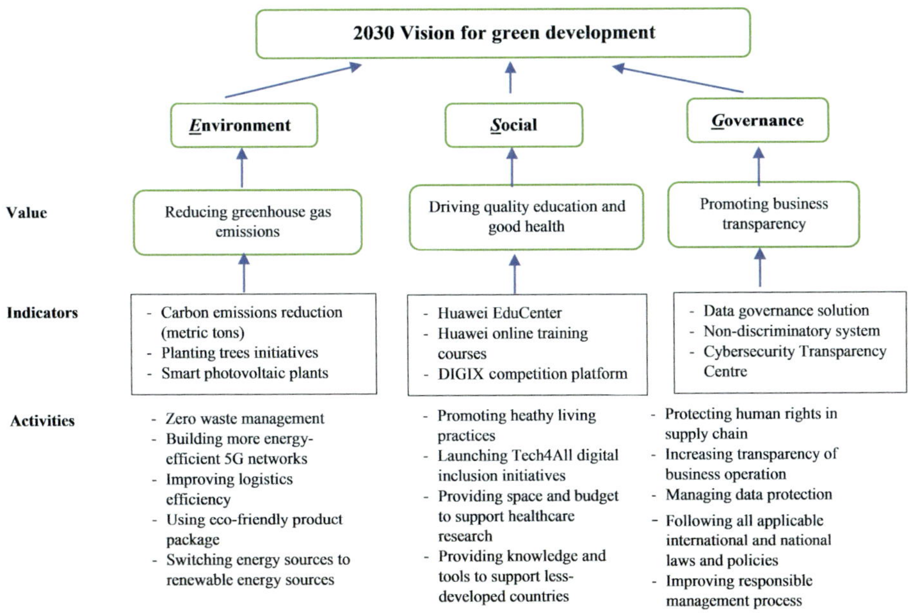

Figure 3.8 Business model innovation – Huawei ESG strategies towards sustainability.

Source: The author's design.

2030 vision for green development. The company was committed to building a sustainable model by pursuing the Tech for a Better Planet strategy focused on reducing carbon emissions, promoting renewable energy, and contributing to a circular economy.

3.5 Conclusions

This chapter is concerned with the analysis of Huawei's strategic positioning, its model of digital transformation in the smartphone market, and its ESG governance. The research was carried out through leveraging machine learning algorithms and interpreted via the lens of innovation diffusion framework. The analyses have shown Huawei's potential to achieve the UN SDGs. The company had demonstrated strong performance with regard to SDGs No. 3, 4, 7, 8, 11, 12, and 16. The research provides a synthesis of Huawei's business model innovations incorporating the ESG strategies to build new digital infrastructure through its 2030 vision for green development. The extent to which Huawei linked corporate strategies to the UN SDGs has reflected its implementation progress.

Notes

1. www.worldbank.org
2. National Bureau of Statistics.

References

Ahmed, S. and Uddin, S. (2018), 'Toward a political economy of corporate governance change and stability in family business groups: A morphogenetic approach', *Accounting, Auditing and Accountability Journal*, Vol. 31(8), pp. 2192–2217.

Balogh, I., Srivastava, M. and Tyll, L. (2022), 'Towards comprehensive corporate sustainability reporting: an empirical study of factors influencing ESG disclosures of large Czech companies', *Society and Business Review*, Vol. 17(4), pp. 541–573.

Cui, F. and Liu, G. (2019), *Global Value Chains and Production Networks: Case Studies of Siemens and Huawei*, Academic Press, London.

Eisenhardt, K.M. (1989), 'Building theories from case study research', *Academy of Management Review*, Vol. 14(4), pp. 532–550.

Fatemi, A., Glaum, M. and Kaiser, S. (2018), 'ESG performance and firm value: The moderating role of disclosure', *Global Finance Journal*, Vol. 38, pp. 45–64.

Fisher, J.C. and Pry, R.H. (1971), 'A simple substitution model of technological change', *Technological Forecasting and Social Change*, Vol. 3, pp. 75–88.

Freeman, R.E. (1984), *Stakeholder management: A strategic approach*, Pitman, Marchfield, M.A.

Merino-Saum, A., Baldi, M.G., Gunderson, I. and Oberle, B. (2018), 'Articulating natural resources and sustainable development goals through green economy indicators: A systematic analysis', *Resources, Conservation and Recycling*, Vol. 139, pp. 90–103.

Neu, D., Warsame, H. and Pedwell, K. (1998), 'Managing public impressions: Environmental disclosures in annual reports', *Accounting, Organizations and Society*, Vol. 23(3), pp. 265–282.

Nuskiya, M.N.F., Ekanayake, A., Beddewela, E. and Gerged, A.M. (2021), 'Determinants of corporate environmental disclosures in Sri Lanka: The role of corporate governance', *Journal of Accounting in Emerging Economies*, Vol. 11(3), pp. 367–394.

Porter, M.E. (1980), *Competitive Strategy*, The Free Press, New York.

Whelan, T., Atz, U. and Casey Clark, C.F.A. (2021), *ESG and Financial Performance*, Centre for Sustainable Business, NYU-Stern.

Yin, R. (2013), *Case Study Research: Design and Methods*, Sage, Beverly Hills.

Chapter 4

From Reporting to Ratings: Understanding the ESG Data Value Chain

Tobias Endress

4.1 Measuring ESG: Data Sources, Methodologies, and Standardization

As sustainability becomes a critical factor in corporate decision-making, businesses face increasing pressure to disclose their environmental, social, and governance (ESG) performance. Investors, regulators, and stakeholders alike seek greater transparency and accountability, making ESG reporting an essential yet complex process. ESG reporting is rapidly evolving, but it is still fragmented. Currently, ESG reports lack comparability, while investor demand for consistency continues to grow. Although many reporting frameworks are voluntary today, mandatory disclosure and global standardization are on the horizon. Digital transformation is another driver in this intersection of digital innovation and much-needed sustainability solutions (Endress & Badir, 2023).

Now is the time to prepare. Understanding the biggest challenges in ESG reporting can help your organization address them before they proactively slow down progress.

Wolters Kluwer's Expert Insights outlines some key challenges in ESG reporting (Cafagna & Tocchini, 2022):

- **Multiple ESG frameworks**—Navigating various reporting standards.
- **Evolving ESG regulations**—Keeping up with changing compliance requirements.

 DOI: 10.1201/9781003528951-4

- **Complex ESG data management**—Collecting, organizing, and analyzing ESG data.
- **Assessing ESG risks**—Measuring and managing ESG-related risks effectively.
- **Enhancing ESG performance**—Using insights to refine sustainability strategies.

Investors and other stakeholders are increasingly interested in companies that invest in ESG and use ESG disclosures to assess their sustainability efforts. Clear regulations and thorough reviews of firms' environmental claims are needed to prevent greenwashing. Governments and non-profit organizations may need to collaborate to set and enforce clear standards for ESG claims, ensuring companies are accountable for their actions and promoting fair competition. Continuous disclosure and monitoring of green initiatives are also essential to determine whether they effectively reduce environmental harm and contribute to a sustainable economy (Sharma et al., 2023). ESG reporting can be challenging because it is still relatively new, constantly evolving, and impacts every financial process. For sustainability-driven investors, the stakes are high, making accuracy and transparency more critical than ever (Cafagna & Tocchini, 2022). Still, some authors estimate that around 70% of ESG data points indicate whether a company has a relevant policy in place. However, having a policy does not necessarily reflect the level of commitment or action taken to follow it (Galipeau & Endress, 2025; Sharma et al., 2023).

Figure 4.1 visually represents a simplified model of how ESG data flows through different stages, connecting organizations, data vendors, and investors. It highlights essential processes such as data collection, analysis, distribution, and decision-making, showcasing how raw ESG data is transformed into valuable insights that drive sustainable investment and business strategies.

Within an organization, ESG data originates from various internal departments, such as sustainability teams tracking carbon emissions, human resources managing workforce diversity, and compliance units monitoring governance practices. These units measure and collect ESG-related data from multiple sources, including internal reports, IoT sensors, employee surveys, and regulatory filings. For example, a company may track its carbon footprint using automated monitoring systems that measure energy consumption across its facilities.

Once collected, this data undergoes a structured analysis process to identify trends, assess risks, and ensure compliance with industry standards. Data analytics teams and sustainability officers employ methodologies such as benchmarking against industry peers, conducting materiality assessments, and integrating machine learning models to predict ESG risks. For instance, an energy company may analyze water usage trends to mitigate potential shortages and regulatory risks.

After analysis, the cleaned and refined ESG data is distributed internally for strategic decision-making and externally to stakeholders such as investors, regulators, and rating agencies. Organizations often use sustainability reports,

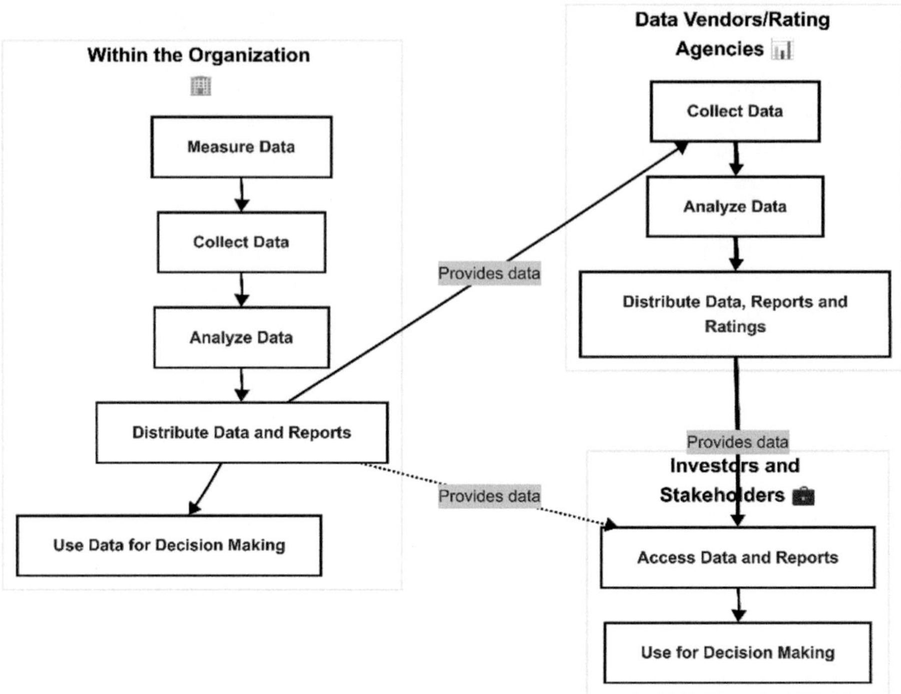

Figure 4.1 Simplified model of the ESG data value chain: From reporting to ratings.

investor presentations, and integrated financial disclosures to share their ESG performance.

ESG data vendors and rating agencies play a crucial role in this value chain by aggregating and standardizing ESG information from multiple organizations. They enhance transparency by providing ESG scores, sustainability indices, and third-party assurance services. For example, a financial data provider like MSCI or Sustainalytics may rate companies based on their ESG performance, helping investors assess sustainability risks before making investment decisions.

Investors and other stakeholders—including asset managers, regulatory bodies, and consumers—access ESG data through annual sustainability reports, ESG indexes, and investment rating platforms. They utilize this information to make informed decisions about portfolio allocations, risk management, and corporate engagement. For instance, an institutional investor may divest from companies with poor ESG scores or engage with businesses to improve sustainability practices.

Overall, managing ESG data requires the coordination of multiple internal and external stakeholders, the integration of various data formats (structured and unstructured), and compliance with global reporting standards such as the Global Reporting Initiative (GRI) (Global Reporting Initiative, 2021), the Task Force on

Climate-related Financial Disclosures (TCFD) (IFRS Foundation, 2023), and the Sustainability Accounting Standards Board (SASB) (SASB, 2022). Through this interconnected value chain, ESG data transforms from raw inputs into strategic intelligence that shapes corporate policies, regulatory compliance, and investment strategies.

4.2 Data Measurement and Orchestration Within the Organization

Data measurement and the implementation of well-orchestrated follow-up processing present significant challenges due to the complexity of ESG data and the diverse stakeholders involved. Within an organization, various departments—including sustainability teams, finance, compliance, operations, and IT—are responsible for gathering and processing ESG-related information. However, these teams often work with heterogeneous data sources that come in multiple formats, such as structured data (e.g., CSV, databases, JSON) and unstructured data (e.g., PDF reports, scanned documents, emails, or handwritten records). Ensuring consistency and interoperability across these formats requires sophisticated data integration and standardization processes, which can be challenging to implement at scale (Endress, 2025). The most suitable platform depends on factors like company size. Large firms need enterprise-grade ESG platforms supporting a wide range of standards, while SMEs might benefit from more straightforward tools.

4.3 The Quality Dilemma: Inconsistencies and Gaps in ESG Data

Managing ESG data across multiple departments and ensuring compliance with various reporting standards can be complex. Additionally, data quality issues—such as missing data, inaccurate entries, outdated information, and corrupt files—can severely impact the reliability of ESG reporting. For instance, the resulting analysis may be misleading if a company's carbon footprint data is incomplete due to missing sensor readings or if human input errors lead to incorrect employee diversity figures. Furthermore, ESG data is often collected from third-party sources, such as suppliers and industry databases, which may have their own inconsistencies or lack timely updates. This introduces challenges in ensuring data accuracy, verification, and alignment with reporting frameworks.

Another obstacle is the lack of standardized measurement methodologies across industries and regions. Different organizations may use varying definitions and metrics for ESG factors, leading to difficulties in benchmarking and comparison. Moreover, regulatory requirements continue to evolve, compelling businesses to continuously update their data collection and processing systems to maintain compliance. Without a well-orchestrated data governance framework, organizations risk making strategic decisions based on unreliable ESG insights, potentially leading to reputational and financial consequences (Elamer & Boulhaga, 2024; Sharma et al., 2023).

To overcome these challenges, businesses must implement robust data management practices, leverage AI-driven automation for data validation, and ensure cross-departmental collaboration to maintain consistency and accuracy in ESG reporting. Establishing clear data ownership, audit trails, and real-time monitoring systems can further enhance the integrity of ESG data processing, enabling organizations to generate more trustworthy insights for investors and stakeholders.

Several platforms help organizations structure, analyze, and report ESG data effectively. Workiva provides a cloud-based system that integrates ESG and financial reporting, supporting frameworks such as GRI, SASB, CSRD, and TCFD, with built-in automation for data collection and audit trails (Workiva, 2025). Sphera ESG Performance focuses on tracking carbon emissions, energy usage, and regulatory compliance, offering integration with ERP systems like SAP and Oracle (Sphera, 2025). Novisto supports ESG reporting and materiality assessments, incorporating AI-driven insights to improve data validation (Novisto, 2025). For organizations in industries with environmental, health, and safety (EHS) considerations, Cority Sustainability Cloud combines risk management, compliance tracking, and data visualization. These platforms provide structured approaches to ESG data management, helping organizations navigate regulatory requirements and improve sustainability reporting (Cority, 2025). These platforms can help to empower businesses to efficiently manage ESG data, enhance transparency, and meet evolving regulatory demands. However, while these tools offer valuable automation and analytical capabilities, the responsibility for interpreting the data, making strategic decisions, and ensuring alignment with broader sustainability goals remains with the organization. Effective ESG management requires not just reliable data systems but also a clear understanding of the underlying domain knowledge, industry context, and company-specific priorities to ensure that insights lead to meaningful action.

4.4 Comparing ESG Ratings: Why Different Agencies Score Differently

ESG rating aims to help investors identify material ESG factors. Various rating agencies provide data analytics services and create rankings and ratings. The following section introduces a few widely used rating approaches. Bloomberg, for example, is widely used in the financial community. Bloomberg ESG provides ESG disclosure scores based on publicly available company-reported data, integrating sustainability factors into financial analysis (Bloomberg, 2025). CDP, formerly known as the Carbon Disclosure Project, is a non-profit organization that develops and operates an ESG disclosure system. CDP Scores assess corporate environmental transparency and performance, focusing on climate change, water security, and deforestation through standardized disclosure questionnaires (CDP, 2025). ISS ESG offers governance-focused ESG ratings, integrating sustainability factors into corporate governance assessments and institutional investor voting policies.

Within the London Stock Exchange Group (LSEG), there are two primary ESG scoring systems. FTSE Russell ESG Ratings evaluate companies across 14 ESG themes, providing industry-specific scores to help investors assess sustainability performance (LSEG, 2025b). The other LSEG (formerly known as Refinitiv) ESG Scores rank companies on a 0-100 scale, analyzing over 630 ESG measures across 10 themes to assess performance and risk exposure. Both scoring systems operate independently within LSEG, offering investors distinct methodologies and insights into companies' ESG practices (LSEG, 2025a).

Other important rating agencies include Morningstar Sustainalytics, which assesses a company's exposure and management of material sustainability issues to measure unmanaged ESG risks (Sustainalytics, 2025). MSCI ESG Ratings evaluate firms' resilience to long-term ESG risks, ranking them on a AAA to CCC scale relative to their industry peers (MSCI, 2025). S&P Global ESG Ratings, based on the Corporate Sustainability Assessment (CSA), gauge ESG performance using a combination of public data and direct company engagement (S&P Global, 2025).

A slightly different approach is taken by RepRisk, which utilizes AI-driven analysis of external sources, including media and NGO reports, to identify ESG risks and controversies in real time. The company emphasizes that the purpose of RepRisk's dataset is not to provide ESG ratings but to systematically identify and assess material ESG risks (RepRisk, 2025). Together, these agencies hold a significant market share and are widely used by major financial institutions. However, it is important to note that many other ESG rating providers exist, some of which may offer high-quality data, particularly in specialized niche areas. For example, Ecovadis for supply chain ESG ratings (EcoVadis, 2025).

Table 4.1 provides a comparison of widely used ESG ratings based on publicly available data and company information. While not an exhaustive analysis, this overview highlights some key features to offer insight into different methodologies. It aims to provide insight into the differences in methodology and approach among ESG rating providers, highlighting how each may be suited to different use cases. Each approach has its own strengths and limitations.

Qualitative data in ESG ratings might provide in-depth insights into company policies, governance structures, and stakeholder engagement, which numerical scores alone may overlook. This allows for a more nuanced evaluation of ESG risks and opportunities, particularly in corporate culture and ethical decision-making areas. However, qualitative assessments can be subjective and inconsistent as they often rely on analysts' interpretations and may vary across rating agencies. Timeliness can also be an issue, as updates to qualitative ESG data are not always frequent or standardized, leading to potential lags in reflecting recent corporate actions,

Table 4.1 Overview of Important ESG Rating Providers

	Bloomberg	*CDP Scores*	*FTSE Russell ESG Ratings*	*ISS*	*LSEG workplace*	*RepRisk*	*Morningstar Sustainalytics*	*MSCI*	*S&P Global*
Values/ Grades Format	*0–100 (best)*	*A (best) to F*	*0–5 (best)*	*1 (best) to 10 and D– to A+ (best)*	*0–100 (best) and D– to A+ (best)*	*AAA (best) to D*	*0–100 (best)*	*AAA (best) to CCC*	*0–100 (best)*
Approach	Proprietary ESG disclosure scores based on publicly available data. Focuses on company-disclosed ESG metrics rather than questionnaires.	Climate change questionnaire based on Disclosure, Awareness, Management, and Leadership	ESG ratings based on 14 themes across environmental, social, and governance pillars	12-level grading system; each pillar has a different weight depending on the regional impact on governance practice	630 company-level ESG measures, which are grouped into 10 categories and standards of reporting	AI-driven approach using external data sources (news, social media, NGO reports).	37 key ESG issues and ten material themes; specific sector weight varies by industry, with a specific weight placed on each issue	Utilizes AI-based scoring and alternative data. Evaluates country. industry, leaders, mutual funds, and ETFs.	S&P Global Corporate Sustainability Assessment (CSA), filled annually by companies, is based on a quantitative analysis
Sector segregation	Cross-sector	Tailored; 12 sectors	Tailored; industry-specific scores	Tailored; 40 sectors	Tailored; 10 sectors	Cross-sector	Tailored; 40 sectors	Cross-sector; 158 sectors	Tailored; 60 sectors
Focuses on	Transparency and ESG disclosure	Transparency and performance	ESG risk and performance benchmarking	Risks management	Transparency and data-driven	Risk exposure to ESG controversies	Risk-based assessment, exposure to unmanaged risks; specific weight on each issue.	Risk-based	Impact; corporate ESG performance

Coverage	~15,000 companies	over 22,000 companies	~8,000 companies	8,100 companies 28,000 funds	~16,000 companies	~290,000 companies (public & private)	over 16,000 companies	over 2,900 companies	over 16,000 companies
Strength	Strong data reliability from financial disclosures	Provides large coverage for emissions data.	Comprehensive scoring framework	Offers detailed governance data.	Offers historical data dating back to 2002.	Real-time monitoring of ESG risks	Considers sector-specific factors and unpredictable risks.	Provides qualitative reports accompanying data collection; feedback is supported to adjust.	Assists companies new to ESG more efficiently.
Weakness	Limited qualitative analysis	Data can be spotty as not every company reports on CDP	Industry weighting may impact comparability across sectors	Has been criticized as being "too strict" by investors and rated companies (McKinsey, 2022)	Reassesses metrics regularly, leading to inconsistent metrics over time	Relies on external sources, not company-reported data	Risk-Based Approach	Low correlation to other ESG ratings; No differentiation among sectors; Risk-based Approach	Industry-specific scores (can't be compared cross-sector)

controversies, or policy changes. Some agencies update their ratings annually (e.g., S&P Global, CDP), while others provide real-time monitoring (e.g., RepRisk, ISS ESG Controversies). Additionally, qualitative data lacks standardization and can be challenging to compare across industries, making it less reliable for benchmarking ESG performance across different sectors (Pillai et al., 2025).

Providers that follow a qualitative analysis, which includes ratings such as Bloomberg ESG, rely heavily on company-reported data, potentially missing qualitative risk factors. Overall, a lack of standardization can be observed. Scores vary widely across providers, leading to a low correlation between ESG ratings from different agencies (Berg et al., 2022; McKinsey, 2022). At the same time, the diversity in ESG ratings might allow for different perspectives on sustainability performance, catering to various investor priorities. While scores vary widely across providers, this variation reflects the evolving nature of ESG assessments and the continuous improvement of methodologies.

Many rating agencies, such as Sustainalytics, and S&P ESG Ratings, offer public access to rating data on their websites. This information is valuable for various stakeholders—employees and job seekers can assess their employers, companies can review their own ratings, and businesses can evaluate competitors or potential partners. Some finance information providers also include ESG ratings in their company profiles, such as Yahoo! Finance, which has ESG ratings from Sustainalytics (Sustainalytics, 2020).

However, the publicly available data comes with limitations. It may not be user-friendly and often lacks advanced functionality. Features such as extended search capabilities, screening tools, and access to historical or, in some cases, the most up-to-date data are typically restricted behind paywalls. This makes conducting comprehensive screenings, sector comparisons, or in-depth analyses challenging. Additionally, publicly accessible ESG ratings often provide only a high-level overview, with more detailed insights locked behind subscription-based services. These premium features—including advanced analytics, detailed reports, and API access—can come at a significant cost. As the demand for up-to-date ESG data grows across various process steps within organizations, accessing professional data services can represent a significant cost for large organizations—though they may be able to manage it due to their greater financial resources. However, for smaller organizations, individuals, and non-profits, these costs can be prohibitive, limiting their ability to access the full data.

Data vendors and rating agencies serve as intermediaries in this process. While most ESG ratings are based on data that companies publicly disclose—such as reports published on corporate websites—it is impractical for individual investors or other stakeholders to gather and analyze this information on a large scale. Initiatives and non-profits like Dataland and CDP contribute to enhancing access to sustainability data, though their impact varies due to differences in scale and comprehensiveness.

Dataland is a relatively new platform that aims to address issues such as data gaps, quality concerns, usage restrictions, and high costs associated with sustainability data. Launched on January 24, 2024, Dataland positions itself as a neutral platform facilitating the exchange of ESG data among users from the financial sector, academia, NGOs, public institutions, and private sector data providers. The platform aspires to create an ecosystem where sustainability data is openly accessible, cost-effective, and standardized, offering an alternative to profit-driven data aggregators. However, as a recent entrant, Dataland's reach and data coverage are still developing (Dataland, 2025).

CDP (formerly the Carbon Disclosure Project) is a well-established international non-profit organization that operates a global environmental disclosure system. Founded in 2000, CDP collects self-reported environmental data from companies, cities, states, and regions, focusing on areas such as climate change, deforestation, and water security (CDP, n.d.). CDP's extensive dataset empowers investors, companies, and governments to make informed decisions regarding environmental action. Despite its broad coverage, the depth and quality of data can vary, as not all companies provide comprehensive disclosures (PCAF & CDP, 2023; Segal, 2024).

In summary, while initiatives like Dataland and CDP play important roles in improving access to sustainability data, their impact is influenced by factors such as the platform's maturity, the scale of data collection, and the comprehensiveness of the data provided. Users seeking sustainability information should consider these factors when utilizing these resources.

The ecosystem and technology are still evolving, and several ways exist to tackle the underlying issue. Chapter 5 of this book presents the data mesh as an alternative to data vendors. Instead of relying on a centralized provider, it adopts a decentralized approach. In this model, domain teams take ownership and responsibility for their data.

Timeliness is another issue in the context of ESG data and corresponding ESG ratings. Some ESG ratings are only updated once yearly, while the update frequency is more often (e.g., weekly or triggered whenever new data is available). However, even if the calculation for the particular ESG rating has a high update frequency, it might still be an issue that the underlying data isn't. A significant amount of data used for ESG rating calculation comes with the company's annual report. As the name "annual report" already suggests, once per year is already not a particularly high frequency. However, preparing the annual reports themselves requires some time in the organization, including various checks, e.g., for quality and legal compliance. This can imply that the reported data is already a few months old on the day of publication, making access to timely information challenging. Some authors argue that current ESG ratings are more descriptive of the past and present status but might have limited predictive quality for future financial performance (Shrestha, 2024).

Risk management is an important driver of the need for timely information. Studies have identified a strong negative relationship between ESG controversies and firm performance, highlighting their detrimental effects on businesses (Elamer & Boulhaga, 2024). Diversifying the data collection process can be a good strategy. Digital listening complements traditional ESG reporting by providing early warnings for crises and reputation risks while offering real-time insights into stakeholder sentiment. Organizations can strategically use this information to make more informed decisions and enhance their ESG strategies and brand management (Xia, 2024).

While it was shown that controversies and firm performance have a negative relationship. It should also be mentioned that this relationship is not uniform and is significantly shaped by corporate governance factors such as board independence, gender diversity, and internal ESG practices (Elamer & Boulhaga, 2024).

Quality and timeliness are crucial for further processing and insight generation. In fact, having complete and timely data available for reporting and exchange with rating agencies can improve the ESG rating. Some rating agencies give a dedicated score for the company's transparency level (e.g., Transparency Level Rating: 0–20%—very low, 20–40%—low, 40–60%—medium, 60–80%—high, 80–100%—very high) or governance scores.

4.5 Beyond Ratings: Integrating ESG Data into Corporate Strategy

Insights gained from ESG data can be a very valuable resource, and their importance for informed managerial decisions shouldn't be underestimated—beyond the mandatory compliance reporting and disclosure obligations. It provides insights into supply chain vulnerabilities, operational inefficiencies, and reputation risks, allowing businesses to address them proactively. Companies with strong ESG performance often gain a competitive edge by appealing to ESG-conscious investors, customers, and partners. Evidence suggests that strong ESG practices enhance investors' perceptions of a company's value creation potential. However, only robust corporate governance can protect stakeholders by mitigating the negative impact of ESG controversies on business performance. While ESG investments can improve market performance and corporate reputation, companies must be mindful that media-publicized controversies are not offset by ESG engagement alone. Additionally, social initiatives may amplify the negative effects of ESG controversies, as market participants may view them skeptically, potentially associating them with social washing rather than genuine commitment (Keidann Soschinski et al., 2024).

Research shows that ESG controversies negatively impact a company's performance. However, strong corporate governance structures and well-implemented ESG strategies can help reduce these negative effects. In some cases, they even turn challenges into opportunities for growth and reputation improvement (Elamer & Boulhaga, 2024).

The Stakeholder Purpose Framework is an example of an impact-driven governance approach, which integrates an organization's purpose with stakeholder interests and uses measurable ESG metrics to assess long-term value creation. This approach aligns with stakeholder capitalism and sustainable business strategies, where companies go beyond financial performance to consider their broader societal and environmental impact. It also reflects principles from corporate purpose alignment, strategic ESG integration, and value-based decision-making in business (Freedman, 2010; Keidann Soschinski et al., 2024).

Firms with a higher proportion of independent directors demonstrate greater resilience to the negative impacts of ESG controversies, while gender diversity on boards also plays a mitigating role. Additionally, well-established internal ESG frameworks can transform these challenges into opportunities, fostering organizational growth and enhancing reputation (Elamer & Boulhaga, 2024).

4.6 Discussion and Recommendations

The evolution of ESG reporting continues to be shaped by multiple regulatory developments, technological advancements, and stakeholder expectations. While demand for standardized ESG data is increasing, significant gaps in data consistency, comparability, and reliability persist. As regulatory frameworks shift toward mandatory disclosures, organizations must proactively address these challenges to improve ESG data quality and enhance investor confidence. Some ask for more detailed and timelier ESG reporting, even discussing including other aspects like tax payment as the fourth pillar in the ESG framework (Koukoulioti, 2024). Others call for reduced reporting requirements to support businesses and stay competitive globally. Overall, it seems advisable to implement adequate measures and pay particular attention to how the data underlying ESG ratings are generated. While ESG ratings serve as a benchmark for sustainability performance, their true value lies in informing strategic business decisions. Companies that effectively integrate ESG insights into their corporate strategy can enhance resilience, drive innovation, and create long-term value for stakeholders.

Organizations should align their ESG reporting with globally recognized standards, such as GRI, SASB, and TCFD, to enhance comparability and transparency. Establishing an internal ESG governance committee can help enforce consistency across business units. The variability in ESG rating methodologies across providers presents challenges for stakeholders attempting to assess corporate sustainability performance. While some agencies emphasize financial disclosures, others rely on alternative datasets or real-time controversies. To mitigate the risks of misinterpretation, companies must take a proactive stance in managing their ESG narrative.

One of the key limitations of current ESG ratings is their retrospective nature. ESG data is often based on annual disclosures, which may not reflect recent sustainability initiatives or emerging risks. To enhance the predictive quality of ESG metrics, companies should prioritize continuous data updates and scenario-based forecasting. As ESG reporting transitions from voluntary disclosure to a regulated framework, companies must proactively adapt to evolving standards and investor expectations. By implementing robust ESG data management practices, engaging strategically with rating agencies, and integrating ESG insights into corporate decision-making, businesses can enhance sustainability performance and drive long-term value creation. Organizations that fail to address these critical aspects risk reputational and financial consequences in an increasingly ESG-conscious investment landscape. ESG management covers various aspects, many of which are long-term, strategic in nature, and of vital importance to the company.

References

Berg, F., Kölbel, J. F., & Rigobon, R. (2022). Aggregate Confusion: The Divergence of ESG Ratings. *Review of Finance*, *26*(6), 1315–1344. https://doi.org/10.1093/rof/rfac033

Bloomberg. (2025). *ESG Data | Bloomberg Professional Services*. https://www.bloomberg.com/professional/products/data/enterprise-catalog/esg/

Cafagna, G., & Tocchini, F. (2022, March 18). *The 5 Biggest Hurdles to Effective ESG Reporting*. Wolters Kluwer's Expert Insights. https://www.wolterskluwer.com/en/expert-insights/the-5-biggest-hurdles-to-effective-esg-reporting

CDP. (n.d.). *CDP's Alignment with Disclosure Frameworks and Standards*. Retrieved March 15, 2025, from https://www.cdp.net/en/about/framework-alignment

CDP. (2025). *Our Question Bank*. https://www.cdp.net

Cority. (2025). *Sustainability Cloud – Cority*. https://www.cority.com/sustainability-cloud/

Dataland. (2025). *Dataland*. https://dataland.com/about

EcoVadis. (2025). *The Leading Sustainability Intelligence Platform for Global Supply Chains*. EcoVadis. https://ecovadis.com/

Elamer, A. A., & Boulhaga, M. (2024). ESG Controversies and Corporate Performance: The Moderating Effect of Governance Mechanisms and ESG Practices. *Corporate Social Responsibility and Environmental Management*, *31*(4), 3312–3327. https://doi.org/10.1002/csr.2749

Endress, T. (2025). Digital Procurement and Sustainability Along the Value Chain. In D. Galipeau & T. Endress (Eds.), *A Practical Approach to Digital Technologies for Sustainability*. Taylor & Francis.

Endress, T., & Badir, Y. F. (Eds.). (2023). *Business and Management in Asia: Digital Innovation and Sustainability*. Springer Nature.

Freedman, D. (2010). *Statistical Models and Causal Inference: A Dialogue with the Social Sciences*. Cambridge University Press.

Galipeau, D., & Endress, T. (Eds.). (2025). *A Practical Approach to Digital Technologies for Sustainability*. Taylor & Francis.

Global Reporting Initiative. (2021). *GRI Standards English Language*. https://www.globalreporting.org/how-to-use-the-gri-standards/gri-standards-english-language/

IFRS Foundation. (2023, July). *IFRS - ISSB and TCFD*. https://www.ifrs.org/sustainability/tcfd/

Keidann Soschinski, C., Mazzioni, S., Baú Dal Magro, C., & Leite, M. (2024). Corporate Controversies and Market-to-Book: The Moderating Role of ESG Practices. *Review of Business Management*, *26*(1), 1–18. https://doi.org/10.7819/rbgn.v26i01.4255

Koukoulioti, V. (2024). T for Taxation: The Fourth Pillar in the ESG Framework. *eJournal of Tax Research*, *22*(3), 420–443.

LSEG. (2025a). *ESG Data | Company Data*. https://www.lseg.com/en/data-analytics/financial-data/company-data/esg-data

LSEG. (2025b, March 10). *FTSE Russell ESG Scores*. https://www.lseg.com/en/ftse-russell/esg-scores

McKinsey. (2022). *ESG Ratings McKinsey and Company 2022*. McKinsey & Company. https://issanet.org/content/uploads/2022/08/McKinsey-ratings_extract.pdf

MSCI. (2025). *ESG Ratings—MSCI*. https://www.msci.com/web/msci/esg-ratings

Novisto. (2025). *Next-Generation Sustainability Management Software*. Novisto. https://novisto.com/

PCAF & CDP. (2023, June). *The Importance of Data Quality in the Journey Toward Decarbonization*. https://cdn.cdp.net/cdp-production/comfy/cms/files/files/000/008/135/original/Importance_of_data_quality_21.6_Final.pdf

Pillai, R., Islam, M. A., Sreejith, S., & Al-Malkawi, H. A. (2025). Comparative Analysis of Environmental, Social and Governance (ESG) Ratings: Do Sectors and Regions Differ? *Journal of Management and Governance*, *29*(1), 69–109. https://doi.org/10.1007/s10997-023-09692-7

RepRisk. (2025). *Repick | Approach*. https://www.reprisk.com/approach

S&P Global. (2025). *Corporate Sustainability Assessment | S&P Global*. https://www.spglobal.com/esg/csa/

SASB. (2022, August 1). About us. *SASB*. https://sasb.ifrs.org/about/

Segal, M. (2024, June 4). *CDP Launches New Sustainability Reporting Platform Aligned with IFRS Climate Disclosure Standard*. ESG Today. https://www.esgtoday.com/cdp-aligns-new-sustainability-reporting-platform-aligned-with-ifrs-climate-disclosure-standard/

Sharma, A., Sheth, U., & Gandhi, N. (2023). How Greenwashing Impairs Environment, Social and Governance (ESG) Investing. *Aweshkar Research Journal*, *30*(2), 69–80.

Shrestha, N. (2024). *The Impact of ESG Scores on the Financial Profitability of Companies in the Automotive Industry* [Master Thesis]. Asian Institute of Technology.

Sphera. (2025). What We Do. *Sphera*. https://sphera.com/company/what-we-do/

Sustainalytics. (2020, July 23). *Sustainalytics Makes its ESG Ratings and Data on More Than 4,000 Companies Publicly Accessible on its Website*. Sustainalytics.Com. https://www.sustainalytics.com/esg-news/news-details/2020/07/22/sustainalytics-makes-its-esg-ratings-and-data-on-more-than-4-000-companies-publicly-accessible-on-its-website

Sustainalytics. (2025). *Company ESG Risk Ratings and scores—Sustainalytics*. Sustainalytics.Com. https://www.sustainalytics.com/esg-ratings

Workiva. (2025). *Workiva | Software for Sustainability, GRC & Financial Reporting*. https://www.workiva.com/

Xia, J. (2024). Building Sustainable Brands in the Digital Age: Integrating New Media and ESG. *Journal of Social Science Humanities and Literature*, *7*(4), 69–75. https://doi.org/10.53469/jsshl.2024.07(04).12

Chapter 5

Utilizing the Data Mesh Paradigm to Address ESG Data Management Challenges

David Feierabend, Jacob Binder, and Dennis Schlegel

The data mesh offers a novel solution to these challenges by moving away from a centralized structure to a decentralized approach. In the data mesh model, ownership and responsibility for data are assigned to domain teams—those closest to the data—who are best equipped to handle and interpret it. This not only resolves scalability and access issues but also ensures that data are used more effectively within its context. By embracing a decentralized, technology-agnostic approach, the data mesh can significantly improve ESG data management, leading to better decision-making and more reliable reporting.

5.1 Introduction

There is a global shift that permanently changes the way ESG data are used. The velocity and continuous development of data requirements and regulatory expectations are significantly increasing. Many companies are struggling because they lack a coherent approach to ESG data management, do not have the necessary

DOI: 10.1201/9781003528951-5

embedded data culture to manage sustainability-related issues, lack an understanding of regulatory requirements and assurance of ESG data, and do not have the necessary technology strategies to address these ESG data-related challenges (ESG Working Group, 2024).

As the importance of ESG data grows, effective ESG data management will become increasingly essential for organizations aiming to report on their use of natural, social, human, intellectual, and financial resources. Accurate ESG data are necessary for organizations to demonstrate how their operations impact society and to show that ESG measures have been successfully integrated into their business processes and strategies. However, there is some skepticism about whether current ESG data and reports truly reflect organizations' ESG performance. Many argue that the quality of the data is often questionable, which also raises concerns about the reporting accuracy (Clark et al., 2019).

This chapter explores the various challenges ESG data present for data management, as well as how the data mesh paradigm may be able to address these challenges. First, we provide a detailed explanation of the data mesh to better understand its potential. Second, we delve into specific issues related to data governance, data quality, data integration and interoperability, and data architecture. These challenges are categorized and defined according to the Data Management Body of Knowledge Framework (DAMA International, 2017). For each challenge, we then propose possible solutions using the data mesh approach.

5.2 Data Mesh

The data mesh approach offers organizations greater flexibility and scalability, enabling them to manage their data more efficiently and adapt to changing demands. Introduced by Zhamak Dehghani in 2019, the data mesh provides a decentralized alternative to traditional, centralized data management systems. This shift is especially relevant for complex data environments like ESG, where data comes from diverse sources and involves multiple stakeholders (Dehghani, 2019). By decentralizing data ownership, the data mesh reduces the strain on central data teams and avoids common issues like bottlenecks and fragile pipelines (McNally & Gorcenski, 2022).

The key idea behind the data mesh is to give ownership for data to the teams closest to it—instead of pooling data in a single centralized storage—and ensuring they can manage, interpret, and use it effectively. This approach is built around four core principles: domain-oriented decentralized data ownership, treating data as a product, self-service data infrastructure, and federated governance (Dehghani, 2020). Together, these principles create a scalable and efficient data management system, which is particularly useful for improving ESG data management.

5.2.1 Domain-Oriented Decentralized Data Ownership and Architecture

Domain ownership is a core tenet of the data mesh. It shifts responsibility from centralized data management teams to decentralized, interdisciplinary teams within specific domains, which, for example, may be organized by business functions such as HR, procurement, or marketing. These domain teams, composed of developers, data engineers, and subject matter experts, are accountable for their data products (Dolhopolov et al., 2024). By giving domain teams ownership of their data products, the data mesh leverages their in-depth, domain-specific expertise to improve data management and decision-making. The goal is to align data structures with the company's organizational structure, allowing for better integration of analytical data (Dehghani, 2020). In this decentralized model, domain knowledge is essential for understanding complex technical relationships and ensures that data is treated as an integral part of the operational ecosystem (Bode et al., 2023).

5.2.2 Data as a Product

In the data mesh, data is treated as a product, meaning domain teams must ensure that their data is usable, reliable, and discoverable by other teams in the organization (Hasan & Legner, 2023). A data product is a combination of data, metadata, code, and infrastructure, used by downstream users to generate business value. It serves as the foundation of the data mesh, enabling businesses to analyze and combine data with business knowledge for data-driven decisions. Data products can range from simple datasets to complex data aggregations and can even produce other data products across domains. Ultimately, they are essential tools for companies striving to answer key questions and drive insights (Tartow & Mott, 2024). Each domain team owns the responsibility for the quality, security, and accessibility of their data products (Driessen et al., 2023). By adopting product thinking, teams ensure that their data serves a specific purpose and is readily available to internal users. This shifts the focus from simply managing data to optimizing its value and usability across the organization (Azeroual & Nacheva, 2023).

5.2.3 Self-Serve Data Infrastructure as a Platform

A self-serve infrastructure is essential for enabling domain teams to build, manage, and operate data products independently. However, replicating infrastructure for each domain would be inefficient. Instead, the data mesh approach promotes the development of a unified data platform layer that reduces complexity and allows teams to focus on creating quality data products rather than the technical details (Dehghani, 2020). This unified infrastructure simplifies the creation, maintenance, and monitoring of data pipelines by hiding repetitive engineering tasks behind an easy-to-use interface (Dolhopolov et al., 2024). A well-implemented self-serve platform allows teams to work autonomously while ensuring that data management remains efficient and scalable (Ashraf et al., 2023).

5.2.4 Federated Computational Governance

Governance is a critical component of data mesh. Federated computational governance ensures that decentralized domain teams adhere to shared policies on data interoperability, security, and compliance. Unlike traditional centralized governance models, which can be rigid and slow to adapt, federated governance distributes decision-making authority across domain teams and ensures that global standards are met (Dolhopolov et al., 2024). Data mesh integrates these governance mechanisms into the infrastructure, enabling automated enforcement of policies (Azeroual & Nacheva, 2023). The balance between decentralization and standardization is crucial for maintaining the flexibility needed for innovation while preventing data silos and ensuring consistency across the organization.

Taken together, the data mesh paradigm offers a paradigm shift in how organizations handle data, moving from centralized to decentralized data management. By aligning data ownership with domain knowledge, treating data as a product, providing self-serve infrastructure, and implementing federated governance, data mesh enables organizations to create scalable, efficient, and adaptable data ecosystems. This approach helps break down monolithic data structures and encourages a more collaborative and decentralized way of managing data, which is especially beneficial for addressing the growing complexities of ESG data management (Dehghani, 2019).

5.3 ESG Data Management Challenges

This section provides an overview of the current challenges in ESG data management and explores how the data mesh paradigm can address these issues. We examine the potential of the data mesh to tackle key obstacles by focusing on four main areas: data governance, data quality, data integration and interoperability, and data architecture. In each of these categories, specific challenges are identified and discussed. An overview is provided in Figure 5.1.

5.3.1 Data Governance

Data governance refers to the exercise of authority and control over data assets, including their planning, monitoring, and management. It serves as the foundation for all other data management activities, ensuring that decisions related to data, people, and processes are made in a structured and regulated way. Effective

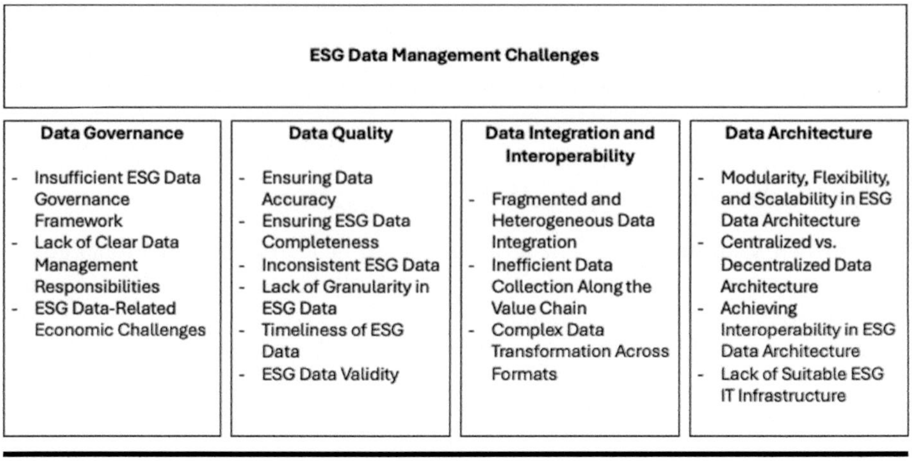

Figure 5.1 ESG data management challenges.

data governance enables organizations to maximize the value of their data while ensuring that operations comply with relevant regulatory requirements (DAMA International, 2017).

5.3.1.1 Insufficient ESG Data Governance Framework

The absence of an adequate data governance framework is a key issue in ESG data management. ESG data require specialized governance structures, but many organizations either lack these or use frameworks unsuitable for handling the complexity and regulatory demands of sustainability data (Liakh, 2021). This deficiency impacts data accuracy, compliance, and accessibility. The complexity of ESG data, coupled with an evolving regulatory landscape, increases pressure on companies to continuously adapt their governance systems (Young In et al., 2019).

Organizations must align their data governance with new legal regulations and frameworks, adding another layer of complexity (Liu et al., 2023). Regulatory requirements, along with the need to communicate ESG performance to stakeholders such as investors, demand robust governance. Traditional centralized governance frameworks often struggle to keep pace with the rapidly changing ESG landscape, leaving organizations ill-equipped to ensure their data management systems support sustainability strategies and regulatory compliance (Hansen et al., 2020).

The data mesh paradigm offers a flexible, decentralized approach to ESG data governance. Unlike centralized systems, data mesh distributes governance responsibilities to data product owners, giving them autonomy over their respective data. ESG data become a product with clear ownership and accountability, enabling local governance decisions that can adapt to regulatory changes and internal policies more easily.

This decentralized model helps ensure that ESG data align with legal and policy frameworks. Federated computational governance within data mesh allows product owners to transparently manage and communicate governance rules, ensuring compliance with external regulations. This transparency is crucial for stakeholders demanding clarity on how ESG data are governed and meet legal standards.

As the relevance of ESG data grows, transparent and accountable governance becomes more critical. The data mesh framework equips organizations with the ability to manage their ESG data effectively, continuously adapting governance practices to meet evolving legal frameworks while ensuring compliance and flexibility.

5.3.1.2 Lack of Clear Data Management Responsibilities

A major challenge in ESG data governance is the lack of clear responsibility across various departments. ESG data span multiple areas, making it difficult to define who is accountable for its management. Clear stewardship roles are essential for overseeing data quality, management, and accessibility. However, differing expectations from various stakeholders make it harder to assign responsibility (Liakh, 2021). Furthermore, ownership of data and associated technologies is often unclear, hindering effective data utilization (Young In et al., 2019).

Without clearly assigned ownership, ESG data often fail to reach those who can turn it into actionable insights (Reisi et al., 2020). This fragmented governance leads to ambiguous goals and missed opportunities to leverage ESG data for strategic decision-making (Park, 2023). Moreover, accessibility remains a significant hurdle, with key decision-makers often lacking the access they need (Peças et al., 2023). The challenge is further complicated by the need to engage both domain experts and operational managers in data governance, a process that is difficult due to the cross-departmental nature of ESG data.

The data mesh paradigm addresses these challenges by decentralizing data ownership and embedding responsibilities within specific data products. Unlike traditional systems, where data ownership is often a by-product of operational activities, data mesh assigns clear ownership to each data product. This ensures that every data product has a designated owner responsible for its storage, quality, and access.

This boundary-driven approach simplifies governance, particularly in federated environments like ESG data. Self-service access through data catalogs or marketplaces further streamlines data accessibility, reducing reliance on IT teams. By making data more accessible to those with domain expertise, data mesh enhances the evaluation, contextualization, and utilization of ESG data.

Through the use of domain-specific knowledge, data mesh improves the quality and usability of ESG data. Domain owners classify data according to quality standards and protection status, making it easier for users to assess its reliability and timeliness. This system ensures that ESG data are not only accessible but also suitable for decision-making, with domain experts providing the context in which the data should be used. As a result, data mesh directly improves data quality and governance, enabling more efficient use of ESG data across the organization.

5.3.1.3 ESG Data-Related Economic Challenges

Managing ESG data are expensive, with costs related to gathering, processing, and governance often outweighing direct financial returns. This makes it difficult to justify the investment, particularly for smaller organizations. Establishing in-house ESG capabilities and governance structures, as well as integrating ESG systems, are costly undertakings (Galeotti et al., 2023). The complexity of managing ESG data, combined with rising costs for compliance and system integration, further exacerbates this financial burden.

For smaller companies with limited resources, these economic challenges make it harder to ensure the availability and quality of ESG data. This financial strain can create an "ESG data gap," where organizations are unable to collect comprehensive and reliable data due to the high costs (Young In et al., 2019). The additional financial requirements for governance programs can overwhelm resource-constrained organizations, especially small- and mid-cap companies (Visalli et al., 2023).

The data mesh offers a solution to these economic challenges by enabling greater financial accountability through federated governance. With data mesh, ownership and management of ESG data are distributed across domains, making it easier to track and manage costs associated with each data product. This decentralized model allows organizations to demonstrate the financial investment required for ESG data while optimizing costs across departments.

A key advantage of data mesh is its ability to introduce federated computational governance, which helps control costs for high-value ESG data projects. By improving cost clarity and cost separation, organizations can allocate resources more efficiently. Additionally, decentralizing ownership and responsibility reduces the formation of shadow IT systems, which can arise from inefficient data management and lead to increased risks and unforeseen costs.

By enhancing compliance and improving governance transparency, data mesh mitigates the financial risks associated with ESG data management. This approach not only reduces costs but also ensures that ESG data are governed effectively, reducing long-term financial burdens while supporting better decision-making.

5.3.2 Data Quality

For successful data management and the provision of data for the respective business needs, the value of the data, i.e., its high quality, is essential and usually an underlying assumption. The goal of all data management disciplines is to contribute to the quality of data (DAMA International, 2017).

5.3.2.1 Ensuring Data Accuracy

Data accuracy is crucial for ESG reporting, as it supports sustainability strategies and reliable decision-making (Liakh, 2021). Inaccurate data can undermine the credibility of reports and lead to flawed insights (Wanner & Janiesch, 2019). Ensuring ESG data accuracy is challenging due to the complex, multi-stakeholder nature of data collection, with errors often occurring along the value chain, distorting the calculation of ESG impacts and making it difficult to draw valid conclusions (Tamym et al., 2023).

The data mesh improves accuracy by decentralizing data ownership to domain experts who best understand the data's context. These experts can assess and classify data accuracy, providing transparent evaluations. Additionally, enhanced collaboration across the value chain reduces errors and misreporting. This results in more accurate ESG data, better insights, and improved sustainability performance. The Mesh also increases accountability, ensuring data is managed with a strong focus on quality.

5.3.2.2 Ensuring ESG Data Completeness

Completeness is key to the reliability of ESG data and its impact assessments. Incomplete data can lead to inaccurate sustainability evaluations (Landolfi et al., 2019). ESG data often come from diverse, federated sources, making it difficult for organizations to ensure that all necessary data is fully captured and populated (Galeotti et al., 2023).

The data mesh decentralizes governance, giving data product owners the responsibility to define and enforce completeness rules. Domain experts can assess which data points are essential, ensuring that all necessary data is included. This approach increases transparency, as users can see whether data is complete or optional. The data mesh improves trust in ESG reporting and helps manage the completeness of datasets more effectively, leading to higher quality sustainability reporting.

5.3.2.3 Inconsistent ESG Data

A key challenge in ESG data management is inconsistency, both within companies and when comparing ESG data across organizations. Differences in reporting frameworks and structures make it difficult to assess and benchmark ESG performance accurately, hindering effective decision-making (Visalli et al., 2023). The lack of standardized reporting adds to the complexity, reducing the reliability of ESG data for both internal use and external comparison (Kotsantonis & Serafeim, 2019).

The data mesh helps address data consistency by enforcing clear governance standards and domain-specific ownership. By assigning data product responsibility to domain experts, ESG data can be standardized before exposure, ensuring uniformity across data sets. The Mesh's focus on standardizing interfaces and protocols improves internal data consistency and facilitates cross-company comparisons. With clear ownership, domain experts can also quickly identify and fix inconsistencies, leading to more reliable ESG data and better decision-making.

5.3.2.4 Lack of Granularity in ESG Data

The demand for more precise and granular ESG data has been widely recognized, yet improvements in this area have been slow (Luoma et al., 2023). Greater granularity is crucial for better decision-making but remains a challenge due to limited precision in current data (Wanner & Janiesch, 2019).

The data mesh can enhance ESG data granularity by promoting better communication between domains about data requirements based on the data-sharing principle. By aligning on the necessary precision and granularity before data products are published, the data mesh ensures that ESG data meet organizational needs and address existing gaps, improving data quality and utility.

5.3.2.5 Timeliness of ESG Data

Timeliness is a critical aspect of ESG data quality, impacting the value of sustainability indicators and the effectiveness of decision-making (Liakh, 2021). It is not just about how up-to-date the data is, but also how relevant it remains over time, depending on its volatility (Galeotti et al., 2023).

The data mesh enhances timeliness by enabling self-service access and domain-specific governance. Domain experts can better assess how time-sensitive the data is, while improved data discoverability reduces dependence on centralized teams, making ESG data available more quickly for decision-makers.

5.3.2.6 ESG Data Validity

Due to the diverse formats and standards of ESG data across companies and countries, ensuring data validity is a significant challenge. The heterogeneity of ESG data makes it difficult to confirm that the data fits within predefined value ranges, formats, and accuracy standards (Visalli et al., 2023).

The data mesh improves data validity through structured governance, where data product owners apply clear, domain-specific rules. Labelling options in the data mesh allow for different gradations of validity, while global governance guidelines ensure it across data products. Domain experts, familiar with the specific context, can best assess ESG data validity.

5.3.3 Data Integration and Interoperability

Data integration and interoperability encompass the processes surrounding the movement and consolidation of data where it is needed. Data integration describes the consolidation of data into consistent forms, and interoperability describes the ability of data to be communicated between different systems (DAMA International, 2017).

5.3.3.1 Fragmented and Heterogeneous Data Integration

ESG data are inherently complex and originate from a variety of sources such as ERP systems, machine-generated data, and external sustainability databases. These data sources are often fragmented and stored across different locations, making it difficult to standardize and integrate them effectively (Koch et al., 2023). As the demand for ESG data increases, companies are forced to manage even more diverse data streams, which complicates their ability to create a comprehensive view of their sustainability performance (Galeotti et al., 2023).

The data mesh approach provides a decentralized solution to these challenges. By introducing self-service data capabilities and democratizing access, organizations can integrate diverse data sources more easily. Standardized APIs and data-sharing mechanisms foster interoperability between previously incompatible data formats. This approach not only simplifies the process of connecting and integrating various data sources but also allows for flexible, dynamic reconfiguration of data pipelines. The result is a system that supports the seamless integration of fragmented ESG data, making it accessible and usable for sustainability management.

5.3.3.2 Inefficient Data Collection Along the Value Chain

ESG data extraction, especially along the value chain, presents a significant challenge due to the labor-intensive, inefficient, and often manual nature of current data collection processes (Landolfi et al., 2019). Many companies lack the digital infrastructure to capture ESG data efficiently, with only a third using specialized software (Liakh, 2021). This problem is further compounded when data is not available in digital form, making it difficult to analyze and calculate the ESG impact of products or services. Achieving a comprehensive view of the ESG performance across a value chain is critical, yet the current methods of collecting and integrating this data remain highly fragmented (Koch et al., 2023).

The data mesh paradigm offers a flexible solution to the challenges of ESG data extraction by decentralizing the process. Its architecture allows for the automation of data collection, tailored to different data sources and formats, making it particularly suited for federated ESG data landscapes. By leveraging the data mesh's decoupled architecture, organizations can dynamically adjust their data extraction processes and incorporate data from across the entire value chain, not just internal or direct supplier data. With a clearer assignment of data ownership and proximity to domain experts, the data mesh also facilitates faster and more accurate data sharing via a centralized catalogue. This reduces the manual burden of data extraction and enables suppliers to share their data products across the value chain, providing a more holistic view of ESG impact while minimizing the effort required for data collection.

5.3.3.3 Complex Data Transformation Across Formats

ESG data often come in various formats—PDFs, images, CSVs—requiring significant transformation to become compatible and interoperable (Jennings-Dobbs et al., 2023). This process is essential to consolidate data from multiple sources into a usable form on digital platforms. Aggregating ESG data for analysis is complex and time-consuming due to the heterogeneous nature of the data, with significant hurdles in achieving integration and interoperability across domains (Reisi et al., 2020).

Data mesh helps simplify data transformation by combining federated governance with standardized processes. While data owners retain autonomy, global governance guidelines ensure that data follows consistent formats, reducing the complexity of transformation. Additionally, quality control mechanisms built directly into the data pipelines by domain teams further ease the transformation process. Automation plays a key role, significantly minimizing manual intervention and the risk of errors. By embedding transformation standards into the data flow and leveraging automation, the data mesh approach makes ESG data transformation more efficient and scalable across heterogeneous sources.

5.3.4 Data Architecture

Data architecture has several tasks which are generally concerned with establishing organized arrangements of components of an overall system. A well-managed data architecture or enterprise architecture is crucial for understanding the current state of the system and for further introducing improvements (DAMA International, 2017).

5.3.4.1 Modularity, Flexibility, and Scalability in ESG Data Architecture

As ESG data demands continue to grow, data architectures must be designed to accommodate this increasing complexity. Current challenges arise from ensuring that data pipelines and architectures can scale computationally to handle large volumes of data, which can slow down processing as datasets expand (Hansen et al., 2020). Moreover, the rapidly evolving landscape of ESG indicators, frameworks, and regulations means that the tools and systems in use need to be flexible enough to adapt to continuous changes in workflows (Poppe et al., 2022).

The data mesh paradigm provides a decentralized and modular solution that addresses these challenges. Its architecture enables domain teams to manage their own data pipelines while adhering to global standards, providing both modularity and flexibility. This approach reduces reliance on centralized systems and shadow

IT, giving domain teams the tools to scale and adapt ESG data management processes to their needs. A decoupled architecture allows for the easy integration of various data sources and the seamless adaptation of data models and pipelines as ESG regulations evolve. The system's flexibility also ensures that components can be reconfigured with minimal impact on the overall architecture, improving reliability by reducing the risk of cascading failures. Scalability, a critical need for ESG data architecture, is enhanced through data mesh, ensuring that large volumes of diverse ESG data can be connected and processed efficiently.

5.3.4.2 Centralized vs. Decentralized Data Architecture

A key debate in data management revolves around whether a centralized or decentralized architecture is better suited for ESG data (Klug & Prinz, 2023). While centralization has traditionally been the standard, with IT teams maintaining control over data management, decentralization has gained attention, particularly with the advent of the data mesh concept. Shifting from a centralized to a decentralized model poses challenges, such as requiring domain teams to develop new IT expertise and manage their own data platforms. Additionally, decentralization may not always present clear advantages over a centralized approach, as each model has distinct trade-offs.

The decentralized nature of the data mesh offers promising potential for ESG data management, but its effectiveness should be considered based on specific use cases. Decentralization can distribute data management responsibilities across domains, enhancing governance, data quality, and interoperability by placing control closer to domain experts. However, it requires a shift in IT competencies and the establishment of robust platform management capabilities within each domain. The trade-off between centralized and decentralized approaches must be evaluated carefully, as decentralization is not a one-size-fits-all solution. In the context of ESG data, the adaptability, scalability, and domain-focused governance provided by data mesh can offer substantial benefits, but success depends on how well these decentralized practices are implemented.

5.3.4.3 Achieving Interoperability in ESG Data Architecture

One of the main challenges in ESG data management is achieving interoperability across heterogeneous data sources. ESG data come in varied formats and from different origins, complicating the ability to exchange and integrate data seamlessly. Semantic interoperability is particularly challenging, requiring alignment across attribute names, input types, outputs, and operations (Reisi et al., 2020). For an ESG data architecture to be effective, it must allow for processing and integrating data from diverse sources without losing its meaning or context. The goal is to create an architecture where ESG data are interoperable, allowing for easy exchange and use across platforms (Koch et al., 2023).

Data mesh provides a solution by establishing decentralized data ownership through its domain-oriented architecture, improving the semantic alignment of ESG data. With clear governance mechanisms, data quality improves, which positively impacts interoperability. Through data catalogs, self-service capabilities, and data democratization, data mesh can create a framework where ESG data products are more easily integrated and exchanged across platforms. Although this implementation will take time, the potential for a fully interoperable ESG data architecture is significant, ensuring better integration of ESG data at a technical level while maintaining the flexibility to adapt to diverse formats and sources.

5.3.4.4 Lack of Suitable ESG IT Infrastructure

One of the critical challenges identified in ESG data management is the lack of a suitable IT infrastructure designed specifically for ESG data (Galeotti et al., 2023). Many companies rely on ad-hoc or outdated systems, making ESG data collection and analysis spontaneous and unreliable (Park, 2023). Effective ESG data management requires an investment in dedicated tools, platforms, and databases to ensure that data is captured and used efficiently. However, many organizations still lack the IT infrastructure to support the necessary processes, and the limited availability of ESG-specific tools remains a significant hurdle (Ajdinović et al., 2024).

The data mesh offers a flexible and decentralized approach that could address the unique challenges of ESG data management. By allowing architecture to adapt dynamically to different data sources, the data mesh enables better integration and more efficient management of ESG data. Through the creation of clear data product boundaries, stakeholders can access and consume ESG data across various domains. The self-service capabilities inherent in the data mesh also empower data owners to become data publishers, reducing reliance on a centralized platform team and distributing the workload.

This decentralized approach allows the IT infrastructure to scale and evolve with the growing demands for ESG data. A sustainability platform built on data mesh principles would transform from a centrally controlled platform to a decentralized system, offering high-quality, easily discoverable ESG data products. This shift would significantly improve the flexibility, scalability, and reliability of the IT infrastructure, making ESG data management more efficient and better integrated into corporate decision-making processes.

5.4 Summary

The data mesh paradigm offers a sociotechnical solution to many of the challenges in ESG data management. While its decentralized and flexible principles hold promise for managing the growing complexity, scale, and regulatory demands of ESG data, implementing the data mesh is not without challenges.

The practical implementation of the data mesh varies depending on the use case, and it is not a one-size-fits-all solution. As a sociotechnical paradigm shift, it requires significant organizational change alongside technical adjustments. A key challenge lies in balancing the integration of new IT solutions with the continued use of existing infrastructure. Additionally, the implementation of a data mesh can strain limited resources—both financial and in terms of competing priorities. Organizations must be cautious not to lose focus on essential data work while dedicating substantial effort to implementing the data mesh itself. The data mesh is not a silver bullet, and its suitability depends on the specific context of each organization, with pros and cons to weigh carefully.

Despite these challenges, the data mesh paradigm provides several transformative benefits for ESG data management. Key principles—domain-oriented decentralized data ownership, data as a product, self-serve infrastructure, and federated governance—offer new ways to handle ESG data. By decentralizing data ownership, domain teams are empowered to manage their data, leveraging their specialized knowledge to improve data quality. This decentralized approach allows for more flexible and scalable management of ESG data, accommodating the increasing variety and volume of data sources, use cases, and access models.

Treating ESG data as a product ensures that it is easily discoverable, accessible, and enrichable, driving greater value across the organization. The self-serve infrastructure enables domain teams to operate ESG data independently, reducing complexity and streamlining operations. Federated governance ensures that, despite decentralization, data products meet global standards for interoperability and compliance. By embracing the data mesh, organizations can transition from technology-centric to sociotechnical data management, ensuring their ESG data is well-governed, interoperable, and scalable.

References

Ajdinović, S., Strljic, M., Lechler, A., & Riedel, O. (2024). Interoperable Digital Product Passports: An Event-Based Approach to Aggregate Production Data to Improve Sustainability and Transparency in the Manufacturing Industry. *2024 IEEE/SICE International Symposium on System Integration, SII 2024*, 729–734. https://doi.org/10.1109/SII58957.2024.10417487

Ashraf, A., Hassan, A., & Mahdi, H. (2023). Key Lessons from Microservices for Data Mesh Adoption. *3rd International Mobile, Intelligent, and Ubiquitous Computing Conference, MIUCC 2023*, 21–28. https://doi.org/10.1109/MIUCC58832.2023.10278300

Azeroual, O., & Nacheva, R. (2023). Data Mesh for Managing Complex Big Data Landscapes and Enhancing Decision Making in Organizations. *Proceedings of the 15th International Joint Conference on Knowledge Discovery, Knowledge Engineering and Knowledge Management*, 202–212. https://doi.org/10.5220/0012195700003598

Bode, J., Kühl, N., Kreuzberger, D., Hirschl, S., & Holtmann, C. (2023). *Towards Avoiding the Data Mess: Industry Insights from Data Mesh Implementations*. https://doi.org/10.1109/ACCESS.2024.3417291

Clark, K. P., Plc, A., Kotsantonis, S., Rehnberg, C., Ward, B., Advisors, K., Serafeim, G., Indahl, R., Gunvor Jacobsen, H., Equity, S., Davis, T., Lescott, B., Business School, H., Lins, K. V., Bizoumi, T., Lazaridis, S., Stamou, N., Ramani, V., Pinney, C., & Capital Management, R. (2019). Four Things No One Will Tell You About ESG Data. *Journal of Applied Corporate Finance*, *31*(2), 50–58. https://doi.org/10.1111/JACF.12346

DAMA International. (2017). *Data Management Body of Knowledge* (2nd ed.). Technics Publications. https://www.TechnicsPub.com

Dehghani, Z. (2019, May 20). *How to Move Beyond a Monolithic Data Lake to a Distributed Data Mesh*. https://martinfowler.com/articles/data-monolith-to-mesh.html

Dehghani, Z. (2020, December 3). *Data Mesh Principles and Logical Architecture*. https://martinfowler.com/articles/data-mesh-principles.html

Dolhopolov, A., Castelltort, A., & Laurent, A. (2024). Trick or Treat: Centralized Data Lake Vs Decentralized Data Mesh. *Communications in Computer and Information Science*, *2022 CCIS*, 303–316. https://doi.org/10.1007/978-3-031-51643-6_22

Driessen, S., den Heuvel, W. J. van, & Monsieur, G. (2023). ProMoTe: A Data Product Model Template for Data Meshes. *Lecture Notes in Computer Science (Including Subseries Lecture Notes in Artificial Intelligence and Lecture Notes in Bioinformatics)*, *14320 LNCS*, 125–142. https://doi.org/10.1007/978-3-031-47262-6_7

ESG Working Group. (2024). *Effective ESG and Sustainability Data Management*. www.edmcouncil.org.

Galeotti, M., Lombardi, R., Principale, S., & Sura, A. (2023). Aligning Integrated Data Management With Corporate Reporting: The Role of Sustainability Reporting. *Management Control*, *2*, 65–81. https://digital.casalini.it/10.3280/MACO2023-002-S1004

Hansen, E. R., Lissandrini, M., Ghose, A., Løkke, S., Thomsen, C., & Hose, K. (2020). Transparent Integration and Sharing of Life Cycle Sustainability Data With Provenance. *Lecture Notes in Computer Science (Including Subseries Lecture Notes in Artificial Intelligence and Lecture Notes in Bioinformatics)*, *12507 LNCS*, 378–394. https://doi.org/10.1007/978-3-030-62466-8_24

Hasan, M. R., & Legner, C. (2023). Data Product Canvas: A Visual Inquiry Tool Supporting Data Product Design. *Lecture Notes in Computer Science (Including Subseries Lecture Notes in Artificial Intelligence and Lecture Notes in Bioinformatics)*, *13873 LNCS*, 191–205. https://doi.org/10.1007/978-3-031-32808-4_12

Jennings-Dobbs, E. M., Forester, S. M., & Drewnowski, A. (2023). Visualizing Data Interoperability for Food Systems Sustainability Research-From Spider Webs to Neural Networks. *Current Developments in Nutrition*, *7*(11), 102006. https://doi.org/10.1016/J.CDNUT.2023.102006

Klug, L., & Prinz, W. (2023). Fair Prices for Sustainability in Agriculture and Food. Requirements and Design Options for a Data-based Transparency System. *24th Annual International Conference on Digital Government Research - Together in the Unstable World: Digital Government and Solidarity (DGO)*, 496–507. https://doi.org/10.1145/3598469.3598525

Koch, D., Waltersmann, L., & Sauer, A. (2023). A Service-Oriented Sustainability Platform—Basic Considerations to Facilitate a Data-Based Sustainability Management System in Manufacturing Companies. In M. Liewald, A. Verl, T. Bauernhansl, & H.

Möhring (Eds.), *Lecture Notes in Production Engineering: Vol. Part F1163* (pp. 791–798). Springer Nature. https://doi.org/10.1007/978-3-031-18318-8_78

Kotsantonis, S., & Serafeim, G. (2019). Four Things No One Will Tell You About ESG Data. *Journal of Applied Corporate Finance, 31*(2), 50–58. https://doi.org/10.1111/JACF.12346

Landolfi, G., Barni, A., Izzo, G., Fontana, A., & Bettoni, A. (2019). A MaaS Platform Architecture Supporting Data Sovereignty in Sustainability Assessment of Manufacturing Systems. *Procedia Manufacturing, 38*, 548–555. https://doi.org/10.1016/J.PROMFG.2020.01.069

Liakh, O. (2021). Accountability through Sustainability Data Governance: Reconfiguring Reporting to Better Account for the Digital Acceleration. *Sustainability, 13*(13814). https://doi.org/10.3390/SU132413814

Liu, X., Yang, Y., Jiang, Y., Fu, Y., Zhong, R. Y., Li, M., & Huang, G. Q. (2023). Data-Driven ESG Assessment for Blockchain Services: A Comparative Study in Textiles and Apparel Industry. *Resources, Conservation and Recycling, 190*, 106837. https://doi.org/10.1016/J.RESCONREC.2022.106837

Luoma, P., Rauter, R., Penttinen, E., & Toppinen, A. (2023). The Value of Data for Environmental Sustainability as Perceived by the Customers of a Tissue-Paper Supplier. *Corporate Social Responsibility and Environmental Management, 30*(6), 3110–3123. https://doi.org/10.1002/CSR.2541

McNally, L., & Gorcenski, E. (2022, December 5). *Data Mesh for ESG: Establishing Accountability and Laying a Foundation for the Generation of High Quality Sustainability Data*. https://www.thoughtworks.com/insights/blog/sustainability/data-mesh-for-esg–establishing-accountability-and-laying-a-foun

Park, A. Y. S. (2023). Beyond Reporting: What Drives Performance Data Use in Sustainability Management? Empirical Evidence from U.S. Cities. *Public Management Review*. https://doi.org/10.1080/14719037.2023.2250356

Peças, P., John, L., Ribeiro, I., Baptista, A. J., Pinto, S. M., Dias, R., Henriques, J., Estrela, M., Pilastri, A., & Cunha, F. (2023). Holistic Framework to Data-Driven Sustainability Assessment. *Sustainability, 15*(4). https://doi.org/10.3390/SU15043562

Poppe, K., Vrolijk, H., de Graaf, N., van Dijk, R., Dillon, E., & Donnellan, T. (2022). Sustainability Monitoring with Robotic Accounting—Integration of Financial and Environmental Farm Data. *Sustainability, 14*(6756). https://doi.org/10.3390/SU14116756

Reisi, M., Sabri, S., Agunbiade, M., Rajabifard, A., Chen, Y., Kalantari, M., Keshtiarast, A., & Li, Y. (2020). Transport Sustainability Indicators for an Enhanced Urban Analytics Data Infrastructure. *Sustainable Cities and Society, 59*(102095). https://doi.org/10.1016/J.SCS.2020.102095

Tamym, L., Benyoucef, L., Nait Sidi Moh, A., & El Ouadghiri, M. D. (2023). Big Data Analytics-Based Life Cycle Sustainability Assessment for Sustainable Manufacturing Enterprises Evaluation. *Journal of Big Data, 10*(170), 1–27. https://doi.org/10.1186/S40537-023-00848-8

Tartow, C., & Mott, A. (2024, July 16). *Data Mesh: Data as a Product*. https://www.starburst.io/blog/data-mesh-and-starburst-data-as-a-product/

Visalli, F., Patrizio, A., Lanza, A., Papaleo, P., Nautiyal, A., Pupo, M., Scilinguo, U., Oro, E., Ruffolo, M., & Vermicelli, P. (2023). ESG Data Collection with Adaptive AI. *Proceedings of the 25th International Conference on Enterprise Information Systems (ICEIS), 1*, 468–475. https://doi.org/10.5220/0011844500003467

Wanner, J., & Janiesch, C. (2019). Big Data Analytics in Sustainability Reports: an Analysis Based on the Perceived Credibility of Corporate Published Information. *Business Research*, *12*, 143–173. https://doi.org/10.1007/s40685-019-0088-4

Young In, S., Rook, D., & Monk, A. H. B. (2019). Alternative ESG Data for Investment Decision Making. *Global Economic Review*, *48*(3), 237–260. https://doi.org/10.2139/ssrn.3380835

Chapter 6

Digital Transformation in the Automotive Industry and ESG

Tracy Dathe

6.1 Emergence of Autonomous Driving Technology

The journey toward autonomous driving evolves through groundbreaking research and innovation. Today, autonomous driving technology represents a rapidly advancing field, driven by safety concerns, technological breakthroughs, and market demand. Below is an overview of the pivotal milestones that shaped the development of autonomous vehicles (AVs).

6.1.1 Key Milestones in the History of Autonomous Driving

The market for autonomous driving is poised to become one of the most significant growth areas in the automotive and technology industries. By 2035, it is projected to generate between \$300 billion and \$400 billion in revenue, underscoring its transformative potential (McKinsey, 2023). This expansion is fueled by advancements in artificial intelligence (AI), connectivity, and sensor technologies, combined with a growing consumer demand for safer, more efficient, and convenient transportation solutions. AVs are not just reshaping how people travel; they are also creating entirely new business models in areas such as mobility-as-a-service (MaaS), logistics, and data monetization.

DOI: 10.1201/9781003528951-6

The journey toward autonomous driving began in the early 20th century, with the concept evolving through groundbreaking research and innovation. Today, autonomous driving technology represents a rapidly advancing field, driven by safety concerns, technological breakthroughs, and market demand. Below is an overview of the pivotal milestones that shaped the development of AVs (Dathe, 2024).

The journey of autonomous driving began as early as 1925 when Francis Houdina amazed New York City by demonstrating a radio-controlled car capable of starting, shifting gears, and braking without human intervention, sparking both fascination and fear (LaFrance, 2016). In 1939, General Motors presented a visionary concept at the New York World's Fair with its "Futurama" exhibit, imagining a world of automated highways and self-driving cars (Tjokro, 2021). By 1953, collaborative efforts between General Motors and RCA led to the development of an automated highway system, using sensors and cables embedded in roads to guide vehicles, showcasing an early glimpse of what would later become the core technologies of autonomous driving (Ackerman, 2016).

The 1980s marked a pivotal shift from concepts to tangible innovation, with projects such as Carnegie Mellon University's NavLab and Mercedes-Benz's EUREKA Prometheus Project pioneering advanced autonomous systems (Mobility21, 2024). These efforts, supported by DARPA, introduced technologies like obstacle detection and lane-keeping, setting the stage for modern developments. However, it was the DARPA Grand Challenge in 2004 and 2005 that truly catalyzed progress. Despite no vehicle completing the inaugural 2004 course, the 2005 event saw Stanford's "Stanley" successfully navigate a 132-mile desert route, proving the viability of autonomous navigation and pushing the boundaries of what these vehicles could achieve (DARPA, n.a.).

As the technology matured, commercial ventures and regulatory milestones began to emerge. In 2009, Google launched its self-driving car project, now known as Waymo, which demonstrated the potential of lidar-equipped vehicles to complete autonomous routes (Waymo, 2020a). By 2011, Nevada became the first state in the United States to permit AV testing, setting a precedent for global legislative frameworks (Nevada Department of Motor Vehicles DMV, 2023). Automakers like Audi joined the movement, showcasing vehicles such as the RS 7 in 2015, capable of autonomous high-speed maneuvers, blending driver-assist technologies with emerging autonomy (Motortrend, 2024).

The transition from experimental to commercial applications accelerated in the mid-2010s, with Uber initiating tests of autonomous ride-sharing in Pittsburgh in 2016 and Waymo launching a fully driverless taxi service in Phoenix, Arizona, in 2020 (Waymo, 2020b; World Economic Forum, 2016). These developments highlighted the industry's rapid progress toward integrating autonomous technologies into everyday transportation, demonstrating their feasibility and appeal to the public (Dathe, 2024).

Underpinning these advancements is a suite of sophisticated technologies. From the evolution of basic cruise control systems to modern adaptive cruise control (ACC), electronic stability control (ESC), and collision avoidance systems (CAS), the integration of sensors like radar, lidar, and cameras has been crucial (Li et al., 2013; Sanjana et al., 2017; Xiao & Gao, 2010). Coupled with the rise of Vehicle-to-Everything (V2X) communication, autonomous systems now leverage real-time data sharing and connectivity to navigate complex environments and ensure safety (Krasniqi & Hajrizi, 2016).

While the potential of autonomous driving is immense, challenges remain. Regulatory uncertainties, public trust, and technological complexities must be addressed to achieve widespread adoption. However, with continued innovation in AI, machine learning, and connectivity, AVs are poised to transform mobility, building on a century-long journey that began with Houdina's "phantom auto" and continues to redefine transportation today.

6.1.2 SAE Levels of Driving Automation

To enhance technical communication, academic research, and the development of robust traffic regulations and legal frameworks for autonomous driving, a standardized classification of automation levels is indispensable (Fraunhofer IKS, 2023; Wang et al., 2021).

Recognizing this necessity, the Society of Automotive Engineers (SAE) introduced the SAE J3016 standard in 2014, titled "Recommended Practice: Taxonomy and Definitions for Terms Related to Driving Automation Systems for On-Road Motor Vehicles," commonly referred to as the SAE Levels of Driving Automation. Updated in collaboration with the International Organization for Standardization (ISO) in 2021, the revised standard solidified its status as a globally accepted framework, underpinning the automotive industry and academia in understanding and advancing AV technologies (SAE, 2021).

The SAE Levels of Driving Automation define six progressive levels of automation, from Level 0 (no automation) to Level 5 (full automation). These levels specify the degree to which a vehicle can operate autonomously, serving as a critical reference for assessing technological capabilities and regulatory requirements (see Figure 6.1).

Level 0 (L0)—no automation

At this level, vehicles rely entirely on human control for driving tasks such as steering, braking, accelerating, and monitoring the environment. Features like emergency braking, blind spot warnings, or lane departure alerts assist drivers by providing warnings but do not assume control of the vehicle (SAE, 2021).

Level 1 (L1)—driver assistance

This is a basic automation level, where systems like ACC or lane-centering assistance manage either steering or acceleration/deceleration, but not both simultaneously. These systems operate under specific conditions, requiring

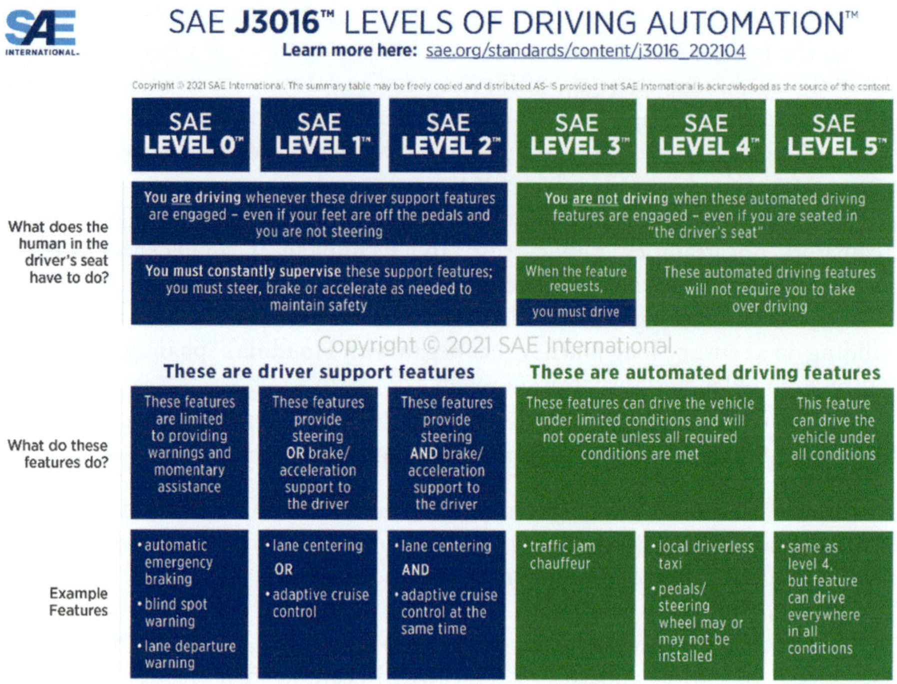

Figure 6.1 SAE J3016™ levels of driving automation.

Source: SAE International (SAE, 2021).

the driver to maintain full responsibility for vehicle control and be prepared to intervene at any moment (SAE, 2021).

Level 2 (L2)—partial automation

At this level, partial automation is achieved, enabling vehicles to manage both steering and acceleration/deceleration simultaneously in certain scenarios, such as highway driving or automated parking. This integration of multiple automated systems allows for smoother operation; however, the driver must monitor the system and be ready to take control when needed (Fraunhofer IKS, 2023; SAE, 2021).

Level 3 (L3)—conditional automation

Vehicles at this level are capable of monitoring their surroundings and executing all driving tasks in specific environments, such as stop-and-go traffic. While the system operates, the driver can engage in non-driving activities but must be ready to take over control upon request. Features like traffic jam chauffeurs exemplify Level 3 functionality (SAE, 2021).

Level 4 (L4)—high automation

At this level, vehicles operate independently without human intervention in pre-defined scenarios, such as urban areas or designated highway routes.

Vehicles at this level can autonomously execute tasks like lane changes and entering highways, enabling passengers to focus entirely on non-driving activities, including relaxing or sleeping. Optional human controls, such as steering wheels and pedals, may still be available (Fraunhofer IKS, 2023; SAE, 2021).

Level 5 (L5)—full automation

Level 5 is the ultimate goal of autonomous driving, where vehicles are capable of handling all driving tasks in any condition, including complex scenarios like navigating intersections. At this level, the vehicle fully replaces the human driver, eliminating the need for any manual controls (Fraunhofer IKS, 2023; SAE, 2021; Wang et al., 2021).

The SAE Levels of Driving Automation provide a comprehensive framework that aids in evaluating technological feasibility, safety considerations, ethical challenges, and the broader social and economic impacts of autonomous driving. By offering a universally recognized standard, this taxonomy plays a pivotal role in shaping the future of mobility and facilitating the seamless integration of AVs into society (Fraunhofer IKS, 2023; Wang et al., 2021).

6.1.3 Prominent Use Cases of Autonomous Driving

Autonomous driving is transforming industries and reshaping the future of mobility, with diverse applications that span passenger vehicles, ride-hailing services, logistics, freight, and public transportation.

6.1.3.1 Passenger Vehicles

Automated driving technology is fundamentally transforming the daily commute by elevating both safety and convenience to unprecedented levels. By addressing human error, which is responsible for the vast majority of traffic accidents, AVs promise a future with safer roads. Equipped with advanced sensors such as lidar, radar, and high-definition cameras, these vehicles achieve real-time 360-degree detection of obstacles, vehicles, and pedestrians. This advanced perception, paired with constant vigilance, ensures that automated systems outperform human capabilities, eliminating risks associated with distractions, fatigue, or impaired driving. Moreover, automated systems adhere strictly to traffic laws, creating a more predictable and secure driving environment (European Union, 2022; Hollinger & Shirazi, 2020).

In addition to safety, convenience is a cornerstone of automated driving's transformative potential. By assuming the driving responsibilities, AVs allow passengers to reclaim time during commutes, whether for relaxation, work, or entertainment. Inter-vehicle communication enables the optimization of traffic flow, reducing congestion and travel times. These capabilities significantly enhance urban mobility, particularly for those unable to drive, including the elderly and individuals with disabilities (Dathe, 2024; McKinsey, 2023).

Automated driving also leverages cutting-edge technological features to further refine the commuting experience. ACC maintains a safe following distance by automatically adjusting speed, while lane-keeping assistance ensures the vehicle remains centered in its lane. In high-density urban traffic, traffic jam assist takes over stop-and-go driving, providing relief from the tedium of congestion. These systems collectively enhance comfort and reduce the cognitive load on human passengers (Bosch, 2024; Garikapati & Shetiya, 2024).

The broader implications of automated driving extend beyond individual benefits. On a societal level, these technologies promise more efficient transportation networks, improved accessibility for underserved populations, and a reduction in the environmental impact of traditional commuting practices. As automated driving continues to advance, it is poised to redefine daily mobility, offering a safer, more convenient, and ultimately more enjoyable experience for all.

6.1.3.2 Ride-Hailing and Robotaxis

Autonomous driving technology has progressed significantly in recent years, driven by key industry leaders innovating across hardware, software, and mobility services. The following examples of robotaxi solutions of Waymo, Tesla, Cruise, and Baidu Apollo demonstrate how these prominent players are shaping the future of AVs through groundbreaking advancements and strategic approaches to technology and market deployment.

Waymo, originally Google's Self-Driving Car Project, launched in 2009 with a mission to achieve full autonomy across diverse road conditions. By 2015, Waymo had completed the world's first public ride without human intervention using custom-built vehicles equipped with lidar, radar, and advanced sensors. This milestone demonstrated the potential of fully autonomous technology to redefine personal and public transportation. In 2016, Waymo became a standalone subsidiary of Alphabet Inc., rebranding itself as an independent leader in the field. Two years later, the company introduced Waymo One, the world's first commercial autonomous ride-hailing service, operating in Phoenix, Arizona. By 2020, Waymo was providing driverless rides without human safety drivers, a first for the industry, while continuing to expand its services across U.S. cities. The company's use of high-resolution lidar, detailed 3D mapping, and extensive real-world testing—totaling over 20 million miles of autonomous driving—underscores its commitment to safety and reliability (Waymo, 2024).

Tesla has taken a distinct approach to autonomous driving, integrating it as part of its broader vision for sustainable mobility. Beginning with the introduction of its Autopilot system in 2014, Tesla revolutionized the driving experience by incorporating advanced driver assistance features like ACC and lane-keeping. The subsequent launch of its Full Self-Driving (FSD) system added automated parking, highway merging, and city navigation capabilities. In 2016, Tesla began equipping all vehicles with hardware for full autonomy, emphasizing scalability and affordability. By 2021, the company transitioned to a camera-only vision system, moving away from lidar and radar to focus on real-time AI-driven image recognition. Despite these advancements, Tesla's FSD package remains classified as SAE Level 2, requiring human supervision due to ongoing technical and regulatory challenges. Tesla's reliance on data from its global fleet allows it to continuously refine its systems, distinguishing its approach from competitors who rely on pre-mapped lidar-based navigation (Schroeder, 2023).

Cruise LLC, founded in 2013 in San Francisco, initially focused on retrofitting vehicles with highway autopilot technology. After its acquisition by General Motors in 2016, the company shifted its efforts toward autonomous ride-hailing services. During the COVID-19 pandemic in 2020, Cruise repurposed its driverless fleet to deliver meals to vulnerable populations and pilot self-driving delivery services for Walmart. By 2022, the company had achieved another milestone, obtaining approval from the National Highway Traffic Safety Administration (NHTSA) to operate vehicles without human controls and beginning public driverless taxi rides. Cruise has also secured significant investments from companies like Microsoft, Honda, and Walmart, enabling it to pursue international expansion plans in Dubai and Japan. Its vehicles use a combination of lidar, radar, and high-definition mapping for navigation, while its emphasis on shared mobility highlights its commitment to sustainable urban transportation (Cruise, 2024; Reuters, 2022).

In China, Baidu Apollo has emerged as a major player in autonomous driving, leveraging its parent company's expertise in AI and big data. Established in 2017, Apollo has rapidly developed technologies that integrate conversational AI, real-time data processing, and proprietary hardware (Baidu, 2017). It operates the robotaxi service Apollo Go, which had completed over 3.3 million rides across major Chinese cities by mid-2023, making it one of the largest deployments of its kind globally (James, 2023). Apollo's success is supported by its partnerships with leading automakers like Ford, Toyota, and Geely, which have enhanced its production and market reach. In 2022, Baidu became the first company in China to receive a government license for fully automated robotaxis, a significant regulatory breakthrough. Apollo's extensive use of search, video, and location data ensures its vehicles are prepared for diverse road scenarios, while collaborations like the Jidu electric vehicle brand with Geely demonstrate its commitment to integrating autonomous driving with sustainable energy solutions (Baidu, 2022; Jaramillo, 2023).

The innovations of Waymo, Tesla, Cruise, and Baidu Apollo highlight the diverse approaches and technologies driving the AV revolution. From Waymo's safety-first design to Tesla's cost-efficient vision-based systems, Cruise's shared mobility focus, and Apollo's AI-driven advancements, each company is redefining mobility to meet the unique demands of global markets. As these players continue to expand, their efforts are collectively reshaping urban transportation, making it safer, more efficient, and accessible.

6.1.3.3 Logistics and Freight

Autonomous trucks and drones are transforming supply chains by fundamentally altering how goods are transported, delivered, and managed. By leveraging advanced technologies, these innovations enhance operational efficiency, reduce costs, and significantly improve delivery times, meeting the growing demands of modern logistics (Xu & Duffy, 2021).

One of the most profound impacts of autonomous trucks and drones lies in their ability to enhance efficiency across the supply chain. Autonomous trucks, unlike traditional vehicles, can operate continuously without requiring rest breaks for drivers. This capacity for 24/7 operation drastically increases the volume of goods that can be transported within shorter timeframes. Moreover, these vehicles rely on advanced algorithms and real-time data to optimize delivery routes, which minimizes travel time and fuel consumption while ensuring consistent and reliable service. Complementing these efforts, drones are redefining last-mile delivery by navigating urban landscapes with ease. These small, agile devices can bypass traffic congestion and deliver packages directly to customers' doorsteps, offering an unparalleled level of convenience and precision in densely populated areas (Xu & Duffy, 2021).

Cost reduction is another critical benefit of integrating autonomous trucks and drones into logistics networks. By eliminating the need for human drivers, companies can achieve substantial labor cost savings, which are traditionally a significant component of logistics expenses. Furthermore, AVs are often equipped with predictive maintenance systems that can identify and address potential mechanical issues before they escalate, thereby reducing the frequency and cost of repairs. Optimized driving patterns and routes also enhance fuel efficiency, leading to lower fuel consumption and further cost savings for businesses (Yang, 2024).

In addition to efficiency and cost benefits, autonomous trucks and drones are revolutionizing delivery times. Continuous operation, enabled by automation, allows for faster and more reliable deliveries, ensuring that businesses can meet the ever-increasing customer demand for rapid service. By communicating with each other and with traffic management systems, AVs can reduce congestion and maintain a steady traffic flow, further improving delivery speeds. Drones play a vital role in speeding up smaller package deliveries, bypassing traditional routes entirely and providing direct, immediate service to customers (Courcoubetis et al., 2024; Dathe, 2024; Xu & Duffy, 2021).

The above advancements are not merely incremental improvements but a complete reimagining of logistics and freight transportation. Autonomous trucks and drones offer solutions to long-standing challenges in supply chains, including labor shortages, rising fuel costs, and urban delivery inefficiencies. By integrating these technologies, companies can build more resilient, cost-effective, and customer-focused logistics systems, setting a new standard for the future of supply chain management.

6.1.3.4 The Role of AI in Mobility

Autonomous driving is reshaping the automotive industry through the transformative application of AI. At the heart of this innovation lies the ability of AI systems to process vast streams of data generated by sensors, cameras, and GPS technologies, enabling vehicles to make split-second decisions in real time. This capability not only disrupts traditional automotive business models but also shifts the industry's core focus from hardware-oriented manufacturing to software-centric development. By integrating sophisticated AI-driven systems, AVs are poised to redefine mobility, efficiency, and safety on a global scale (Dathe, 2024).

The role of AI in autonomous driving extends across a range of critical functions. AI enables perception, decision-making, and vehicle control, which are foundational to AV operation. Machine learning (ML) and deep learning (DL) models empower these systems with the ability to identify patterns, predict scenarios, and adapt to varying traffic conditions. Additionally, computer vision technology allows AVs to detect objects, interpret traffic signs, and analyze complex traffic scenarios, ensuring safe navigation. Efficient data processing, facilitated by edge and cloud computing, further enhances the ability of AVs to handle high volumes of information seamlessly and reliably, even in high-demand environments (Fraunhofer IKS, 2023; Wang et al., 2021).

To navigate unpredictable environments and ensure reliability, AVs depend on advanced solutions addressing key technical challenges. One such area is sensor and sensor system integration, which combines data from multiple sources to create a comprehensive understanding of the environment. Sensor fusion technology plays a pivotal role here, enabling AVs to integrate inputs from cameras, radar, lidar, and ultrasonic sensors into a cohesive framework for decision-making. The development of robust actuators and control systems enhances the ability of AVs to respond effectively to unexpected road conditions. Algorithms for efficient path planning and predictive decision-making are equally critical, providing the computational foundation for AV maneuverability and safety (Fraunhofer IKS, 2023; Krasniqi & Hajrizi, 2016).

Another crucial aspect of autonomous driving is the integration of advanced radio technologies for cellular communication, which ensures seamless data exchange between vehicles and their surroundings. Dedicated Short-Range Communications (DSRC) and 5G technology are two leading innovations in this domain. DSRC facilitates high-speed, two-way data transmission for V2X communications, which enhances safety and coordination among vehicles. However, it requires significant investment in new roadside infrastructure. Conversely, 5G technology leverages existing infrastructure while enabling faster data rates, lower latency, and broader application scopes, including infotainment systems, remote diagnostics, and firmware updates. Together, DSRC and 5G provide a redundant communication network, ensuring reliability in critical operations (Fraunhofer IKS, 2023; Krasniqi & Hajrizi, 2016).

In addition to communication technologies, advanced mapping materials are indispensable for AVs. These maps must be highly detailed, allowing AVs to recognize surrounding objects and obstacles, such as other vehicles, pedestrians, and road signs. By creating precise virtual representations of real-world environments, AVs can navigate with accuracy and adapt to dynamic changes in their surroundings. Detailed maps also enable AVs to identify and respond to potential hazards in real time, enhancing safety and operational efficiency (Krasniqi & Hajrizi, 2016).

Finally, the robustness of the software running these systems cannot be overstated. Ensuring the reliability and fault-tolerance of AV software is essential to preventing malfunctions, which could compromise safety and operational integrity. The combined advancements in AI, sensor integration, communication technologies, and mapping systems illustrate the multifaceted nature of autonomous driving as a disruptive innovation. As these technologies mature, they promise to revolutionize transportation, logistics, and urban mobility on an unprecedented scale (Krasniqi & Hajrizi, 2016).

6.2 ESG Impacts of Digitalization in the Automotive Industry

The rise of autonomous driving technology brings profound changes across environmental, economic, and social dimensions. By integrating advanced AI, real-time data processing, and sustainable mobility strategies, AVs have the potential to optimize transportation efficiency, reduce emissions, and reshape urban infrastructure. However, alongside these benefits come challenges such as energy consumption, economic disruption, and ethical considerations. This section explores the environmental, economic, and social impacts of autonomous driving, analyzing both its transformative potential and the critical factors that will determine its long-term success.

6.2.1 Environmental Impact

Autonomous driving holds considerable promise for reducing greenhouse gas emissions and contributing to a more sustainable transportation system. By leveraging advanced technologies, these vehicles can optimize traffic flow, decrease idling times, and enable efficient ride-sharing, leading to significant environmental benefits. However, the extent of these advantages depends heavily on the energy sources powering AVs and the lifecycle environmental impacts of manufacturing AV-specific components, such as LiDAR systems, sensors, and other advanced hardware (Krasniqi & Hajrizi, 2016).

One of the primary ways AVs reduce environmental impact is by improving traffic flow. Through real-time data processing and predictive algorithms, AVs can communicate with each other and traffic management systems to optimize driving patterns, reduce congestion, and eliminate stop-and-go traffic. This leads to smoother traffic dynamics, less energy waste, and reduced fuel consumption. For instance, by avoiding unnecessary braking and acceleration, AVs can minimize the inefficiencies typically associated with human driving behavior (Silva et al., 2022).

Autonomous driving also contributes to lower greenhouse gas emissions. Many AVs are designed to be electric, which significantly reduces tailpipe emissions compared to internal combustion engine vehicles. Combined with efficient routing and smoother driving patterns, this can further decrease the overall carbon footprint of the transportation sector. For example, intelligent navigation systems in AVs ensure that vehicles take the most efficient routes, avoiding high-traffic areas and minimizing the time spent on the road, which translates to lower emissions per trip (Krasniqi & Hajrizi, 2016).

Additionally, AVs improve fuel efficiency through precise control of speed and acceleration. Unlike human drivers, who may engage in inefficient driving habits such as aggressive braking or rapid acceleration, AVs are programmed to maintain optimal driving patterns. This precision not only conserves energy but also reduces wear and tear on vehicles, leading to lower maintenance requirements and a longer operational lifespan (Courcoubetis et al., 2024; Dathe, 2024; Silva et al., 2022).

Despite these potential benefits, the environmental impact of AVs must be evaluated holistically, including the energy sources used for charging electric AVs and the production of specialized components like LiDAR systems. The production of advanced sensors and computing hardware involves resource-intensive processes that may offset some of the environmental gains from operating the vehicles. Furthermore, the shift to electric AVs depends on the availability of clean energy sources. If the electricity powering these vehicles comes from fossil fuels, the environmental benefits will be diminished (Krasniqi & Hajrizi, 2016).

Therefore, while autonomous driving represents a significant step toward sustainable mobility, its environmental impact will depend on broader systemic factors. These include the adoption of renewable energy, advancements in sustainable manufacturing practices, and policies encouraging efficient use of shared autonomous fleets. By addressing these factors, autonomous driving can become a transformative force in reducing greenhouse gas emissions and promoting a greener future for mobility.

6.2.2 Economic Impact

Autonomous driving is poised to redefine transportation by reducing accidents, optimizing traffic flows, and minimizing carbon emissions. This transformative potential has made AVs a priority for governments, investors, and industry leaders worldwide. The urgency to capture this market is driven not only by the economic benefits but also by the societal advantages, including enhanced mobility for underserved populations and the creation of smarter urban environments. Companies that combine technological leadership with adaptable, forward-thinking business strategies will be best positioned to thrive as the autonomous driving era unfolds (McKinsey, 2023).

AVs also hold the promise of reducing costs and improving efficiency in urban transportation systems. By eliminating the need for human drivers, ride-hailing and robotaxi services can significantly reduce labor expenses, which represent a major cost for traditional taxi operators. Furthermore, optimized fleet management enabled by AI and real-time data analysis can reduce the number of vehicles required to meet demand while minimizing idle time. Advanced diagnostic systems and predictive maintenance technologies will also lower repair and maintenance costs, ensuring vehicles operate efficiently for longer periods (Yang, 2024).

While automation may disrupt traditional employment in driving-related sectors, it will simultaneously generate demand for roles in AI development, data analytics, vehicle maintenance, and infrastructure planning. Cities will also need to adapt to the widespread adoption of AVs, driving investments in smart infrastructure such as advanced roadways, communication networks, and traffic management systems. These changes are expected to contribute to economic growth while fostering innovation in urban planning and mobility solutions (McKinsey, 2023).

The broader implications of autonomous driving for urban transportation are equally transformative. Innovations in traffic optimization, ride-sharing, and fleet operations are paving the way for smarter cities, where mobility solutions are not only environmentally sustainable but also cost-effective. By enhancing logistics efficiency, reducing fuel consumption, and addressing congestion, AVs stand to generate significant economic and societal benefits. However, realizing this vision will require substantial investments in research and development, infrastructure, and workforce retraining, underscoring the need for a coordinated effort among industry stakeholders, policymakers, and technology providers (Krasniqi & Hajrizi, 2016).

In summary, autonomous driving technologies offer transformative opportunities to reduce costs and enhance efficiency in urban transportation. Innovations in ride-hailing, fleet management, and vehicle maintenance, coupled with advanced traffic optimization capabilities, are paving the way for smarter cities and better mobility solutions.

6.2.3 Social Impact

The social implications of autonomous driving extend beyond technological advancements, influencing mobility, employment, ethics, and data security. While AVs have the potential to create more inclusive transportation systems, reduce traffic congestion, and improve road safety, they also raise concerns about job displacement, ethical decision-making, and cybersecurity threats. Understanding these multifaceted impacts is crucial for ensuring that autonomous driving benefits society as a whole.

6.2.3.1 Multifaceted Influences

The social impact of autonomous driving is multifaceted, with both significant opportunities and challenges. AVs have the potential to create a more inclusive transportation system by enhancing mobility for the elderly, disabled, and non-drivers. These groups, traditionally underserved by conventional transportation options, could benefit greatly from the independence and accessibility provided by AVs. By integrating ride-hailing services and robotaxis, AVs promise to reduce transportation barriers and promote social equity in mobility (Courcoubetis et al., 2024; Dathe, 2024).

However, the shift toward automation also raises critical concerns about job displacement. Professional drivers, including those in taxi services, trucking, and delivery, face potential job losses as autonomous technologies become mainstream. The scale of this impact could affect millions of workers globally, requiring proactive measures to address this economic disruption. Policymakers and businesses must collaborate to provide retraining and upskilling programs that prepare displaced workers for emerging roles in the evolving mobility ecosystem, such as those in AI development, vehicle maintenance, and data management (Krasniqi & Hajrizi, 2016; Krieger-Lamina, 2016).

Autonomous driving also carries broader societal implications. For example, while AVs can optimize traffic flow, reduce congestion, and lower urban pollution levels through efficient driving patterns, the environmental and social benefits are not evenly distributed. Wealthier individuals or communities may have earlier access to AV technology, exacerbating existing inequalities. Affordability remains a pressing issue, as the high initial costs of AV adoption could marginalize disadvantaged groups (Krasniqi & Hajrizi, 2016).

The integration of AVs into urban infrastructure also raises ethical and logistical questions. Cities will need significant upgrades to support AVs, including smart roadways and traffic systems. Determining how to fund these developments, particularly in regions where car ownership is declining, presents a challenge. Debates over whether non-drivers should contribute to these costs highlight the complexity of ensuring fairness in transportation policy (Krasniqi & Hajrizi, 2016).

In conclusion, while autonomous driving presents transformative opportunities for enhancing mobility, reducing environmental impact, and driving economic growth, its social implications require careful management. Addressing issues of equity, job displacement, ethics, and infrastructure funding will be critical to realizing the potential of AVs in a way that benefits society as a whole. Achieving this balance will require a collaborative effort among governments, industry leaders, and communities.

6.2.3.2 Ethical/Legal Dilemmas in Decision-Making

AVs represent a technological frontier that promises safer, more efficient transportation systems. However, as machines designed to navigate human environments, AVs face a unique set of ethical challenges, particularly in unavoidable accident scenarios. Unlike human drivers, who often act reflexively, AVs must rely on pre-programmed algorithms, which require developers to anticipate and encode responses to complex moral dilemmas.

A quintessential illustration of these ethical complexities is the "Trolley Problem," a thought experiment that poses a grim choice: should an AV continue on its path and harm a group of pedestrians or swerve, potentially causing harm to its occupants or a single bystander? While human drivers rely on split-second instincts, AVs must execute pre-defined decisions. This distinction magnifies the moral weight of such situations.

Programming decisions for AVs in these scenarios are not merely a technical issue; they involve deep ethical responsibility. For instance, a utilitarian approach might prioritize the greatest good for the greatest number, sacrificing one life to save many. While seemingly logical, this approach raises profound concerns about the quantification and valuation of human lives. Who decides whose life is more "valuable"? Should demographic factors, age, or perceived social contribution be considered?

Moreover, legal implications further complicate this issue. For example, if an AV's algorithm deliberately prioritizes one group over another, could the manufacturer or programmer be held liable for wrongful death or even manslaughter? Existing legal frameworks, often based on human accountability, struggle to address these new complexities.

To address these dilemmas, it is essential that AV decision-making principles are not determined unilaterally by manufacturers or policymakers. Instead, inclusive public dialogue must shape these systems, ensuring they reflect societal values and norms. Public trust in AVs depends significantly on the transparency of their decision-making algorithms.

Developing ethical AI for AVs also necessitates interdisciplinary collaboration, blending insights from engineers, ethicists, legal experts, and social scientists. Ethical training for engineers, particularly in corporate social responsibility (CSR), is vital. By embedding ethical considerations into the development process, engineers can better anticipate and address potential societal impacts.

Governments and international bodies need to play an active role in shaping the regulatory environment for AVs. These frameworks should provide clear guidelines for ethical programming, emphasizing accountability without stifling innovation. Additionally, regulatory bodies must establish protocols for incident analysis, ensuring that liability is fairly assigned between manufacturers, software developers, and vehicle operators.

Societal acceptance of AVs hinges on addressing these ethical challenges comprehensively. Public forums, citizen panels, and stakeholder engagement initiatives can foster consensus on how AVs should handle moral dilemmas. For example, governments could facilitate large-scale surveys or deliberative workshops to gauge public opinion on AV decision-making priorities.

Furthermore, continuous education and dialogue about the capabilities and limitations of AV technology are crucial. Misinformation or lack of understanding can lead to misplaced fears or unrealistic expectations, undermining societal trust in AVs (Dathe, 2024; Krieger-Lamina, 2016).

6.2.3.3 Cybersecurity and Data Privacy Concerns

The emergence of AVs offers unprecedented possibilities for connectivity and efficiency. However, the integration of advanced technologies into AVs brings with it significant challenges related to cybersecurity and data privacy, issues that are central to public trust and the safe adoption of this transformative technology.

AVs rely on complex networks of sensors and systems to navigate and operate efficiently. These systems generate and process vast amounts of data, encompassing everything from location tracking and environmental monitoring to user behavior and vehicle performance. This data is crucial for enabling the high levels of precision required for autonomous navigation and communication with external systems. Yet, the sheer volume and sensitivity of the information collected raise serious privacy and security concerns.

The data collected by AVs can paint an intimate portrait of an individual's life, including their daily routines, frequented locations, and personal preferences. The potential misuse of such information poses ethical and security risks. For example, unauthorized access to movement data could enable criminal activities, such as targeted theft or surveillance. Additionally, commercial exploitation of this data without informed user consent undermines personal privacy, creating tension between technological advancement and individual rights.

AVs, as part of an ecosystem that includes other vehicles, road infrastructure, and service providers, are particularly vulnerable to malicious attacks. Cybersecurity breaches could compromise not only individual vehicles but entire networks, leading to safety incidents or systemic disruptions. The risk of hacking, whether to access sensitive data or manipulate vehicle functions, underscores the critical importance of robust security measures to protect both users and infrastructure.

Addressing these challenges requires a multifaceted approach. Technological solutions must be paired with legal frameworks to govern data use and ownership. The question of who controls the data generated by AVs remains unresolved, with competing claims from vehicle owners, manufacturers, and third-party providers. Resolving these ambiguities is essential for establishing accountability and safeguarding user rights.

Regulatory efforts have begun to tackle these issues. In some regions, initiatives have been launched to ensure transparency in data handling and to provide users with greater control over their information. These efforts aim to strike a balance between leveraging data for innovation and protecting individual privacy. However, the complexity of AV data ecosystems demands ongoing collaboration between governments, industry stakeholders, and civil society.

The role of automotive manufacturers is particularly significant. Companies must adopt a proactive stance, embedding data privacy and cybersecurity considerations into the design of AV systems from the outset. This involves not only technical safeguards, such as encryption and intrusion detection, but also ethical commitments to prioritize user protection over commercial gain. By fostering a culture of responsibility and transparency, manufacturers can help build the trust necessary for widespread acceptance of autonomous technology.

Public engagement is also critical. Educating consumers about the data collected by AVs and their rights regarding its use is key to empowering individuals and fostering informed consent. Public discourse can also help shape the ethical principles underpinning AV design, ensuring that societal values are reflected in technological development.

The integration of AVs into daily life offers immense potential to revolutionize transportation, but this promise can only be realized if cybersecurity and data privacy are addressed comprehensively. By building resilient systems, enacting clear regulations, and engaging transparently with the public, the automotive industry and policymakers can navigate these challenges, laying the foundation for a secure and ethical autonomous future (Dathe, 2024; Krieger-Lamina, 2016).

6.3 Outlooks: Future Trends and Developments

The future of autonomous driving is poised to transform the automotive industry, redefining mobility through advances in AI, V2X communication, and the adoption of sustainable technologies. These developments promise innovative solutions, such as AI-driven traffic management systems and autonomous flying vehicles, which could alleviate urban congestion, revolutionize logistics, and even play critical roles in disaster response scenarios (Dathe, 2024; Hu et al., 2021).

In today's era of mobility, the focus has shifted toward in-vehicle infotainment systems that enhance user experience with advanced connectivity and applications. This shift has attracted non-traditional players into the automotive ecosystem, including software developers and third-party content providers, intensifying competition and diversifying the industry's value chain. As V2X technologies evolve, the integration of next-generation wireless communication, Internet of Things (IoT) devices, and robotics will ensure seamless interaction between vehicles and infrastructure. For instance, cooperative control of connected systems may optimize traffic flow, improve road safety, and reduce energy consumption. These technologies are not limited to automotive applications; they also hold promise for sectors such as agriculture and defense, demonstrating their far-reaching potential (Hu et al., 2021; Krasniqi & Hajrizi, 2016).

Automakers are rethinking their roles, shifting from solely producing vehicles to becoming providers of integrated mobility services. Some business models are even enabling customers to monetize their vehicles by subletting them within their communities. This aligns with the broader trend of the shared economy, where efficiency and accessibility are prioritized (Butcher, 2022; Lawrence, 2019). While these changes promise environmental and cost benefits, they also raise challenges, such as managing the transition period during which private and shared AVs coexist. Achieving Level 5 autonomy will likely accelerate the adoption of MaaS and further disrupt traditional vehicle ownership models (Lawrence, 2019).

The rise of AVs is driving a paradigm shift in mobility, favoring service-oriented business models over traditional car ownership. This transition is particularly evident in urban centers where shared mobility solutions, such as autonomous ride-hailing and delivery services, are gaining traction. For instance, Baidu's "Apollo Go" service is pioneering the deployment of driverless robotaxis in cities like Beijing, which underscores the potential for MaaS to reduce private vehicle ownership. These recurring income streams not only diversify traditional business models but also offer scalability and long-term growth opportunities. Moreover, the transition to autonomous mobility is driving innovation in vehicle design, manufacturing processes, and smart infrastructure, igniting a race among companies to secure leadership positions in a rapidly evolving market (Butcher, 2022; Lawrence, 2019).

Success in this competitive landscape requires a multifaceted approach. Rapid technological innovation is essential for developing cutting-edge systems that ensure safety, efficiency, and user trust. Strategic partnerships can help address complex challenges, from regulatory compliance to infrastructure integration. Additionally, consumer adoption will depend on delivering exceptional user experiences, emphasizing reliability, convenience, and safety. Companies that excel in integrating AI capabilities with smart city ecosystems and uphold rigorous ethical standards in autonomous technologies will likely lead the charge in defining the future of mobility.

Emerging innovations like autonomous flying vehicles are poised to revolutionize urban transportation by addressing challenges such as congestion and disaster response. These vehicles, which integrate advanced driving technologies with vertical mobility capabilities, could redefine mobility in cities. Industry projections suggest commercialization efforts will mature by the early 2030s, with applications ranging from air taxis to cargo transport. Companies such as Volocopter and others are leading this charge, focusing on pilot testing and infrastructure development to ensure scalability and safety. However, significant hurdles remain, particularly around regulatory approvals, infrastructure readiness, and consumer adoption (Economist, 2019).

The increasing sophistication of AVs also demands adaptation from the automotive insurance industry. Liability is shifting from individual drivers to manufacturers, leading to changes in policy frameworks and claims handling. Additionally, policymakers are tasked with modernizing traffic laws, taxation systems, and deciding how to allocate the costs of upgrading infrastructure to accommodate AVs. Collaboration among public and private stakeholders will be crucial to addressing these challenges effectively (Krasniqi & Hajrizi, 2016).

Autonomous driving also introduces profound implications for Environmental, Social, and Governance (ESG) considerations. Environmentally, AVs promise significant reductions in emissions and energy use through optimized traffic flows and fuel-efficient designs. Socially, they hold the potential to democratize mobility, providing greater access for non-drivers, including the elderly and disabled. However, these benefits must be weighed against potential job losses and societal disruptions. From a governance perspective, transparency in AI algorithms, cybersecurity protocols, and data privacy standards is essential to fostering public trust (Krasniqi & Hajrizi, 2016; Taeihagh, 2025).

While AVs offer substantial advantages, including enhanced road safety, reduced congestion, and lower transportation costs, challenges such as increased maintenance expenses, privacy concerns, and ethical dilemmas in decision-making remain. The balance of these factors underscores the importance of thoughtful regulation, ethical oversight, and robust cybersecurity measures. Governments and industry leaders must work together to ensure that the societal benefits of autonomous mobility are maximized while mitigating its adverse impacts (Krasniqi & Hajrizi, 2016; Krieger-Lamina, 2016).

China remains at the forefront of AV development, with services such as Baidu's Apollo Go exemplifying the country's leadership in robotaxi deployment. These driverless services are scaling rapidly across urban areas, offering cost-effective mobility solutions. However, this growth raises critical concerns about employment, particularly for workers in public transportation and delivery sectors. To address these disruptions, governments are pressed to implement robust retraining programs and support frameworks that enable workers to transition into roles suited to an evolving job market (McKinsey, 2023).

Tesla, on the other hand, is ramping up its robotaxi ambitions with plans to mass-produce millions of AVs. CEO Elon Musk has positioned Tesla's robotaxi initiative as a cornerstone of the company's strategy, emphasizing the potential to redefine urban mobility through sustainable, electric-powered AV fleets. Tesla's advancements not only accelerate competition in the sector but also highlight the interplay of private innovation and public infrastructure development required for large-scale deployment (Reuters, 2024).

Geopolitically, the AV race is emblematic of broader technological competition between the U.S. and China. Each nation leverages policies, investments, and standards-setting efforts to secure leadership. Concerns over data governance and supply chain dependencies are central to this rivalry, particularly as AVs generate vast amounts of sensitive information, necessitating robust cybersecurity and privacy protections.

Autonomous driving represents a cornerstone of digital transformation in the automotive industry. Its influence extends beyond transportation, reshaping economic models, urban planning, and societal dynamics. By addressing technical, ethical, and regulatory challenges with foresight and collaboration, the promise of autonomous driving can be realized in a way that aligns with global sustainability and equity goals.

References

Ackerman, E. (31 August 2016). Self-Driving Cars Were Just Around the Corner—in 1960. Retrieved from IEEE Spectrum: https://spectrum.ieee.org/selfdriving-cars-were-just-around-the-cornerin-1960, accessed 23.11.2024.

Baidu. (2017). DuerOS—Conversational AI Platform. Retrieved from Duer: https://dueros.baidu.com/en/html/dueros/index.html, accessed 23.11.2024.

Baidu. (29 December 2022). Baidu to Add 200 Fully Driverless Robotaxis to Fleet in 2023, Aiming for World's Largest Fully Driverless Ride-hailing Area. Retrieved from PR Newswire: https://www.prnewswire.com/news-releases/baidu-to-add-200-fully-driverless-robotaxis-to-fleet-in-2023-aiming-for-worlds-largest-fully-driverless-ride-hailing-area-301711296.html, accessed 23.11.2024.

Bosch. (2024). Automated Driving. Retrieved from https://www.bosch.com/stories/topics/automated-driving/, accessed 23.11.2024.

Butcher, L. (6 May 2022). Baidu Secures Permits for Autonomous Ride-Hailing Operations in Beijing. By Autonomous Vehicle International: https://www.autonomousvehicleinternational.com/news/robotaxis/baidu-secures-permits-for-autonomous-ride-hailing-operations-in-beijing.html, accessed 23.11.2024.

Courcoubetis, C., Li, Y., Gao, S., & Huang, Q. (2024). The impact of ride-hailing in city transportation. *Frontiers of Engineering Management*, https://doi.org/10.1007/s42524-024-4198-0

Cruise. (2024). History of Cruise. Retrieved from Cruise: https://getcruise.com/about/, accessed 23.11.2024.

DARPA. (n.a.). What is the Urban Challenge? Retrieved from Urban Challenge: https://www.grandchallenge.org/grandchallenge/overview.html, accessed 23.11.2024.

Dathe, T. (2024). Automated driving and AI in mobility. In M. Helmold, A. K. Yilmaz, & T. Dathe, *The digital champion. Best practices and insights for the successful transformation and digitization roadmap*. Singapore: World Scientific Publishing Co. Ptd. Ltd.

Economist. (2019). Flying Cars are Almost Here, But They Don't Look Like Cars - The First Ones Available are Most Likely to Run as Taxis. Retrieved from Economist.com: https://www.economist.com/technology-quarterly/2019/05/30/flying-cars-are-almost-here-but-they-dont-look-like-cars?utm_medium=cpc.adword.pd&utm_source=google&ppccampaignID=18151738051&ppcadID=&utm_campaign=a.22brand_pmax&utm_content=conversion.direct-resp, accessed 23.11.2024.

European Union. (24 March 2022). Artificial Intelligence in Automated Driving: An Analysis of Safety and Cybersecurity Challenges. Von HAMON Ronan; JUNKLEWITZ Henrik; SANCHEZ MARTIN Jose Ignacio; FERNANDEZ LLORCA David; GOMEZ GUTIERREZ Emilia; HERRERA ALCANTARA Antonio; KRISTON Akos: https://publications.jrc.ec.europa.eu/repository/handle/JRC127189, accessed 23.11.2024.

Fraunhofer IKS. (2023). Autonomous Driving. Retrieved from Fraunhofer Institute for Cognitive Systems IKS: https://www.iks.fraunhofer.de/en/topics/autonomous-driving.html, accessed 23.11.2024.

Garikapati, D., & Shetiya, S. S. (2024). Autonomous Vehicles: Evolution of Artificial Intelligence and the Current Industry Landscape. *Big Data and Cognitive Computing*, *8*(4), 42. https://doi.org/10.3390/bdcc8040042

Hollinger, K. V., & Shirazi, H. (December 2020). Management of Safety Risk in Automated Driving Systems. Retrieved from MITRE: https://www.mitre.org/sites/default/files/2021-11/prs-20-3326-management-of-safety-risk-in-automated-driving-systems.pdf, accessed 23.11.2024.

Hu, J., Bhowmick, P., Jang, I., Arvin, F., & Lanzon, A. (2021). A Decentralized Cluster Formation Containment. *IEEE Transactions on Robotics*, *37*(6), 1936–1955.

James, A. (7 September 2023). Baidu's Apollo Go robotaxi Fleet in Wuhan Goes from Five to 300 Vehicles – In One Year. Retrieved from Autonomous Vehicle & International: https://www.autonomousvehicleinternational.com/news/robotaxis/baidus-apollo-go-robotaxi-fleet-in-wuhan-goes-from-5-to-300-vehicles-in-one-year.html, accessed 23.11.2024.

Jaramillo, E. (23 February 2023). Top 10 Chinese Autonomous Driving Companies to Watch. Retrieved from The China Project: https://thechinaproject.com/2023/02/23/ten-chinese-autonomous-driving-companies-to-watch/, accessed 23.11.2024.

Krasniqi, X., & Hajrizi, E. (2016). Use of IoT Technology to Drive the Automotive Industry from Connected to Full Autonomous Vehicles. *IFAC-PapersOnLine*, *49*(29), 269–274. https://doi.org/10.1016/j.ifacol.2016.11.078

Krieger-Lamina, J. (2016). *Vernetzte Automobile - Datensammeln beim Fahren – von Assistenzsystemen zu autonomen Fahrzeugen*. Vienna, Austria: Institut für Technikfolgen-Abschätzung der Österreichischen Akademie der Wissenschaften.

LaFrance, A. (29 June 2016). Your Grandmother's Driverless Car. Retrieved from The Atlantic: https://www.theatlantic.com/technology/archive/2016/06/beep-beep/489029/, accessed 23.11.2024.

Lawrence, L. (25 February 2019). From Car Owning to Ride-Sharing: How MaaS Could Change the Way We Travel. Retrieved from Smart Mobility Hub: https://www.smart-mobility-hub.com/car-owning-to-ride-sharing-how-maas-could-change-the-way-we-travel/, accessed 23.11.2024.

Li, L., Jia, G., Song, J., & Ran, X. (2013). Progress on Vehicle Dynamics Stability Control System. *Journal of Mechanical Engineering*, *49*(24).

McKinsey. (6 January 2023). Autonomous Driving's Future: Convenient and Connected. Retrieved from https://www.mckinsey.com/industries/automotive-and-assembly/our-insights/autonomous-drivings-future-convenient-and-connected, accessed 23.11.2024.

Mobility21. (2024). The Road Ahead for Self-driving Cars. Retrieved from Mobility21 News: https://mobility21.cmu.edu/the-road-ahead-for-self-driving-cars/, accessed 23.11.2024.

Motortrend. (2024). 2015 Audi RS 7 Expert Review. Retrieved from Reviewed by Stefan Ogbac: https://www.motortrend.com/cars/audi/rs-7/2015/, accessed 23.11.2024.

Nevada Department of Motor Vehicles DMV. (2023). Autonomous & Alternative Electronic Transportation System Vehicles. Retrieved from https://copilot.microsoft.com/chats/GxBzg2dYboYu8hnDBec1Z, accessed 23.11.2024.

Reuters. (18 February 2022). GM Seeks U.S. Approval to Deploy Self-driving Vehicles. By David Shepardson: https://www.reuters.com/business/autos-transportation/gm-seeks-us-approval-deploy-self-driving-vehicle-2022-02-18/, accessed 23.11.2024.

Reuters. (24 October 2024). Tesla Promises Paid Robotaxis Next Year, But Significant Hurdles Remain. By Chris Kirkham: https://www.reuters.com/business/autos-transportation/tesla-promises-paid-robotaxis-next-year-significant-hurdles-remain-2024-10-24/, accessed 23.11.2024.

SAE. (3 May 2021). SAE Levels of Driving Automation™ Refined for Clarity and International Audience. By Society of Automotive Engineers: https://www.sae.org/blog/sae-j3016-update, accessed 23.11.2024.

Sanjana, T., Fuad, K. A., Habib, M. M., & Rumel, A. A. (2017). Automated Anti-Collision System for Automobiles. International Conference on Electrical, Computer and Communication Engineering (ECCE) (S. 16-18). Cox's Bazar, Bangladesh: IEEE.

Schroeder, S. (7 July 2023). Elon Musk Says Tesla Might Achieve Fully Autonomous Driving 'later this year'. By Mashable: https://mashable.com/article/elon-musk-tesla-fully-autonomous-self-driving, accessed 23.11.2024.

Silva, Ó., Cordera, R., González-González, E., & Nogués, S. (2022). Environmental Impacts of Autonomous Vehicles: A Review of the Scientific Literature. *Science of the Total Environment, 830*, 154615. https://doi.org/10.1016/j.scitotenv.2022.154615

Taeihagh, A. (2025). Governance of Generative AI. Policy and Society, *44*(1), 1–22, https://doi.org/10.1093/polsoc/puaf001, accessed 18.12.2025.

Tjokro, M. (20 April 2021). Why Self-Driving Cars: From Horseless to Driverless. By Mobility21 News: https://mobility21.cmu.edu/why-self-driving-cars-from-horseless-to-driverless/, accessed 23.11.2024.

Wang, J., Huang, H., Li, K., & Li, J. (2021). Towards the Unified Principles for Level 5 Autonomous Vehicles. *Engineering, 7*(9), 1313–1325. https://doi.org/10.1016/j.eng.2020.10.018

Waymo. (22 April 2020a). In the Driver's Seat: Footage from Our 2009-2010 1,000 Autonomous Mile Challenge. By Nathaniel Fairfield: https://waymo.com/blog/2020/04/in-the-drivers-seat-1000-mile-challenge/, accessed 23.11.2024.

Waymo. (8 October 2020b). Waymo Is Opening Its Fully Driverless Service to the General Public in Phoenix. By John Krafcik (CEO): https://waymo.com/blog/2020/10/waymo-is-opening-its-fully-driverless-service-in-phoenix/, accessed 23.11.2024.

Waymo. (2024). Starting at Mile One - Waymo Story. Retrieved from Waymo: https://waymo.com/about/#story, accessed 23.11.2024.

World Economic Forum. (19 August 2016). Uber Is Rolling Out Its First Self-Driving Cars (with Humans Behind the Wheel). By Rosamond Hutt: https://www.weforum.org/stories/2016/08/uber-s-rolling-out-its-first-self-driving-cars-although-they-ll-still-have-humans-at-the-wheel/, accessed 23.11.2024.

Xiao, L., & Gao, F. (2010). A Comprehensive Review of the Development of Adaptive Cruise Control Systems. *Vehicle System Dynamics, 48*(10), 1167–1192. https://doi.org/10.1080/00423110903365910

Xu, Z., & Duffy, V. (2021). A Systematic Review of Autonomous Driving in Transportation. *HCI International 2021 - Late Breaking Papers: HCI Applications in Health, Transport, and Industry*. Cham: Springer. https://doi.org/10.1007/978-3-030-90966-6_28

Yang, Z. (23 January 2024). What's Next for Robotaxis in 2024. Retrieved from MIT Technology Review: https://www.technologyreview.com/2024/01/23/1086936/whats-next-for-robotaxis-2024/, accessed 23.11.2024.

Chapter 7

Pragmatic Approaches to Lending Decisions in the Context of Climate and ESG Risks and Their Technical Perspectives

Benjamin Tobias Peylo

7.1 The Risk-Based Perspective

There has always been a close, if not always harmonious, relationship between finance and sustainability. As early as 1760, the realization that the potential for profit tempted many, if not most, investors to disregard ethical considerations led John Wesley to establish non-financial principles for the use of money – essentially defining the first systematic exclusion criteria (Sparkes 2006). He thus became one of the founding fathers of sustainable investing, also known as socially responsible investing (SRI) because of its strong ethical component (for different etymologies and their characteristics, see Eccles & Viviers 2011). The core principle of SRI is to align investment decisions with ethical, environmental, and social considerations, thereby promoting a broader assessment of the long-term value of a company or project and its contributions – or detriments – to society and the planet (Statman 2007).

For many years, SRI remained a small niche in investment practice, but it was the only scientifically considered manifestation of sustainable finance. However,

 DOI: 10.1201/9781003528951-7

the focus was almost exclusively on whether sustainable investing meant sacrificing monetary returns (for an overview, see Bauer et al. 2005 or Orlitzky et al. 2003). For a long time, the question of whether this had an actual impact, i.e., a positive effect on sustainability-related goals, remained a niche within a niche. Where it has been examined, the impact has been assumed rather than assessed, taking into account the chain of effects via reputational effects and shareholder engagement that motivate companies to adopt sustainable practices (e.g., Oekom research 2013). Indeed, for the financial instruments considered (i.e., mutual funds), a more direct impact seems unlikely, as they are firmly embedded in the secondary market and thus more suited to move money between investors than to channel it into the transformation of companies or sustainable projects in the interest of sustainable development.

In contrast to this traditional anchoring of sustainability in investments, references to sustainability in lending are more recent. Here, the first systematic definition of exclusion criteria emerged, particularly in connection with the ecological damage caused by the oil industry: The Equator Principles (Scholtens & Dam 2007). In adopting these principles, banks "… seek to ensure that the projects we finance are developed in a socially responsible manner and reflect sound environmental management practices" (from the preamble of the Equator Principles, www.equator-principles.com). This was never intended to be a fundamental change in lending policy, but simply an attempt to prevent the worst of the worst from being financed.

The realization that it is not only possible to make concessions in the use of money, but also to consciously achieve the promotion of sustainable goals through the targeted channeling of money, was already reflected in the Brundtland Report, where the pursuit of sustainable development also considers "the direction of investment" (United Nations Brundtland Commission 1987, paragraph 30 of the report). Given the context, the term "investment" is used in a broader sense to include primarily primary market investments and lending/financing – as this is clearly aimed at enabling transformation rather than reflecting personal values in secondary market investment decisions.

These two perspectives, i.e., investment decisions based on sustainability criteria and the use of money as a catalyst for sustainable development, have long dominated the framework for sustainable finance. In a recent attempt to systematize different forms of sustainable finance, they are referred to as "value-based sustainable finance" and "action-based sustainable finance" (Peylo 2024). Especially in the wake of the EU's "Action Plan: Financing Sustainable Growth" (European Commission 2018), the latter in particular left its niche existence and was catapulted into the mainstream with the help of the Green Deal and the Green Taxonomy. However, there is a third important perspective to consider, which is currently on the verge of overtaking all others in importance: Risk-based sustainable finance, which focuses on assessing and managing climate-related risks and protecting loan portfolios from environmental, social, and governance (ESG)-related losses.

One of the reasons why this latter perspective has taken some time to emerge is the simple truth that the then Governor of the Bank of England, Mark Carney, aptly described in September 2015 as the "tragedy of the horizons" (Carney 2015): The disconnect between long-term climate-related impacts and short-term investment horizons. It allowed investors and banks who were not intrinsically motivated to neglect the issue – simply because it was not relevant to the time horizon in which they were investing. Under the label of "stranded assets" (i.e., the potential loss of value of fossil resources due to a changing market), both investors and regulators began to discuss the issue in a loose way, but this consideration initially remained rather abstract (BaFin 2019a).

Again as a result of the EU's "Action Plan: Financing Sustainable Growth" (European Commission 2018), however, an unprecedented spiral of action by central banks and supervisors worldwide has created considerable momentum: From the first papers with an emphasis on "recommendation" (e.g., BaFin 2019b) to a comprehensive, binding regulatory framework (e.g., ECB 2021) that is currently even enforced with substantial fines (Reuters 2024), the development of the risk perspective has accelerated enormously. By 2020, as confirmed by the Basel Committee on Banking Supervision in its "Stocktake Report", regulatory initiatives on ESG and climate risk regulation have multiplied and reached a global scale (BIS 2020).

Both the development itself and its urgency can be explained by the fact that there is strong evidence that the horizon of rapid climate warming and increasing economic impacts may not be so far away after all (Granoff 2023): "Climate risks like abrupt responses to policy and consumer demands – or the now-inevitable early shockwaves of physical climate impacts – are far more relevant to the economics of business decisions today". And indeed, the expected consequences for 2050 are even bleaker, with high percentage GDP declines for many countries (Swiss Re Institute 2021). Climate risk is already material and must be considered a significant threat to global financial stability (Basel Committee on Banking Supervision 2022).

7.1.1 Climate Risks and ESG Risks in Regulatory Frameworks

Unlike SRI, which promotes Sustainable Finance from a value-based perspective, the risk-based approach is not rooted in morally defined principles that can sometimes be criticized as being rather arbitrary (Peylo & Villhauer 2021). Similarly, unlike action-based sustainable finance, which centers on the Sustainable Development Goals (SDGs) as a transformative agenda, this perspective does not represent a forward-looking commitment to change. Instead, it reflects a collective awakening of financial markets triggered by the tangible and immediate threats of climate change, which have long been foreseen but are now undeniably real.

According to the "Action Plan: Financing Sustainable Growth" (European Commission 2018), the concept of risk-based sustainable finance has been further developed through several publications by financial institutions. These do not immediately give the impression of a coordinated approach, and often use different wording (e.g., referring to the risks in question as either "sustainability risks", "ESG risks", or "climate risks"), but they nevertheless convey a coherent picture of the action needed: In Europe, the German banking regulator BaFin published the "Guidance Notice on Dealing with Sustainability Risks" (2019b) almost simultaneously with the European Banking Authority's (EBA) "Action Plan on Sustainable Finance" (2019). The EBA later built on this with the detailed "Discussion Paper on Management and Supervision of ESG Risks for Credit Institutions and Investment Firms" (2020). Similarly, the European Central Bank (ECB) published a draft "Guide on Climate-Related and Environmental Risks" in 2020, which was finalized in 2021. Most notably, the Bank for International Settlements (BIS) capped these efforts with its "Principles for the Effective Management and Supervision of Climate-Related Financial Risks" in 2022, following up on its earlier stocktaking report (Basel Committee on Banking Supervision 2020) and potentially paving the way for future Basel developments (Basel Committee on Banking Supervision 2022). Other central banks and supervisors worldwide have also contributed to their own publications.

Despite slightly different labels and definitions, recent international publications tend to use the term "ESG risk" rather than "climate risks", "climate-related risks", or "sustainability risks" (EBA 2024, but also NBG 2024 and CBA 2024), so this term will also be used here in this paper. The closest thing we have to a general definition is the explanation provided by the EBA (2024): "Climate change, environmental degradation, social issues and other environmental, social and governance (ESG) factors are posing considerable challenges for the economy. The impact of acute and chronic physical events, the needed transition to a low carbon, resource efficient and sustainable economy as well as other ESG challenges are causing and will continue to cause profound economic transformations that impact the financial sector" (ibid, 5). Despite this broad approach, the prominence of climate risks is also made clear: "Environmental risks, including climate-related, are expected inter alia to become even more prominent going forward through transition and physical risk drivers. This may affect all traditional categories of financial risks to which institutions are exposed".

As a first response to the threat to financial stability, many supervisors have formed the Network for Greening the Financial System (NGFS, https://www.ngfs.net/en), whose main contribution to the implementation of risk-based sustainable finance has been the definition of climate scenarios for stress testing. Because of the tie-in to conventional stress testing as a proven tool of financial regulation, they are welcomed by many regulatory institutions – but they are also criticized by the scientific community for significant and potentially highly influential flaws. The renowned Institute and Faculty of Actuaries at the University of Exeter, in its pointed publications "The Emperor's New Climate Scenarios", formulates a "warning for financial services" (Institute and Faculty of Actuaries 2023): "It is concerning to see these same economic models being used to underpin climate-change scenario analysis in financial services, leading to the publication of implausible results in the Task Force on Climate-related Financial Disclosures (TCFD) reporting that show benign, or even positive, economic outcomes in a hot-house world".

Judging by the results of the ECB's second economy-wide climate stress test (ECB 2023), it could indeed be argued that the impact of the assumed risks does not fully reflect the full extent of the crisis highlighted, for example, by the Swiss Re Institute (2021). However, the findings that "Frontloading green investment significantly reduces medium-term costs and risks facing households and firms" and "further delaying transition means missing Paris Agreement goals and exacerbating impact of costly physical risks" are less distorting than predicted by the Institute and Faculty of Actuaries (2023) and provide a strong basis for the next step of regulation: After raising awareness of the issue and conducting an economy-wide assessment, the focus is now on systematic and comprehensive management of ESG risks in financial institutions. And for many banks, this is where the problems begin.

7.1.2 Demand-Based vs. Solution-Based Regulation

The current approach in European banking supervision – as reiterated in the "Draft Guidelines on the management of ESG risks" (ECB 2024) – can be described as a "demand-based approach". In this approach, supervisors set objectives, such as the effective measurement and management of ESG risks, but leave it to institutions to determine their own methods of achieving these objectives. Institutions are required to present their results and justify their validity, but regulators typically take their time before identifying and endorsing particular solutions as "best practices". While this approach encourages innovation and adaptation to specific institutional contexts, it can create challenges, particularly for smaller institutions with limited resources and expertise, as they must develop solutions that meet regulatory expectations on their own or purchase them at significant cost.

An alternative approach that could address these challenges is a "solutions-based approach". Here, supervisors take a more active role in developing, training, and disseminating standardized tools and guidance for ESG risk assessment and management. These resources are then made freely available to institutions, particularly smaller ones. This approach greatly helps to address several issues: For smaller institutions, it reduces the burden of independently developing complex ESG risk management systems, enabling them to implement high-quality practices for whom regulatory acceptance is secured without imposing additional financial burdens. For supervisors, on the other hand, it streamlines the identification of effective solutions and facilitates a more consistent implementation of ESG risk standards across the banking industry. This, in turn, accelerates the establishment of robust ESG risk management practices, thereby improving the sector's resilience to climate and other sustainability risks.

The work of the National Bank of Georgia (NBG) is an excellent example of an institution taking the latter approach: The NBG sets high standards for the country's banks, but also provides them with the tools to implement these standards in a pragmatic way – while still leaving room for individual solutions. As a pragmatic tool for ESG risk assessment at the portfolio level, the first version of what was then called the "Climate-related Risk Radar" (NBG 2022) was published in 2022. In 2023, the ESG Guidelines broadened the scope to include loan-level applications. In 2024, the new version of the now-named "ESG Risk Radar" was published, with a much more refined and detailed approach to risk assessment (NBG 2024). The tool is based on the author's research and concepts (described in Peylo & Nuß 2024) and was implemented in cooperation with the Deutsche Sparkassenstiftung für Internationale Kooperation DSIK (engl. German Sparkassenstiftung for International Cooperation, https://www.sparkassenstiftung.de), which in turn cooperates with the University of Applied Sciences Kempten (https://www.hs-kempten.de) in the topic of sustainable finance. The NBG has contributed significantly to the development of the loan-level assessment, while the Central Bank of Armenia was instrumental in the development of the second version of the tool, which has now been published in its application for the country of Armenia as well (CBA 2024).

The ESG Risk Radar, presently used by a dozen institutions on five continents, is a strong example of how ESG risk assessment and management can be approached pragmatically, even in contexts where individual banks and financial institutions face challenges such as limited data availability and lack of prior experience. These tools demonstrate that, with a focus on practicality and ease of implementation, it is possible to support banks and financial institutions in effectively integrating ESG considerations into their risk management frameworks.

It is important to note, however, that highlighting the ESG Risk Radar as a positive example is not intended to suggest that it is the best tool available or that it outperforms other commercial or open source solutions. Rather, its value lies in the positive feedback it has received and its demonstrated ability to meet specific criteria of accessibility, adaptability, and usefulness, particularly in data- and information-constrained environments. This example underscores the potential for regulators and financial institutions to make meaningful progress in ESG risk management by leveraging pragmatic, user-friendly approaches.

7.1.3 The ESG Risk Radar

For most banks, the practical implications of ESG risks are most evident in their impact on the loan portfolio, which is their core business (see NBG 2022 for this and subsequent discussions). Here, banks are at a significant disadvantage compared to securities investors: Since publicly traded companies already provide a wealth of information relevant to ESG assessment due to their size and both formal regulation and informal expectation, investors can either conduct their own research or rely on professional rating agencies that provide standardized ESG ratings (e.g., see ISS 2021). However, most bank customers are small and medium-sized enterprises (SMEs) or individuals for whom professional ESG ratings are not available and who are often not even aware of the concept of ESG, let alone able to provide adequate data.

As a result, the traditional approach to risk assessment in the credit process (i.e., gathering risk-relevant information from the bottom up, directly from the client) is often not feasible for ESG risk assessment. As a result, a top-down approach is often taken, analyzing the ESG risk situation in the client's industry to gain insight into the ESG issues related to the client's overall business model. This approach can be seen, for example, in Germany's two largest banking groups – the savings banks group and the cooperative banks group. Their tools, the "S-ESG Score" (published, e.g., by Haspa 2024) and the "VR-ESG-RisikoScore" (discussed by Jackes 2023), respectively, aggregate statistical data to generate sector-based ESG risk scores.

While the sector-based approach has many merits and solves the problem of a lack of information on the part of the customer, a detailed analysis of the two examples at hand shows that the criteria used within the scoring sometimes do not clearly distinguish between a sustainability assessment with its ethical or moral considerations and an ESG assessment with its strictly economic focus. While sustainability and ESG have a large overlap, they differ significantly in that ESG only considers the financial, risk-relevant consequences and can thus be seen as the "financialization of sustainability" (Delgado-Ceballos et al. 2023). It is therefore of paramount importance that ESG ratings focus only on ESG and do not dilute this view with less focused considerations related to a broader sustainability context where economic impacts may be less well established. In addition, with tools solely relying on statistical data, there's always the question of whether the key figures on which the scoring is based are really suitable for conveying the information that the concept hopes for.

Beyond these more specific considerations – which will clearly improve over time given the current steep global learning curve – scores based on statistical information rely on a substantial supply of data that cannot be taken for granted in most countries yet. This is where the concept of the ESG Risk Radar comes in, as it uses the top-down approach, but is based on a strong foundation of qualitative research that neither requires statistical data nor runs the risk of using metrics that ultimately do not reflect what they are intended to measure.

The ESG Risk Radar was first developed in Germany, where it preceded the statistically based approaches mentioned above, and has been implemented in more than 100 savings and cooperative banks there. Since then, it has been further developed (to a large extent in cooperation with teams from the NBG and the CBA, and to a lesser extent with other international partner institutions) and implemented by the German Sparkassenstiftung DSIK in projects on five continents.

As a scoring-based approach, it qualifies as an example of the "exposure method" in the EBA typology (EBA 2020, p. 68). As it allows banks to directly assess the ESG risks of the portfolio and individual clients, the EBA highlights the exposure method as "the most practical and easy to implement of the three approaches" that are given there (ibid.). In general, the exposure method uses a scoring system to assess the potential impact of ESG factors on a counterparty. This scoring framework is intended to provide an assessment of the extent to which these factors could negatively affect a client's ability to meet their financial obligations, thereby exposing the bank to the risk of increased loan defaults. The important part of any application, therefore, is the identification of the relevant ESG factors.

At its core, risk management always involves identifying and assessing potential threats in order to gain a clear understanding of them and make informed decisions. However, as Borge (2001) aptly states, "Risk management is not and will never be a magic formula that will always give you the right answer. It is a way of thinking that gives you better answers to better questions, and in doing so, helps you shift the odds in your favor". In many risk areas, this process often relies on the analysis of historical data. However, ESG risks, which are both forward-looking and largely unprecedented, lack the robust data sets required for complex mathematical modeling. As a practical alternative, a qualitative approach, coupled with a structured and thorough consideration of all relevant factors, serves as a critical starting point in the development of ESG risk management.

To address this challenge, the ESG Risk Radar has been deliberately designed to be practical, easy to understand, and transparent. Its mechanics are fully disclosed, avoiding any "black box" ambiguity often given with commercial tools that have to hide their core algorithm in order to protect their USP. The sector scoring methodology allows users to clearly see and, if necessary, adjust the risk ratings in order to reflect regional peculiarities. As a result, the tool is designed to be a streamlined yet effective risk management tool, adaptable to the unique context and requirements of the bank and the country in which it operates.

The selection used by the ESG Risk Radar is shown in the scorecard in Figure 7.1, which is the core of the methodology. The selection of criteria and their weighting are described in great detail in the methodology published by CBA (2024), but suffice it to say here that the score, which ranges from 0 to 12, is made up in equal parts of physical climate risks (both acute and chronic), transition risks, and other ESG risks. Each of these three parts consists of different elements: For example, the assessment of transition risks is based, on the one hand, on the sector's contribution to emissions (as this is a key factor in determining the extent to which the sector will come under pressure to change) and, on the other hand, on the intensity of transition of the given sector, which in turn consists of the likelihood and impact of regulatory changes, the availability of new technologies and their acceptance by market participants.

The selection of these items is based on the stakeholder model of socio-economic rationality (Schaltegger et al. 2003) and aims at a consistent modeling of the

NACE Code	Sector Name			Scoring			Reference
	Physical Climate Risk	Acute		0-4, Weight 50%		0-4	1
		Chronic		0-4, Weight 50%			2
	Transition Climate Risk	GHG-Emission Contribution		0-4, Weight 50%		0-4	3
		Transitional Intensity	Probability of Regulatory Change	0-4, Weight 25%	0-4, Weight 50%		4
			Economic Impact of Regulatory Change	0-4, Weight 25%			5
			Technological Change	0-4, Weight 25%			6
			Customer Behavior	0-4, Weight 25%			7
	Other ESG Risks	Loss of Biodiversity		Add-on Factor	0-1, Weight 25%	0-4	8
		Other Environmental Risks		Add-on Factor	0-1, Weight 25%		9
		Possible Human Rights Issues		Add-on Factor	0-1, Weight 25%		10
		Other Social Risks		Add-on Factor	0-1, Weight 25%		11
					ESG-Risk Score at Sector-Level:	0-12	

Figure 7.1 The main scorecard of the ESG Risk Radar (From Peylo, B. T. & Nuß, C. (2024). Two Sides of the Same Coin: ESG Risk and Opportunity Management in the Investment and Lending Business. In *Sustainable Wealth Management: Directing Capital Towards Sustainability* (p. 127). Springer International Publishing).

driving forces behind transition processes in sustainable development. The score that the item receives ranges from 0 to 4, where 0 can be interpreted as a *theoretical* consideration, and 1 includes *perceptible* developments that will cause some damage in individual cases. A score of 2 would indicate a development/risk that is *obvious* and must be detrimental to business; a score of 3 would indicate a development/risk that is *significant* and will cause serious and widespread damage. Finally, a score of 4 indicates an *existential* development/risk whose potential damage is very high and may prove fatal for many companies in the sector. By applying a weighting, the item of each part is aggregated to an overall score between 0 and 4 for each of the three parts, which is then summarized to the total score accordingly ranging between 0 and 12.

While in the first version of the ESG Risk Radar, the score for each item was assessed by a researcher, documenting both the decision and the sources on which the assessment was based, this was found to be arbitrary and scores could vary between different researchers. Therefore, in version 2 of the tool, the assessment of each item is now done in sub-scores, where six indicators are defined and scored. For example, the item of "acute physical climate risk" is assessed via the indicators "observed loss of assets/property", "expected impact on revenue", "expected impact on costs", the likelihood of these indicators increasing in the future, "lack of business model adaptability", and the consideration of whether sectors in the supply chain have already received a high risk score that could act as a "contagion" and affect the sector under scrutiny. Whether these indicators are given or not is determined by the availability of sources that report them, taking into account both the emphasis (indicator "present" or "strong") and the quality of the source (three levels ranging from social media at the lowest level to peer-reviewed journals and laws at the highest level), resulting in an indicator-score between 0.25 and 1. The overall score is truncated at a maximum of 4 and then fed back into the parent scoring table as shown in Figure 7.1.

This methodology has been shown to produce consistent, intersubjectively understandable results based on a wealth of research. It needs to be done sector by sector for each country where it is implemented – with a higher level of precision and documentation for potential high-risk sectors and a more pragmatic approach for medium or low-risk sectors. Obviously, the initial effort of this method is considerable. However, the major advantage is that it does not require quantitative data (which is often missing) and produces a body of documented knowledge on ESG risk in a country's sectors that can be useful in understanding and managing ESG risk in a bank well beyond the scoring itself. Because of its strictly defined methodology, it removes as much subjectivity as possible, and because everything is well documented, the results are easily accessible. In fact, this "open box" approach is one of the success factors of the ESG Risk Radar. Where "black box" approaches hide the assessment process in an algorithm and simply present the result that one has to *accept*, the transparent, well-documented process of the radar opens the eyes for the interrelationships and mutual influences, and in this way makes it possible to evaluate and *understand* the results.

As part of the tools implementation in the banks, a workshop is held to present both the methodology and the results to the staff of the partner organizations. The results of the assessment of the economic sectors are displayed on a bulletin board, and the participants are asked to indicate with colored stickers their agreement (green sticker), doubt (yellow), or disagreement (red) directly on the assessment sheets. The result is always quite mixed, with a lot of resistance, especially to high-risk results. The next step is to formalize working groups that go through each assessment in detail, re-evaluate the sources, and do their own research. From experience, there have been cases where the working groups have raised the risk ratings – for example, by adding native-language sources. But there has not yet been a case where the score was lowered after this research. Instead, the now well-informed bankers were able to explain to their colleagues the emergence of ESG risks and their great relevance to the bank.

This awareness and ownership can be seen as an even greater outcome than the list of sector scores alone. While the latter can now be used to analyze risk at the portfolio level (i.e., the "heat map", see Basel Committee on Banking Supervision 2022) and to formulate thresholds and strategies, it is the knowledge and awareness of the staff that enables the level of consideration and competent management intended and required by supervisors.

It is also a prerequisite for an independent re-evaluation of the results after a certain period of time, since the research must naturally be renewed and the sources re-evaluated after 2–3 years. However, this does not have to be done by individual banks: As the scores are valid at the country level, both the initial research and the ongoing updating process can be organized and carried out either by a central bank (as is the case in three of the countries where the tool has been implemented) or, for example, by a banking union. Regardless of who carries out the reassessment, it makes sense to plan for the training aspect at the same time: banks need the application and general knowledge of ESG risk management, and this is currently not available to the extent needed: Given the challenges and the small, slow steps in which the overall topic of sustainability is anchored in the university context (Žalėnienė & Pereira 2021), this process naturally poses an even greater challenge for the highly specialized topic of sustainable finance. For this reason, the banks and their associations will have to implement further education and training in this area themselves for the foreseeable future before the education system can deliver the high level of knowledge required. Here, the tool also lends itself to the design and delivery of learning units to maintain a consistently high level of expertise in the banks using it.

Finally, while the tool allows for a sector-level risk assessment of the loan portfolio, it does not yet provide direct control over the lending process (except for limits at the portfolio level, which should be viewed with caution due to their high level of abstraction). It is therefore necessary to define a systematic overall process that enables ESG risk management at the borrower or loan level.

7.1.4 The ESG Due Diligence

Looking at the scorecard above, some readers may have noticed that governance, the last component of ESG, is not included there. This is not because governance issues are less important than environmental or social issues, but because it is not appropriate to measure them at the sector level: Organizational structures, responsibilities, and the embedding of compliance issues in strategy and processes are company-specific issues that can only be considered on an individual basis. The same is true for the aspects of individual adaptation to other ESG aspects, which can sometimes differ significantly from the industry average at the level of individual companies. An example of this is the automotive industry, where the transition to electric mobility, together with the applicable regulations and market changes to be observed, represents a significant ESG risk for the conventional automotive industry, but a significant opportunity for companies such as Tesla or BYD due to their strategic positioning.

It is therefore essential for the lending process to now move from the sector and portfolio level to the individual client and their loans in order to complete the ESG assessment. Here, the duality of the two perspectives can be coherently assigned to the concept of dual materiality (Delgado-Ceballos et al. 2023), which encompasses the assessment of the economic impact of external and internal ESG factors. The outside-in perspective captures developments at the sector level, which represents the general framework for all and thus the level on which all companies in a sector operate. The extent to which the company adapts its strategy, products, and processes, the level of resilience it achieves or already has, and the resulting degree of adaptation represent the inside-out level. From this analysis, a coherent assessment concept can be derived, as presented by the NBG (2023) in its "ESG Guidelines through double materiality perspective", summarized schematically in Figure 7.2.

The outside-in perspective can be adequately assessed by the ESG Risk Radar. In a second step, now the inside-out perspective is implemented, closely linked to the radar concept and referred to as "ESG Due Diligence": Here, for the same risk components that were assessed in the scoring at the sector level (namely "physical climate risk", "transition risk", and "other ESG risks"), an individual assessment is now added as an extension. Additionally, for larger companies, the aspect of governance is also considered. For this purpose, questionnaires with a manageable

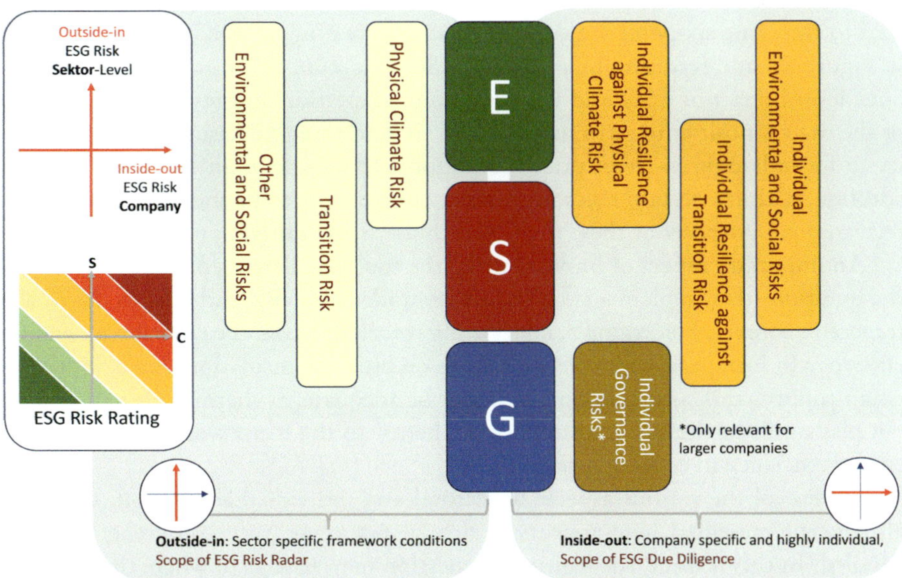

Figure 7.2 ESG risk assessment under the dual materiality perspective (own presentation similar to NBG 2023, p. 22).

number of questions have been defined to analyze the extent to which the specific client is exposed to the risks identified at the industry level and how it has already adapted to them.

Since many customers are not well informed, the approach could be labeled "a maximum risk baseline assessment": Starting with the highest risk score, the score decreases as verified mitigating factors are identified. Thus, a client who cannot answer any of the risk mitigation- or adaptation-related questions will receive the highest risk score. An informed and well-prepared client will be able to provide compelling information to mitigate their ESG risk score.

Each ESG risk component has six indicators that are translated into mitigation/adaptation questions. The question is compared to the status quo of the client's situation. The mitigation factors are given as a guide. They are not exhaustive and can be expanded with similar considerations. If the mitigating factors are fully considered, the client receives a score of "1". If they are partially present, the resulting score is "0.5"; otherwise, the score is "0". The loan level risk score is reduced accordingly.

The indicators considered in this assessment comprise, for the example of physical climate risk, "location of client facilities" and their protection status quo, "water supply resilience", "energy supply resilience", "supply chain resilience", "information management", and "adequate insurance". Each has the potential to reduce the individual physical risk score by up to 1, so the final score can range from 0 to 6. As an average of all four ESG risk components, the client then receives an individual ESG score. This can be combined with the sector score (which is normalized to the same six-point scale for simplicity), creating an ESG matrix as shown in Figure 7.3 and resulting in an overall ESG risk score that now reflects both the outside-in impact of ESG and the inside-out adaptation and resilience. The score or the matrix-positioning can now be used to guide credit decisions, with the ability to formulate limits, loan prices/conditions, or require additional collateral. In addition, within a certain risk range, it may make sense to finance only taxonomy-relevant loan purposes as these then contribute to risk mitigation.

An important aspect of implementing the tool in different countries is to make the questions that implement the indicators understandable and easy to use in the respective context. For example, concerning transition risks, the question on energy efficiency in European countries may focus on building insulation. For a Southeast Asian context, this specification would not be adequate, as thermal insulation does not play a role in the climatic conditions there – so the focus would have to be on energy efficiency in cooling processes.

In view of the various aspects of sectoral and individual assessment, the overall concept presented here appears at first glance to be very comprehensive and detailed. In this respect, the legitimate question may arise as to where the pragmatism emphasized at the beginning comes into play. This pragmatism is based on the fact that the adaptation processes described above are a one-time effort, after which the ESG Risk Radar scores at the sector level can simply be used by all banks in a

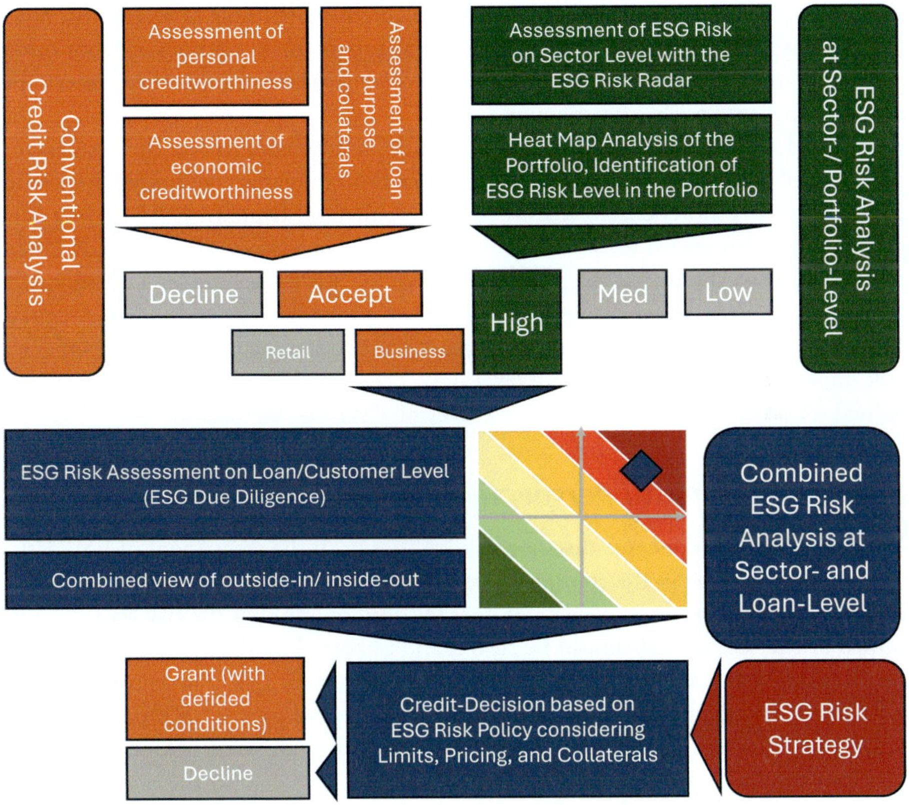

Figure 7.3 Overview over the ESG Risk Management Process using ESG Risk Radar and ESG Due Diligence.

country to assess ESG risks at the loan portfolio level without any further effort. Similarly, adapting the questionnaires of the ESG Due Diligence is a one-off process, after which those questionnaires are available to all banks in a country. They must be applied individually to each loan, but since that assessment only has to be carried out for loans in high-risk sectors above defined volume limits, it is ensured that the effort is only expended where it is directly necessary to protect the bank from high ESG risks. In this respect, the application process is very pragmatic and keeps a close eye on the cost-benefit ratio.

Another important aspect that should be mentioned lastly is that all aspects of the data process are currently limited to corporate and commercial banking. This is in line with the focus of regulation and supervision, which only considers ESG at this level so far. However, this implies that retail exposures are not relevant in terms of ESG risks.

Two considerations argue against this: First, retail customers are often dependent employees of larger companies that may experience difficulties because of

ESG risks, which may subsequently affect the creditworthiness of retail customers through layoffs or wage cuts. Second, retail customers finance homes, cars, or other assets that are subject to ESG (and especially climate) risks and therefore need to be considered from an ESG perspective as well.

It would therefore be important to include retail customers in the assessment process and to address the issue of collateral in this context accordingly. This could also require a comprehensive re-evaluation of collateral from an ESG perspective, particularly with regard to retail real estate. These considerations are already taken into account in the tool implementation projects (with the provision of adequate scorings for mortgages and auto financing), but it is to be expected that the regulatory focus on these issues will only take place once the immediate problems of ESG risk management at the corporate level have been solved and experience has been gained – i.e., certainly in the "second wave" of ESG risk regulation.

7.1.5 The Technical Perspectives

It is clear from the concepts discussed above that both the assessment of ESG risks and their application in the credit process involve a wide range of technical demands in addition to the business aspects. It goes without saying that the risk scores determined at the sector level should be stored and analyzed by the IT systems so that, for example, the creation of the "Heat Map" and ESG risk management at the portfolio level are not a manual, but a largely automated process. Similarly, it must be ensured that the ESG Due Diligence questionnaires are accessible in the system and that the rating result is not only stored in and connected to the account of the client, but that it can also be aggregated at portfolio level in order to modify and, if necessary, correct the results initially determined at sector level on the basis of the individual findings. The later point will largely improve the ESG risk analysis on the portfolio level, because it will take into account how individual adaptations and transformation processes mitigate the ESG risk that has been initially assumed on the basis of a pure sector analysis.

These aspects are all conventional banking IT requirements, where, of course, neither the effort nor the challenges should be underestimated. From a technical point of view, however, a much more far-reaching question arises today, and this concerns the use of artificial intelligence.

In principle, there are several levels of consideration:

1. Artificial intelligence could be used in a first stage at the design level. ESG Risk Radar is about identifying the right risk components, scoring items and indicators, while ESG Due Diligence is about the indicators and the questions used to determine them. Which is "right" and adequate has so far been defined by humans, but it could also be defined by AI.
2. In a second stage, artificial intelligence could be used to support research to assess the individual indicators.

3. In the third stage, artificial intelligence would perform the entire evaluation based on the defined system and present the results in the most transparent way possible.

The first two stages have already been partially implemented with the tools in their current status quo. All components of the concept have been discussed with several AI models as "sparring partners" and, in the case of the ESG Due Diligence, have already been slightly adjusted on the basis of the results. In addition to conventional research methods, AI models have also been included in the research process for the sector assessments with the ESG Risk Radar.

Based on this application experience, it can be said that even in the current status quo, there are already considerable benefits from the use of AI. In all cases, however, a direct adoption of the results as delivered would have led to gross distortions: At the methodological level, a mixture of different facts and levels of observation could be observed; at the research level, a lack of differentiation of the local context and, in some cases, even the use of invented sources was present. However, when used selectively, the inclusion of AI brought new aspects that enriched the conventional methodology.

Individual attempts at a more comprehensive evaluation, as described for stage 3, have produced results that were not only difficult to understand on their own but also highly inconsistent. Especially, the results have changed largely with even minor modifications of the prompts. In this respect, stage 3 is not recommended based on the current state of the art; the first two levels are, however, interesting and will certainly lead to increasingly better results as the technology matures.

Interestingly, in the context of ESG and climate risk assessment, there are institutions who are already focusing primarily on a purely AI-based analysis. Given the high level of effort involved in the methodology as described above, this approach is entirely understandable. However, in addition to the already mentioned aspects of "black box" and erratic variations, it should also be considered with caution for two reasons: First, the complexity of the topic requires a fundamental and, above all, standardized understanding, which is not yet given in the source situation available on the Internet. Different institutions and authors have different basic understandings, goals, and perspectives when it comes to the many facets of sustainable finance (as discussed in detail in Peylo 2024). The example of the different naming of ESG risks in regulatory institutions described above shows that a human researcher with knowledge of the facts and the perspective of the publishers can work out overlaps and contradictions so that both the synonymity of different terms and different understandings of the same terminology can be understood and considered. AI often does not demonstrate that same ability in the status quo.

But the second, perhaps most important aspect is this: Above all, risk management requires a deep understanding of the subject matter. And human learning is strongly linked to the acquisition of knowledge as well as to its application – effective learning involves a dynamic interplay between the two, where acquired knowledge is applied, reflected upon, and refined through experience. For this reason, it is particularly important in risk management to ensure that the knowledge on which decisions are based is largely self-acquired and therefore deeply understood. Where IT and AI can provide support, this support should be considered and applied in a balanced way. However, the final step of combining and synthesizing the knowledge should be the responsibility of human beings and will, over time, contribute not only to a significant improvement in ESG risk management, but also to a balanced implementation in combination with ESG opportunity management – especially in terms of transition financing.

References

BaFin. (2019a). *BaFin Perspektiven: Nachhaltigkeit (engl. BaFin Perspectives – Sustainability).* Bundesaufsichtsamt für Finanzdienstleistungsaufsicht BaFin. https://www.bafin.de/SharedDocs/Downloads/DE/BaFinPerspektiven/2019/bp_19-2_sustainable_finance.html

BaFin. (2019b). *Guidance Notice on Dealing with Sustainability Risk.* Bundesaufsichtsamt für Finanzdienstleistungsaufsicht BaFin. https://www.bafin.de/SharedDocs/Downloads/EN/Merkblatt/dl_mb_Nachhaltigkeitsrisiken_en.pdf?__blob=publicationFile&v=5

Bauer, R., Koedijk, K., & Otten, R. (2005). International Evidence on Ethical Mutual Fund Performance and Investment Style. *Journal of Banking & Finance, 26*(29), 1751–1767. http://dx.doi.org/10.1016/j.jbankfin.2004.06.035

Basel Committee on Banking Supervision. (2020). *Climate-related Financial Risks: A Survey on Current Initiatives.* Bank for International Settlements (BIS). https://www.bis.org/bcbs/publ/d502.htm

Basel Committee on Banking Supervision. (2022). *Principles for the Effective Management and Supervision of Climate-related Financial Risks.* Bank for International Settlements (BIS). https://www.bis.org/bcbs/publ/d532.pdf

Borge, D. (2001). *The Book of Risk.* John Wiley.

Carney, M. (2015). *Breaking the Tragedy of the Horizon - Climate Change and Financial Stability.* Lloyds, London, United Kingdom. https://www.bankofengland.co.uk/speech/2015/breaking-the-tragedy-of-the-horizon-climate-change-and-financial-stability

CBA (Central Bank of Armenia). (2024). *ESG Risk Radar for Armenia – Assessment of Climate-related and Other ESG Risks.* Central Bank of Armenia.

Delgado-Ceballos, J., Ortiz-De-Mandojana, N., Antolín-López, R., & Montiel, I. (2023). Connecting the Sustainable Development Goals to Firm-Level Sustainability and ESG Factors: The Need for Double Materiality. *BRQ Business Research Quarterly, 26*(1), 2–10. https://doi.org/10.1177/23409444221140919

EBA (European Banking Authority). (2019). *Action Plan on Sustainable Finance.* European Banking Authority. https://www.eba.europa.eu/sites/default/documents/files/document_library/EBA%20Action%20plan%20on%20sustainable%20finance.pdf

EBA (European Banking Authority). (2020). *EBA Discussion Paper on Management and Supervision of ESG Risks for Credit Institutions and Investment Firms.* European Banking Authority. https://www.eba.europa.eu/sites/default/documents/files/document_library/Publications/Reports/2021/1015656/EBA%20Report%20on%20ESG%20risks%20management%20and%20supervision.pdf

EBA (European Banking Authority). (2024). *Draft Guidelines on the Management of ESG Risks.* European Banking Authority. https://www.eba.europa.eu/activities/single-rulebook/sustainable-finance/guidelines-management-esg-risks

ECB (European Central Bank). (2021). *Guide on Climate-related and Environmental Risks.* European Central Bank. https://www.bankingsupervision.europa.eu/legalframework/publiccons/pdf/climate-related_risks/ssm.202005_draft_guide_on_climate-related_and_environmental_risks.en.pdf

ECB (European Central Bank). (2023). *The Road to Paris: Stress Testing the Transition Towards a Net-zero Economy.* European Central Bank, Occasional Paper Series No. 328. https://www.ecb.europa.eu/press/pr/date/2023/html/ecb.pr230906~a3d6d06bdc.en.html

Eccles, N. S. & Viviers, S. (2011). The Origins and Meanings of Names Describing Investment Practices that Integrate a Consideration of ESG Issues in the Academic Literature. *Journal of Business Ethics, 104*(3), 389–402. http://dx.doi.org/10.1007/s10551-011-0917-7

European Commission. (2018). *Action Plan: Financing Sustainable Growth.* European Commission. https://eur-lex.europa.eu/legal-content/EN/TXT/?uri=CELEX:52018DC0097

Granoff, I. (2023, May 4). *The Tragedy on the Financial Horizon is Closer Than You Think.* Columbia Law School Sabin Center for Climate Change Law. https://blogs.law.columbia.edu/climatechange/2023/05/04/the-tragedy-on-the-financial-horizon-is-closer-than-you-think/

HASPA Hamburger Sparkasse. (2024). Der S-ESG Score (engl. The S-ESG Score). https://www.haspa.de/fi/home/nachhaltigkeit/s-esg-score.html

Institute and Faculty of Actuaries. (2023). *Emperor's New Climate Scenarios – A Warning for Financial Services.* Institute and Faculty of Actuaries, University of Exeter. https://actuaries.org.uk/emperors-new-climate-scenarios

ISS (Institutional Shareholder Services). (2021, September 26). *ESG Corporate Rating.* Institutional Shareholder Services. https://www.issgovernance.com/esg/ratings/corporate-rating/

Jackes, P. (2023, June 30). VR-ESG-RisikoScoring – ESG-Risiken werden bewertbar (engl. VR ESG risk scoring - ESG risks become assessable). FCH AG Blog. https://www.fch-gruppe.de/Beitrag/22192/vresgrisikoscoring–esgrisiken-werden-bewertbar?ID=22192

NBG (National Bank of Georgia). (2022). *Climate-related Risk Radar for Georgian Economic Sectors.* National Bank of Georgia. https://nbg.gov.ge/en/page/climate-risk-radar

NBG (National Bank of Georgia). (2023). *ESG Guidelines.* https://nbg.gov.ge/en/page/esg-guidelines

NBG (National Bank of Georgia). (2024). *ESG Risk Radar for Georgia.* National Bank of Georgia. https://nbg.gov.ge/en/page/climate-risk-radar

Oekom research. (2013). *Der Einfluss nachhaltiger Kapitalanlagen auf Unternehmen (the influence of sustainable investment on companies).* Oekom research.

Orlitzky, M., Schmidt, F. L. & Rynes, S. L. (2003). Corporate Social and Financial Performance: A Meta-analysis. *Organization Studies, 24*(3), 403–441. https://doi.org/10.1177/0170840603024003910

Peylo, B. T. & Villhauer, B. (2021). Clustering of Negative Criteria. A Pragmatic Approach for the Implementation of SRI. In K. Wendt (Ed.), *Theories of Change – Change Leadership Tools, Models and Applications for Investing in Sustainable Development* (pp. 109–121). Springer Nature.

Peylo, B. T. (2024). The Green Siblings: Exploring the Emerging Structure of Sustainable Finance. In *Sustainable Wealth Management: Directing Capital Towards Sustainability* (pp. 169–181). Springer International Publishing.

Peylo, B. T. & Nuß, C. (2024). Two Sides of the Same Coin: ESG Risk and Opportunity Management in the Investment and Lending Business. In *Sustainable Wealth Management: Directing Capital Towards Sustainability* (pp. 169–181). Springer International Publishing.

Reuters. (2024, September 24). *ECB Started Issuing Fine Notices to Banks not Meeting Climate Expectations.* https://www.reuters.com/sustainability/ecb-started-issuing-fine-notices-banks-not-meeting-climate-expectations-2024-09-24/

Schaltegger, S., Burritt, R., & Petersen, H. (2003). *An Introduction to Corporate Environmental Management: Striving for Sustainability*. Greenleaf Publishers.

Scholtens, B., & Dam, D (2007). Banking on the Equator. Are Banks that Adopted the Equator Principles Different from Non-Adopters? *World Development*, *35*(8), 1307–1328. https://doi.org/10.1016/j.worlddev.2006.10.013

Swiss Re Institute. (2021). *The Economics of Climate Change: No Action Not an Option*. Swiss Re Management Ltd., Swiss Re Institute. https://www.swissre.com/institute/research/topics-and-risk-dialogues/climate-and-natural-catastrophe-risk/expertise-publication-economics-of-climate-change.html

Sparkes, R. (2006). A Historical Perspective on the Growth of Socially Responsible Investment. In R. Sullivan & C. Mackenzie (Eds.), *Responsible Investment* (pp. 39–54). Greenleaf Publishing.

Statman, M. (2007). Socially Responsible Investments. *Journal of Investment Consulting, 8*(2), 17–37. http://dx.doi.org/10.2139/ssrn.995271

United Nations Brundtland Commission. (1987). *Report of the World Commission on Environment and Development: Our Common Future*. The United Nations. https://www.un.org/en/academic-impact/sustainability

Žalėnienė, I. & Pereira, P. (2021). Higher Education For Sustainability: A Global Perspective. *Geography and Sustainability*, *2*(2), 99–106. https://doi.org/10.1016/j.geosus.2021.05.001

Chapter 8

Exploring Climate Blended Finance for Climate Mitigation Projects: A World View Versus National Perspective

Tareq Mahbub

8.1 Introduction

Currently, climate finance stands at a critical juncture. Climate blended finance transactions form a strong theme with the blended finance market. Although global climate finance flows have grown consistently over the past decade, they still lag far behind what is needed to meet the goals of the Paris Agreement, which is limiting global warming to 1.5°C. A study by the International Energy Agency (IEA, 2001) estimates that for delivering the net-zero targets would require US$6 trillion of climate finance annually between 2023 and 2030 and over US$7 trillion by 2050. The same study suggests that over US$1 trillion per year will need to be invested in emerging markets through 2030 to get these countries on track toward net-zero emissions by 2050. It is argued that emerging markets alone cannot

DOI: 10.1201/9781003528951-8

meet such investment needs to meet their net-zero goals. This problem could be compounded by the complex and challenging macro-economic landscape, rising inflation, mounting debt burdens, and geopolitical stabilities, especially the Russia-Ukraine war.

Recent trend suggests that though the public financing for climate deals is increasing, overall they are in decline, coupled with the prospect of dwindling private climate financing. It has been suggested that the aggregate blended finance flows from private sector investors are in decline, as have been from Development Finance Institutions (DFIs) and Multilateral Development Banks (MDBs) for climate mitigation and adaptation projects (Convergence, 2023). Some of the reasons for this trend are: rising interest hikes and capital flight; currency depreciations across the low and middle-income developing countries, which are disinclining private investors from investing in high-risk developing countries (Convergence, 2023; Juneja, 2024). As private investors seek more stable environments with comparable returns, which incline them to diversify resources away from riskier markets. Therefore, it underscores the need for an urgency for increased concessional capital from donor and philanthropic sources to attract the trillions in commercial investment to steer these countries toward net-zero targets.

8.2 What Is Blended Finance?

Blended finance is a strategic development finance for the mobilization of additional finance toward sustainable development in developing countries. This concept, which emerged at the beginning of the Sustainable Development Goals (SDGs) era, has its central aim into channeling private capital into sectors of high-development impact that address climate and diversity crises, social inequality, poverty, and other societal challenges while at the same time delivering risk-adjusted returns. In this vein, blended finance serves as a catalyst for private capital investments in projects that create societal value that otherwise would not have been financed (Development Initiatives, 2016; Flammer et al., 2024; OECD, 2018). In particular, the inbuilt de-risking apparatus enables this approach to attract private capital flow to finance "risky" interventions with an unfavorable risk-return investment profile – that would not have been possible in the absence of such a mechanism (EU, 2020; IFC, 2024). It has helped in financing a broad range of projects on renewable energy, climate technology, nature-based solutions, and social inclusion, among others. Figure 8.1 shows a typical blended finance mechanics and structure.

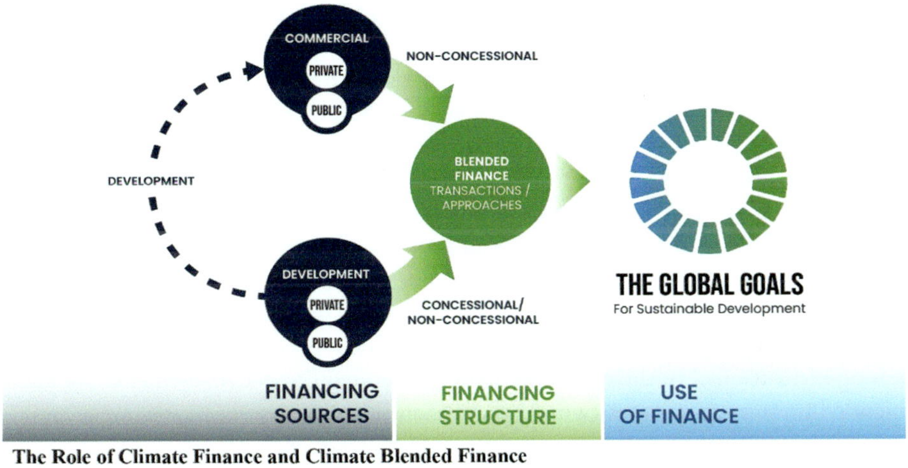

Figure 8.1 A simple blended finance model.

Source: Author's own representation.

8.3 The Role of Climate Finance and Climate Blended Finance

Climate finance refers to financial resources that comprise local, national, or transnational financing drawn from public, private, and alternative sources of financing that are used to support action on climate change. It draws its origin from the Convention – The United Nations Framework Convention on Climate Change (UNFCCC), the Kyoto Protocol, and the Paris Agreement call for lending more financial assistance to Parties that are less endowed and climate vulnerable (UNFCCC, 2024). Therefore, climate finance is required for mitigation and adaptation actions including large-scale capital investments to reduce significant greenhouse gas (GHG) emissions coupled with helping climate-vulnerable countries to adapt to the effects of climate change. It has been recognized that the capacity for contributing capital, preventing and coping with the consequences of climate change vary among these countries. Climate blended finance forms a central theme within the blended finance market and is reaching scale more consistently than other segments. In this vein, they consist for about half (49%) of the blended finance market in terms of deal count and 57% of the aggregating financing.

8.4 The Role of Climate Blended Finance in Targeting Climate Outcomes and Meeting SDG Goals

Blended finance uses public-sector development finance and ODA to attract supplementary private investment in order to achieve development goals, such as reducing poverty, promoting economic growth, and creating jobs (Attridge & Engen, 2019). It can be used to mitigate existing and emerging risks and threats in achieving SDG targets by attracting required investments and has tremendous potential to finance the sizeable SDG investment gap in developing countries. It is highly aligned with the SDG goals (Sial, 2024). For example, blended finance is highly aligned with goals such as 18 (Decent work and economic growth) and Goal 13 (Climate action), while less aligned with SDGs such as Goal 16 (Peace, justice and strong institutions). In the overall makeup of blended finance investments, climate-blended finance constitutes two-thirds of such investments.

8.5 The Three Lenses of Climate Blended Finance

The overall makeup of climate blended finance could be addressed through three investment lenses, which are mitigation blended finance, adaptation blended finance, and hybrid mitigation-adaptation blended finance (Climate Policy Initiative, 2023; Convergence, 2023, 2024; OECD, 2023; Sial, 2024). Mitigation blended finance aims to reduce carbon dioxide (CO_2) and other GHG emissions from human-made sources into the atmosphere. The majority of climate blended finance is focused on mitigation projects. For example, since 2013, approximately 58% of the annual climate deals have been majorly focused on mitigation, which represents US$64.2 billion in total mitigation finance. Mitigation transactions tend to be more attractive to investors than other blended finance deals as they are easier to define and linked to a reduction of GHG emissions targets with a clear understanding to their impacts and ready revenue-generation activities. Adaptation blended finance refers to financial resources aimed at helping communities, companies, and regions adapt to the impacts of climate change. Examples of such deals include financing the relocation of an infrastructure project away from areas with rising sea levels, supplying drought-resistant seeds for farming, or building a dam with a larger retention basin for increasingly variable rainfall. Some caveats for this type of deal are (i) a perception among investors' community as such deals are riskier and present lower rates of returns; (ii) they are too small to meet investor criteria; (iii) the timeline for investment could be too long; and (iv) a lack of standardization criteria for measuring outcomes for these projects. Lastly, hybrid mitigation-adaptation blended finance refers to financial transactions that contain elements of both mitigation and adaptation finance. It also refers to sectors that combine both mitigation and adaptation outcomes such as the agriculture sector. For example, in the case of sustainable agriculture, which can combine both climate mitigation and adaptation outcomes by improving soil health and increasing carbon sequestration (i.e., storing carbon) through organic material while at the same affording food security to vulnerable populations. Evidence suggests that around 45% of institutional investments into climate finance are hybrid solutions compared to 35% in mitigation and 20% in adaptation (Convergence, 2023).

8.6 The Five Primary Vehicles of Climate Blended Finance Transactions

There are five primary vehicles for climate blended finance transactions. These are briefly enumerated as follows. These are (i) bonds; (ii) companies; (iii) facilities; (iv) funds; and (v) projects (Convergence 2024; Earth Security, 2021; OECD, 2018, 2023).

Projects. Projects constitute the largest share of total financing volume to climate blended finance. These projects are structured around either greenfield or brownfield investments. It has been estimated that projects as one of the primary vehicles for climate blended finance transactions constitute 40% of total climate finance deals conducted per year. For example, from 2020 to 2022, projects accounted for US$4.4 billion of climate finance annually, which is followed by funds, the second most effective mobilizers of climate finance at about US$2.1 billion. Among the climate blended finance projects, renewable energy comprises the majority of such projects including the creation of new renewable energy assets. However, currently there is a decline of such projects, which has dropped from US$347 million (2017–2019) to US$171 million (2020–2022). The reasons for a drop of such projects are (i) a large number of utility-scale renewable energy projects have been replaced by wholly commercial financing; (ii) the current macroeconomic landscape fueled by geopolitical tension (i.e., Russia-Ukraine conflict); (iii) inflationary pressures; and (iv) mounting debt impacting the Emerging Markets and Developing Economies (EMDEs).

Bonds. Blended bonds which include sovereign and corporate bonds are an influential vehicle for financing climate finance projects. These include (i) energy asset financing; (ii) green infrastructure; and (iii) sector-agnostic green financing. This sort of climate blended finance transaction is gaining traction and has increased its volume from 2017 (i.e., from 2% of total climate blended finance in 2018 to 9% in 2022). Their momentum is increasing to 11% of climate blended finance transactions per year from 2020 to 2022. The benefits from using bonds are they help for mitigating credit risk to institutional investors whilst providing cost of capital relief to borrowers. This is particularly beneficial for attracting climate finance projects in developing countries (i.e., EMDs) whose risk profiles continue to increase with changing macroeconomic landscape.

Funds. Blended funds in climate finance represent (i) limited partnership private equity and debt funds, as well as funds-of-funds. Currently, there is an overall decline in blended funds for climate projects, which in 2022 constituted 11% of total climate blended finance deals worldwide. These fall into private equity, venture capital, and private debt fund activities. Their decline is owed to the growing macroeconomic challenges confronting many developing countries causing lower valuation of assets and a tendency for private investors to move funds abroad (i.e., capital flight). Additionally, many of these funds are concentrated to a few private investors, which further compounds the ability for new fund managers to raise additional new funds. In this context, it is argued that Technical Assistance (TA) funding that provides targeted support to various aspects of climate projects (i.e., knowledge and skills training including capacity building to identify, assess, and manage risks effectively) significantly raises the operational viability of projects. These help for de-risking potential investment in new or uncertain markets by drawing additional funding from investors. For example, Ivory (2023), in an analysis of 270 blended finance deals, reports about a quarter of these transactions are in the financial services, energy, and agricultural sectors with 64% being commonly associated with concessional capital transactions.

Company. Company-level blended finance refers to direct private equity and debt financing of businesses on both market-rate and below-market-rate terms. This form of blended finance has grown steadily during the last few years and is currently considered one of the most influential vehicles for climate blended finance. It is particularly important in the agricultural sector.

Facility. A facility is an earmarked allocation of public development resources (sometimes including support from philanthropies) for help investing in development projects through a range of instruments for mobilizing additional finance through its operations. An example is the NEPAD infrastructure Project Preparation Facility (NEPAD-IPPF), a 98-million US$ multi-donor facility – a special fund mobilized by The African Development Bank and KfW (Germany) established to boost regional infrastructure in Africa (AfDB, 2023).

8.7 Investors' Landscape in Climate Blended Finance

There are five types of investors by class involved in climate blended finance. These are: commercial investor; development agency; DFI/MDB; Foundation/NGO; and impact investor. For example, commercial investors represent institutional investors or private sector investors in blended finance projects. These are (i) corporate; (ii) financial institutions; (iii) asset managers; (iv) pension fund; and (v) insurance companies. Corporates have been the most active commercial investor class in climate blended finance projects. Corporate financing is primarily channeled through equity. Estimate suggests that about 96% of corporate investment between 2020 and 2022 was equity stakes. The second largest sponsor for climate blended finance projects in the commercial investor class is commercial banks. Their primary mode of commitment is through senior debt. However, there is a decline in such funds from 2020 to 2022 for sponsoring climate finance deals, which is owed to a contraction of global economic activity during the COVID-19 pandemic for which many banks faced a significant liquidity crisis (Convergence, 2023). One of the biggest initiatives to mobilize funds for meeting net-zero targets in this regard is The Glasgow Financial Alliance for Net Zero (GFANZ), which is a global coalition of 45 countries representing 450 leading financial institutions supporting country-led financing platforms through the use of blended finance to align with the net-zero targets (GFANZ, 2021). In this instance at COP 27, GFANZ has committed to providing US$10 billion from private financial institutions toward the Indonesian Just Energy Transition Partnership (JETP) (PwC, 2024). Development agencies and multi-donor funds are significant sources of concessional capital in blended finance transactions. Some of the leading agencies that commit such funds are (i) the private infrastructure development group (PIDG), Global Climate Fund (GCF), Clean Technology Fund, Global Environment Fund (GEF), and the Canadian Climate Fund. These represent 50% of the top ten investors which finance climate outcomes through direct or indirect means (Convergence, 2024). DFI/MDB are key suppliers of capital to climate blended finance projects mobilized through paid-in capital from bilateral public providers and multilateral institutions including raising additional capital from the capital market. Typically, MDB finance are larger in size and are targeted toward larger-scale climate change mitigation and adaptation projects (OECD, 2023). From 2017 to 2022, they supplied US$2.2 billion of commercial capital per year to climate blended finance deals. In alignment with net-zero and sustainability targets, both International Finance Corporation (IFC) and Multilateral Investment Guarantee Agency (MIGA) under the World Bank have committed to align 100% of their Board-approved real sector operations with the Paris Agreement by 1 July 2025. In this context, the Asian Development Bank (ADB) is playing the lead in piloting Energy Transition Mechanisms (ETMs), which draw on blended finance to support the fossil-fuel plants to be converted to renewables. Similarly, Fin Dev Canada and Mitsubishi UFJ Financial Group (MUFG) announced the launch of the project GAIA, a US$1.5 billion blended finance platform to help drive climate-focused investment into developing countries mobilized through the Green Climate Fund (Jessop et al, 2023). Further the backing of DFI and MDBs in projects raises the creditworthiness of such deals and helps de-risk investors' concerns who have strict investment-grade mandates for emerging country markets. Foundations are taking on a central role in climate finance. They are the only investor class with more than 50% of investment directed toward transaction of adaptation focus (both adaptation and hybrid deals). These financial transactions could also be subsumed under philanthropic investors and consist a small share of the climate blended finance market though their influence is growing. As of 2020–2022, concessional investment from foundations to adaptation projects has dropped from 15% to 13% vis-à-vis 8% to 5% in mitigation projects (Convergence, 2023). Some of the biggest philanthropic investors in this category are (i) Shell Foundation; (ii) The Rockefeller Foundation; (iii) Omidyar Network; and (iv) David and Lucille Packard. For example, the Rockefeller Foundation has recently announced a US$1 billion commitment to fund climate solutions including lending further support for the Global Energy Alliance for People and Planet (GEAPP) while in the advancement of COP 28. Similarly, Bloomberg Philanthropies and the International Renewable Energy Agency (IRENA) have formed a partnership to accelerate renewable energy deployment for emerging economies worldwide. Lastly, the impact investor represents a minor investor group in the overall makeup of climate finance deals. They provide a dual role of being fund managers and providers of both concessional and commercial capital for blended finance transactions. Some of the leading investors in this regard are: Ceniarth LLC, Responsibility Investments AG, Calvert Impact Capital, and the Land Degradation Neutrality Fund.

8.8 Geographical Distribution of Climate Blended Finance Worldwide

Energy transactions form the basis in climate mitigation projects having the lion share of overall climate blended deals constituting a total of 319 deals till 2023 with a volume of US$101 billion. Project finance is the primary vehicle for energy blended finance. The majority of these energy deals are concentrated in Sub-Saharan Africa (SSA), which comprises 43% of transactions between 2021 and 2023, followed by the Middle East and North Africa (KPMG, 2024). Eastern Europe has seen the largest regional increase in energy deals with a 90% boost in total volume. There has been a spike in a series of utility-scale projects in Uzbekistan and Ukraine. The rise of utility-scale solar projects in Uzbekistan has been attributed to the local government's support program mediated by IFC (the primary lending arm of the World Bank) to incentivize the acceleration of Independent Power Projects (IPPs) in Uzbekistan (IFC, 2024). In terms of a single country focus, Nigeria has been the top destination country having 10 transactions in power projects for which 50% were bonds. It is to be mentioned that in the last two years (2021–2023) blended bonds and notes with proceeds directed toward clean energy projects have been the dominant transaction medium to cater for clean energy projects, and their share in financing green projects is rising. Figure 8.2 presents the regional distribution of energy deals by proportion from 2018 to 2023.

8.9 The Role of Renewable Energy in Climate Blended Finance

Energy blended finance is primarily focused on renewable energy asset creation (OECD, 2023). Between 2021 and 2023 renewable energy transactions

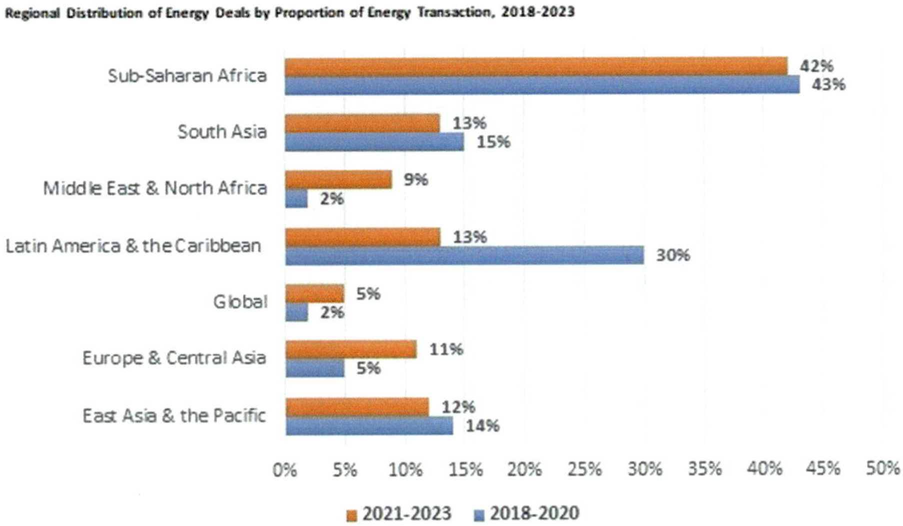

Figure 8.2 Regional distribution of energy deals by energy transactions from 2018 to 2023.

Source: Author's own representation from data gleaned from Convergence (2024).

accounted for 86% of all energy deals, reaching as high as 91% in 2023. Solar dominates renewable energy investment in both the frequency of projects and aggregate financing (Convergence, 2024). Wind power plants comprised 23% of renewable energy deals between 2021 and 2023. In terms of investment archetypes, concessional debt and equity instruments are the most frequently used transaction vehicles to finance renewable energy projects. Additionally, a major determinant of financing renewable energy projects is the use of TA funds which have risen since 2021. This could be blended with other concessional funds including green bonds and green loans to help finance power projects. For example, Finance in Motion's LAGreen Fund, a US$175 million fund that invests in participations in green bonds and green loans, includes a TA component which provides structuring support to issuers and policy and market strengthening support for local bond markets. A case in point is the 20 MW Neo 1 Solar project in Lesotho (MIGA, 2016), which received structuring TA from AfDB via their Africa Climate Technology Centre, to cover legal and other design costs.

In terms of investor classes, DFIs/MDBs consist the lion share of financing energy blended deals. Additionally, there is a growing number of donor capital pool administered by the MDBs (i.e., the Canadian Climate Fund for the Private Sector in the Americas and the IFC-Canada Climate Change Program), which are contributing to renewable energy finance. Some of these donor capital pools represent (i) the Green Climate Fund and (ii) Private Infrastructure Development Group (PIDG). These form the very basis of concessional funding to renewable energy deals. Alongside Corporates account for about half (48%) of financial commitments channeled through the private sector. Lastly, institutional investors are currently increasing their role to finance renewable energy deals owing to the growing usage of capital markets for financing renewables and energy efficiency deals (IRENA, 2020). Here Box 8.1 presents a case that illustrates a blended finance transaction for climate mitigation projects (i.e., Vietnam – Quang Tri Wind Farm Project).

BOX 8.1 VIETNAM – QUANG TRI WIND FARM PROJECT: THE ROLE OF MDBS IN SECURING FINANCING

The attraction of investment in renewable energy, including wind energy, is a priority policy in Vietnam. A core part of the strategy is transforming the Quing Tri region into an energy hub by 2030. The Lotus Onshore Wind Power Project with a capacity of 144MW is the largest internationally project-financed wind-power project in the country.

It was developed under a PPP arrangement with a cost of US$247 million with financial closure reached in October 2021. The project involved significant foreign participation through equity and debt financing but no government guarantee. It was formulated with viable risk allocation for international lenders. The project financing is 30% equity, 60% of it contributed by PCCI (a local company) and the rest Renova (Japan). The project was financially structured and arranged by the Asian Development Bank, other international stakeholders (advisees, equipment suppliers, and energy purchase contractors) have also played a key role.

The financing for the project was secured through two stages. First was the role of the Asian Development Bank conducting structuring, due diligence, and loan syndications. The Bank mobilized long-term, limited-recourse financing in United States dollars from commercial banks (i.e., B loans) and other development finance that was not available locally. The second part constituted a supportive national policy, including tax incentives and a 20-year PPA with the off-taker – the State-owned energy company EVN. EVN covered energy production at a favorable price and other subsidies

Source: UNCTAD (2023).

8.10 Some Risks and Opportunities of Climate Blended Finance

Climate blended finance possesses some risks and opportunities. Especially, this kind of financing instrument often implies debt, which must be paid back. Additionally, there are issues around transparency and accountability regarding how the funds are used. This is particularly important when a growing number of developing countries are facing serious debt crises (i.e., the global macroeconomic headwinds after the COVID-19 pandemic, rising inflation, and the Russia-Ukraine conflict), which makes relying on debt-creating instruments very challenging. However, there are multiple opportunities which could signify a shift toward mobilizing considerable capital for sustainable development.

In terms of risks, it has been argued that blended finance can perpetuate climate coloniality. There are two reasons to support this view. One consideration is that developing countries sometimes depend on the global north countries for external financing, which is often tied to their colonial origins, set against their current economic condition and their inability to move out of poverty. Second, the nature of blended finance is not entirely concessional, as it is an interest-bearing capital tied to investors of the global north. For example, the process of exporting "green hydrogen" from the global south to the global north countries is deemed as extractive and at the expense of resource depletion of the global south. A case in point is the EUs the "Critical Raw Materials Act" (entered in 2024), which is focused on ring-fencing the bloc's access to raw materials,[1] such as the Global Gateway under which France has recently announced an investment of Euro 50 million in the Democratic Republic of Congo for raw material extraction (i.e., raw resources like lithium, cobalt, manganese and other rare earths) (Trade Mark Africa, 2023) is critiqued as a subsidy to the global north for perpetuating neo-colonial extraction. Additionally, profits for such projects are also repatriated to the global north countries.

Another consideration is that mobilizing private blended finance sometimes requires major overhauls in recipient countries' regulations and domestic policy frameworks to adapt to the investors' needs; sometimes these projects become expensive at the expense of increased cost of households and the local government. Further the additional layers of security afforded to the private investors sometimes makes an existing solution more complex, which otherwise could have been accommodated by simple reforms of the public sector utility or infrastructure per se (Sial, 2024).

A third consideration is that blended finance projects have been subject to criticism due to a lack of transparency and accountability. This is due to the complex interaction of different reporting measures as well as the general inclination to ensure access to information for the public. Though the DFIs and IFCs are mandated to disclose project information and reporting to the public, however, due to a lack of harmonization about a common definition and methodology of "blended finance transactions" sometimes reporting remains subjective (Pereira, 2017).

In regard to investment opportunities, currently, there are standards for best practices and impact assessment measures to evaluate blended finance projects. For example, the OECD DAC approved the OECD-UNDP Impact Standards for Financing Sustainable Development (OECD, 2023). However, these standards are voluntary and are not legally binding. Therefore, there are opportunities for developing appropriate legislations (Choi & Seiger, 2020; Isah et al., 2023; Sheriffdeen et al., 2022) that bind all project investors and implementers to ensure development and penalties for failure of implementation of blended finance projects. Additionally, such legislation should also take heed of human rights issues and the protection and rehabilitation of local communities impacted by such projects. Another consideration is that blended finance can play a critical role in directing (external) concessional finance to strengthen public finance in developing countries. In this instance, National Banks of developing countries with their wider mandate of responding to public needs and nationally determined development strategies are often better positioned in supporting climate-resilient infrastructure and public services (Isah et al., 2023; McHugh, 2021). For example, evidence suggests that in many countries of the global south, the national development public banks when well governed and adequately resourced play a critical role in supporting climate resilient infrastructure and public services. These banks had been the most important actors in improving and cushioning the impacts of the COVID-19 health crisis for their wider mandate beyond profit-seeking and taking the risks to meet public need. Lastly, blended finance projects facilitated through grants can support renewable energy infrastructure. This can spur the transfer of technology and technological know-how to the host countries. Additionally, the allocation of grants for the transfer of technology and technological know-how, coupled with host government support, cooperative research and co-production agreements between countries including education and training could accelerate domestic investment and manufacturing of technology including developing a local supplier base.

Having reviewed some of the concepts of climate blended finance in terms of its definition, its significance in the overall universe of blended finance, its role of targeting climate outcomes and meeting the SDG financing gaps, the investment lenses or archetypes through which climate blended finance deals are conducted including investor types, their geographical spread and the role of climate blended finance in climate mitigation especially in creating renewable energy assets – the ensuing text focuses on "Bangladesh" a country vulnerable to the impacts of climate change as the unit of analysis for attracting climate blended finance in its renewable energy sector. In this vein, it will discuss some of the salient aspects of attracting climate blended finance in Bangladesh's renewable energy sector including the opportunities, challenges, and potential caveats for attracting significant capital with implication in future payment obligations and balance of payment effects. Additionally, it will discuss some brief recommendations in the overall universe of blended finance in order to attract sustainable climate blended finance for the emerging countries.

8.11 Exploring Climate Blended Finance in the Bangladeshi Renewable Energy Sector

From the Bangladeshi perspective, climate blended finance initiatives have been predominantly mobilized by domestic sources. These include the Bangladesh Climate Change Trust Fund (BCCTF) and the Refinancing Scheme of Bangladesh Bank for Renewable Energy and Green Financing. As of 2022–2023, some Bangladesh Taka (BDT) 3919 crore has been allocated to the climate change trust fund. The yearly allocation for climate causes has been increasing each year. In terms of attracting global funds for financing climate finance projects, GCF is the principal source of funding for climate finance projects. Among others are the Least Developed Country Fund (LDCF) mobilized by GEF, MDBs, and bilateral sources. Since 2014, Bangladesh has received US$503 million to implement eight climate projects from the GCF and other development partners. In 2022–2023, Bangladesh received US$1 billion Special Drawing Rights (SDR) as budget support from the International Monetary Fund (IMF) under its Resilience and Sustainability Facility (RSF) fund (i.e., the first Asian country to access the RSF) for providing climate change adaptation and mitigation support which include renewable or sustainable energy development (Yusuf & Sohel, 2024).

The author carried out a series of interviews with consisted (i) research and policy institutes; (ii) non-governmental financial institutions; (iii) developmental agencies; and (iv) academics.

The scientific rationale for conducting these interviews was to gain an understanding of the investment dynamic, the institutions which are involved in conducting blended finance transactions, the sectors which are the primary beneficiaries for blended finance transactions, and potential challenges and impediments for mobilizing climate blended finance in climate mitigation projects, especially renewable energy.

From the Bangladeshi perspective, it was known that "blended finance" is relatively new. Though it is widely discussed, however, the government has yet to adopt a working definition of the term, as different agencies use this term arbitrarily to suit their needs. Also it was found that there is no single dedicated agency in charge of blended finance initiatives, as when there is a new initiative/project that requires innovative financing on non-conventional terms it takes a long time to get such projects off the ground. Government officials seem ambivalent for approving such deals as there are no regulations and guidelines in place for approving such new projects. Currently, among international financiers, IFC has the largest blended finance operation in Bangladesh. Other than IFCs, other IFCs that are engaged into blended finance in Bangladesh are: ADB, IDB, KFW, and CDC. Amongst the government agencies which are playing critical roles in dealing with blended finance in Bangladesh are: The External Resources Division (ERD) under the Ministry of Planning, the Public Private Partnership Authority (PPPA), the Bangladesh Investment Development Authority (BIDA), the Bangladesh Bank, and the Finance Division in the Ministry of Finance. In terms of the domestic financial companies which are involved in blended finance, these include the Infrastructure Development Company Limited (IDCOL), Bangladesh Infrastructure Finance Fund Limited (BIFFL), and Investment Promotion and Financing Facility II (IPFF II).

From the field interviews, it was revealed that infrastructure sector holds the majority of current and future blended finance investment in Bangladesh. These include transport and communications, the energy and power sector, port facilities, and so forth. Apart from infrastructure, other sectors that can attract significant blended finance are: high-tech parks, logistics industry (warehousing facilities), and export-oriented thrust sectors such as leather and footwear, pharmaceuticals, ICT, plastic, and light engineering. It was also revealed that industries such as waste treatment plants that have high development impact including the health sector are a potential attractive avenue for attracting blended finance.

Since Bangladesh is a fast-growing developing country, it is assumed that it will receive less concessional financing for developmental projects in the future, as more funds need to be mobilized and utilized from its internal sources. In this context, blended finance has the potential to attract investment in areas that are critical for meeting the SDG goals. Since renewable energy development is directly aligned with the SDG 7: By 2030, ensure universal access to affordable, reliable and modern energy for all, it has strong potential to draw blended concessional finance. Additionally, it was revealed that renewable energy projects are good investments for IFIs, as they are bound by "power purchase agreement" (PPA) by the off-taker – the Bangladesh Power Development Board (the government agency that buys power from private power producers) with a guaranteed financial return on investment which makes such financing much secure.

Information gleaned from the interviews revealed that there is no regulatory guideline or institutional framework for the adoption and implementation of blended finance initiatives in Bangladesh. The different government agencies that play a critical role in mobilizing blended finance lack coordination, and the very idea about which agency takes charge of this initiative remains blurry. Additionally, expert interviews with IDCOL – the principal lending arm of GCF in Bangladesh, which specializes in both adaptation and mitigation projects, revealed that it takes large amounts of paperwork including security documents and a lengthy disbursement process, which makes access to these funds for project developers increasingly difficult.

Additionally, it was also revealed that in the course of disbursing funds from the IFIs; sometimes these funds get cancelled, which affects the future development of the pipeline projects per se. Lastly, getting approved for these finances by the IFIs and other lending agencies takes significant time (i.e., a good number of years), which does not facilitate a quick uptake and disbursement of these funds when expeditiously needed for project developers for completing their projects.

It has been suggested that there are potential caveats on relying on additional blended finance for renewable energy power projects. The rationale for this stems from the belief that since these loans are indexed in US dollars, it will create additional pressure for the power companies including the government for meeting their future debt service in foreign currency resulting in higher foreign exchange obligations for the government and contribute to a recipient country's indebtedness. Additionally, there could be risks of substituting domestic financing with blended finance initiatives, which could crowd out the domestic financial sector including having a drawdown effect on the local financial market. Therefore, due diligence is needed in approving the projects that are implemented with the blended finance initiative.

Here the author presents some of the salient recommendations mostly geared toward private investors for mobilizing additional blended finance. These recommendations have been gleaned from the overall blended finance literature that seems realistically and critically expedient for drawing sustainable blended finance for mitigating SDG gaps in emerging country markets.

The blended finance ecosystem has witnessed remarkable transformation over the last couple of years, which has manifested in large-scale collaborative initiatives among governments, development partners, and MDBs across the various investors' spectrum for mobilizing considerable capital for climate blended finance projects geared toward the developing and climate-vulnerable economies. These recommendations are a way forward in deepening international cooperation and mechanisms to crowd-in more private investments for helping developing countries create an enabling domestic environment with the private sector for drawing additional finance into climate projects.

As DFI and MDBs play a crucial role in mobilizing private sector investment to achieve the SDGs, it is recommended that there should be a unified collaborative approach based on the alignment of mutual interests and incentives based on targeted KPIs for greater involvement of the private sector in climate mitigation finance. In this vein, the MDBs and DFIs could spearhead a de-risking partnership with donor governments and philanthropic foundations consistent with their existing mandates, which would incline private investors to invest more in risky emerging markets thus help create a stable environment with comparable returns.

Second, it is suggested that private investors should not give too much emphasis on the sovereign credit ratings to assess the creditworthiness of such projects for developing countries, as these sometimes give an erroneous notion of exaggerated risks vis-à-vis the actual project risk per se. In this instance, an improved risk assessment methodology that better captures the unique characteristics of blended finance investments per se coupled with offering guarantees along with TA assistance for building local capacity could help assuage the concerns of private investors to invest in commercially viable projects in developing countries.

Third, there is a need for improved impact tracking and monitoring of blended finance transactions so that there is less variability of selecting projects that have diverse and unclear outcomes to projects that are consistent, stringent to high-reaching outcomes. In this vein, establishing a standardized impact measurement, tracking, and reporting system based on outcome metrics would inform investors about the comparability of projects and sectors and make informed decisions for future investing. In this vein, future development projects could be modeled on previous successful projects that could be advanced or expanded on a replicable basis. Additionally, the use of TA in projects that provide targeted support and capacity building would go a long way for increased blended finance transactions and reaching high developmental impacts.

Fourth, there is a need for data transparency when underwriting investments from private investors so as to dispel the assumption that emerging markets carry significant risks vis-à-vis the developed markets. Evidence suggests that developing markets demonstrate a significant return on investment compared to the developed markets. In this instance, greater data transparency and disclosure would close the gap between perceived and actual risk on the ground when investing in a developing country and help for evidence-based decision making. For this, having a uniform reporting standard with impact metrics can guide future investment decision-making. In this instance, data must guide the replication and standardization of projects with proven financial structure and solutions.

Finally, there is a need for supportive policies and regulations to identify, develop, and implement bankable blended finance projects with the involvement of various stakeholders. It is argued that many local governments in emerging markets lack the knowledge, capacity, and expertise to effectively mobilize blended finance transactions. Additionally, there is a need for the engagement of institutional investors such as pension funds and insurance companies along with the development of capital markets for mobilizing large domestic capital aligned with the needs and preferences of domestic investors. It is assumed that greater collaboration, innovation, and ongoing learning would create a more supportive ecosystem for blended finance.

8.12 Conclusion

This book chapter has evaluated the role of climate blended finance from a number of perspectives. It has attempted to explore the dynamics of blended finance and the role of climate blended finance in the overall universe of blended finance. In that vein, it has explored the role of climate blended finance in meeting the SDG targets, especially delving into the roles of different investment lenses through which climate blended finance deals are conducted, their geographical spread, the key IFIs and MDBs and other multilateral organizations involved in disbursing these finances, the role of private finance in the overall mix of blended finance and some key recommendations for attracting additional and sustainable blended finance for the emerging countries. In that instance, it has also explored the opportunities and challenges of attracting blended finance in the renewable energy sector in Bangladesh as a unit of analysis through primarily obtaining data for comparing and contrasting the available information and seeking new information from emerging markets which are seeking to attract concessionary blended finance in their respective power sectors with potential caveats.

In the final analysis, it could be argued that more private capital finance should be crowded in into the aggregate mix of blended finance for meeting the SDG goals and help developing countries meet their future net-zero targets. This comprises private equity, venture capital, and private debt fund activities, as the volume of these funds in the overall makeup of blended finance funds is declining. It is suggested that successful projects include the right combination of debt, equity, or grant financing, the right seniority of investors in terms of absorbing losses and earning returns, and appropriate risk-mitigation products. For channeling additional private capital, there should be a mix of sustainable, optimal, and innovative strategies in collaboration with the private sector, the host government, and the MDBs and DFIs with technical support that would ensure greater investment. Additionally, private investors should be encouraged to take greater levels of risk on emerging markets' projects for which previously they have not been exposed to, which will help recalibrate their risk perceptions (i.e., as their perception of risk comes down) for greater engagement in developing countries.

Note

1. The Critical Raw Materials Act (CRM Act) will ensure EU access to a secure and sustainable supply of critical raw materials, enabling Europe to meet its 2030 climate and digital objectives. It puts a disproportionately high focus on raw materials to produce rare-earth magnets, as well as battery-grade lithium (*Source*: Institute of Materials, Minerals & Mining, 2023).

References

AfDB, (2023). Germany provides €10 million to NEPAD Infrastructure Project Preparation Facility (NEPAD-IPPF) to boost infrastructure development in Africa, https://afdb.africa-newsroom.com/press/germany-provides-euro10-million-to-nepad-infrastructure-project-preparation-facility-nepadippf-to-boost-infrastructure-development-in-africa?lang=en (accessed 9 September 2024).

Attridge, S. and Engen, L. (2019). *Blended finance in the poorest countries: The need for a better approach*. Overseas Development Institute.

Climate Policy Initiative, (2023). Global landscape of climate finance 2023, Global-Landscape-of-Climate-Finance-2023.pdf (accessed 14 October 2024).

Convergence, (2023). State of blended finance in 2023: Climate edition, https://www.convergence.finance/api/file/a49fc01d786ce2b97fa3aead2eb107ff:c318cbcb287bf94e1e003b67c0f58fc323c215ac838a9bd932b29e7fb5c28b18afde6459fff72eb943250e0e6a9419a0c78a1d22d90dadc26110a72ca1eff3e292fd85d7a16b2fdb1c2a4653e02e02d-dbcf4cccef2560c1ce27f98153793f6a774d588e865f3c60b7ffc281d7ee0f1ba7b-0f6459ed0d40ebb94cb1e0628d4db29f1c30a7cb7db40a502e5ec55c98f0fe (accessed 18 July 2024).

Convergence, (2024). State of blended finance, https://www.convergence.finance/api/file/d703af732381b70ced8ca428936bc0f4:cb9ba34d2f5a2f20bcdb07137554b296c5e86676cf361c6e406d66b88190c2553a06fcd70f1149ff1a1de61994c60ccb4e6d6723b98ed26ba054a96089bc814169dccb65249359f9dcf50ecbee5f3ed239769653035fd46aa323d861c2ef8d7f7e0a55ce6ec554bfbfcc4a865bd51bd188646e7a09b-dafff38b15f08bc2fe2fd0d35359379d0524475ee48b1e47e40a2 (accessed 18 July, 2024).

Choi, E. and Seiger, A. (2020). Catalyzing capital for the transition toward decarbonization: Blended finance and its way forward, https://sfi.stanford.edu/publications/catalyzing-private-investment/catalyzing-capital-transition-toward-decarbonization (accessed 9 September 2024).

Development Initiatives, (2016). Blended finance: understanding its potential for agenda 2030, https://www.convergence.finance/api/file/d8d7d977aa23bf38be4462caa9f556af:ef74b001a18ab1a50041a274c018b858c18e5147356b29d416173e69ec3f310b4e8b8d15e7cb4e9fd987d55724ac22b7e658dc5c7801462512aca755a3d-79f7859e7d0f56a8ebb55c5d07ac5e26cbaf2526bc816d598d2e724c3442e-733b7eb32e33b6768c50604fd196d44a4558fd994413a7330409de77b1bd5a001dc7394a0918446b1d740f644441a36ed5f45d9938636310abae43873a-519553b407186e692d060790f62689c70e11037de948057878c2dbdd84c5d-0479e5dc317b44eaf (accessed 10 October 2024).

Earth Security, (2021). The blended finance playbook for nature-based solutions.

EU, (2020). The use of development funds for de-risking private investment: how effective is it in delivering development results? https://www.europarl.europa.eu/RegData/etudes/STUD/2020/603486/EXPO_STU(2020)603486_EN.pdf (accessed 10 September 2024).

Flammer, C., Girourx, T., and Heal, G. (2024). Blended Finance. NBR Working Paper Series. https://www.nber.org/system/files/working_papers/w32287/w32287.pdf (accessed 14 October 2024).

GFANZ. (2021). The Glasgow financial alliance for net-zero: On progress and plan towards a net-zero global economy, https://assets.bbhub.io/company/sites/63/2021/11/GFANZ-Progress-Report.pdf (accessed 15 October 2024).

IEA, (2001). Scaling up private finance for clean energy in emerging and developing economies, https://iea.blob.core.windows.net/assets/a48fd497-d479-4d21-8d76-10619ce0a982/ScalingupPrivateFinanceforCleanEnergyinEmergingandDevelopingEconomies.pdf (accessed 20 July 2024).

IFC, (2024). Uzbekistan to build new solar plant and first battery energy storage system with World Bank support, https://www.ifc.org/en/pressroom/2024/uzbekistan-to-build-new-solar-plant-and-first-battery-energy-storage-system-with-world-bank-group-support (accessed 10 October 2024).

Institute of Materials, Minerals & Mining, (2023). EU Critical Raw Materials Act receives raw critique, https://www.iom3.org/resource/critical-raw-materials-act-receives-raw-critique.html (accessed 10 September 2024).

IRENA, (2020). Renewable energy finance: Institutional capital, https://www.irena.org/-/media/Files/IRENA/Agency/Publication/2020/Jan/IRENA_RE_finanace_Institutional_capital_2020.pdf (accessed 15 October 2024).

Isah, A., Dioha, M.O., Debnath, R., Abraham-Dukuma, M.C., and Butu, H.M. (2023). Financing renewable energy: Policy insights from Brazil and Nigeria. *Energy Sustainability and Society*, *13*(2). https://doi.org/10.1186/s13705-022-00379-9

Ivory, R. (2023). Blending with technical assistance: Data brief, https://assets.ctfassets.net/4cgqlwde6qy0/1cPyptaju6esN7ktzUO6Pt/721e7e168c43e3e0cf1d22c3bcd265e9/DB_TechnicalAssistance-FINAL-Oct_18__1_.pdf (accessed 9 September 2024).

Jessop, S., Binnie, I., and Thomas, L. (2023). MUFG, partners launch 1.5 billion climate finance platform, https://www.reuters.com/sustainability/sustainable-finance-reporting/mufg-partners-launch-15-bln-climate-finance-platform-2023-06-22/ (accessed 23 September 2024).

Juneja, M.K. (2024). How blended finance can reorient cautious private investors to infrastructure, https://blogs.worldbank.org/en/ppps/how-blended-finance-can-reorient-cautious-private-investors-to-i (accessed 23 September 2024).

KPMG, (2024). Doing deals in Sub-Saharan Africa: Key insights from dealmakers, https://assets.kpmg.com/content/dam/kpmg/ci/pdf/doing-deals-in-sub-saharan-africa.pdf (accessed 10 October 2024).

McHugh, C.A. (2021). Mobilizing private funding of development finance. *Journal of Development Studies*, *57*, 1979–2001.

MIGA, (2016). Project brief Neo 1 20 MW solar PV Plant, https://www.miga.org/sites/default/files/2022-07/Appendix%20A-Neo%20I_NES_Project%20Brief.pdf (accessed 5 October 2024).

OECD, (2018). Blended finance definitions and concepts, https://www.oecd-ilibrary.org/docserver/9789264288768-7-en.pdf?expires=1729001123&id=id&accname=guest&checksum=BEE4B639D2D7F128101A1ED45D6629FA (accessed 12 September 2024).

OECD, (2023). Scaling up the mobilization of private finance for climate action in developing countries: Challenges and opportunities for international providers, https://www.oecd-ilibrary.org/environment/scaling-up-the-mobilisation-of-private-finance-for-climate-action-in-developing-countries_17a88681-en (accessed 14 July 2024).

Pereira, J. (2017). Blended finance: What it is, how it works and how it is used, https://oxfamilibrary.openrepository.com/bitstream/handle/10546/620186/rr-blended-finance-130217-en.pdf;jsessionid=7E022733A8246CE668B2332EA1A42181?sequence=1 (accessed 6 October 2024).

PwC, (2024). Tapping into the power of blended finance, https://www.pwc.com/gx/en/issues/esg/the-energy-transition/sustainable-energy-infrastructure/tapping-into-the-power-of-blended-finance.html (accessed 20 September 2024).

Sial, F. (2024). Blended finance for climate action: Good value for money, https://assets.nationbuilder.com/eurodad/pages/3326/attachments/original/1714126924/01_blended-finance-report-FINAL_%281%29.pdf?1714126924 (accessed 20 September 2024).

Sheriffdeen, M., Nurrochmat, D.R., Perdinan, and Abubakar, H.K.A. (2022). Effectiveness of emerging mechanisms for financing national climate actions: Examples of the Indonesian climate change trust fund. *Climate and Development* (2), 81–92. https://doi.org/10.1080/17565529.2022.2057905

Trade Mark Africa, (2023). EU to invest €50 million in infrastructure and mining in DRC, https://furtherafrica.com/2023/03/09/eu-to-invest-e50-million-in-infrastructure-and-mining-in-drc/ (accessed 6 September 2024).

UNCTAD, (2023). World Investment Report 2023: Investing in sustainable energy for all, https://unctad.org/system/files/official-document/wir2023_en.pdf (accessed 22 September 2024).

UNFCCC, (2024). Introduction to climate finance, https://unfccc.int/topics/introduction-to-climate-finance (accessed 10 September 2024).

Yusuf, M.A. and Sohel, A.K.M. (2024). https://today.thefinancialexpress.com.bd/30th-anniversary-issue-2/scaling-up-climate-finance-for-bangladesh-options-to-consider-1700904860 (accessed 13 October 2024).

Chapter 9

Future Climate and Sustainability Duties in the Financial Industry: Opportunities, Risks, Ideas

Marc Nathmann

9.1 Introduction

The financial industry is increasingly being called upon worldwide, especially within the European Union ("EU"), politically and in the media to make a greater contribution to climate protection efforts. In recent years, it appeared that there was also a consensus within the financial industry that politically desired efforts to achieve climate protection goals were supported within the financial industry and worldwide.

Using a word from climate reporting, the question is now increasingly being asked at the beginning of 2025 whether the year 2025 will reach a "tipping point" within the financial industry. For the first time, there are signs that the attitude that climate protection and sustainability are core issues for the industry's future strategy may not be so uniformly shared. On the one hand, there are increasing considerations, particularly in EU-dominated Europe, to force financial market players to contribute to climate protection by legal

DOI: 10.1201/9781003528951-9

means. Meanwhile, on the western side of the Atlantic in particular (from a European perspective), the climate policy wind is shifting, and core players such as BlackRock are abandoning climate protection initiatives. Polito, economically speaking, industry opinion is swinging in a different direction in line with politics.

The future will show whether climate protection and sustainability can and will prove to be sustainable as a strategic core objective within the financial industry. In any case, opinions on this are becoming more diverse within the industry and also in politics, and therefore among legislators, which is certainly conducive to an appropriate debate. At the same time, however, the question arises as to what strategic orientation is required, so the world is also becoming more difficult in this area (Endress & Badir, 2023; Galipeau & Endress, 2025).

This article therefore presents the current developments surrounding climate protection considerations in the field of financial markets and examines which efforts are foreseeable, particularly from a regulatory perspective. From this, opportunities and risks are derived that arise on the basis of the regulatory playing field.

9.2 Background of So-called Climate Change and Measures

Climate change, sustainability, and related measures are central to the discussion; therefore, revisiting these terms for clarity might be helpful.

9.2.1 *Climate Change*

Based on a commonly referenced definition, climate change refers to long-term changes in temperatures and weather patterns on Earth (Pielke, 2004; Werndl, 2016). These changes can be of natural origin, such as fluctuations in solar activity. Since the 19th century, however, climate change has mainly been caused by human activities, in particular the burning of fossil fuels such as coal, oil, and natural gas, which release greenhouse gases.

The whether, how, and why of the need to limit climate change is not discussed here. The opinions about this can hardly be adequately presented according to scientific standards. Assuming that the main causes of climate change are manifold, but can mainly be traced back to human activities, some of the most important factors can be identified:

- Burning fossil fuels: The use of coal, oil, and natural gas to generate energy releases large quantities of carbon dioxide (CO_2) and other greenhouse gases.
- Deforestation of forests: Forests absorb CO_2 and store it. Deforestation releases this CO_2, which increases the greenhouse effect.

- Agriculture: Livestock farming and certain agricultural practices release methane (CH_4) and nitrous oxide (N_2O), which are also powerful greenhouse gases.
- Industry: Various industrial processes, including cement production, contribute to the release of greenhouse gases.
- These activities increase the concentration of greenhouse gases in the atmosphere, which leads to global warming and the associated climate changes.

There are various measures to combat climate change that are being discussed at both the individual and political levels. Essentially, the following measures are called for:

- Switch to renewable energies: The use of solar, wind and hydropower can significantly reduce greenhouse gas emissions (Council of the European Union, 2025).
- Increase energy efficiency: Energy consumption can be reduced by using energy-efficient technologies and improving building insulation.
- Reforestation and forest protection: Forests play an important role in storing CO_2. Reforestation projects and the protection of existing forests are therefore crucial.
- Sustainable agriculture: Practices such as reducing the use of fertilizers and promoting organic farming can reduce emissions from agriculture.
- Promotion of public transport: The expansion and use of public transport and the switch to low-emission vehicles can reduce CO_2 emissions in the transport sector.
- Reducing meat consumption: A plant-based diet has a smaller ecological footprint and can reduce methane emissions from livestock farming.

9.2.2 Sustainability

A key element in combating climate change should be more *sustainability*. The term *sustainability* has a complex and multifaceted conceptual history. The word sustainability is derived from the verb sustainable, meaning "to last or remain for a long time". Nowadays, there are essentially three different meanings:

The original meaning of "a long-lasting effect", the special forestry meaning as a "forestry principle according to which no more wood may be felled than can grow back in each case", the modern, comprehensive meaning in the sense of a "principle according to which no more may be consumed than can grow back or regenerate and be made available again in the future" (Grober, 2013; Rödel, 2013). In current usage, different understandings of the term compete with each other:

- an everyday understanding that something can or should last, exist, continue to have an effect, or be for a long time after it has been built, started, and/or set in motion;

- different political views that vary from this basic understanding of sustainability, according to the position of different interest groups. This expansion initially resulted from the global environmental and development policy debate since the Second World War, in particular with the definitions by the World Commission on Environment and Development (Brundtland Commission) set up by the United Nations in 1983, the Club of Rome, and the Enquete Commission of the German Bundestag. The following can be observed
  - the three-dimensional concept of sustainability, which sees sustainability as a bundle of objectives that strives for ecological, social, and economic goals in equal measure; this concept is popularized by the Brundtland Commission and Agenda 21, the final document of the 1992 UN Conference on Environment and Development in Rio de Janeiro
  - the business-oriented concept of sustainability, which refers to business or economic stability
  - the environmentally oriented concept of sustainability, which identifies sustainability with environmental justice
  - the socio-ecological concept of sustainability, which defines sustainability as a bundle of ecological and social goals.

(Jessen, 2025)

All measures to combat climate change and achieve greater sustainability often require a combination of political decisions, technological innovations, and behavioral changes at an individual level. In essence, implementation requires first and foremost investment. It is precisely this need for investment that suggests a direct or at least implicit commitment from the financial industry to participate. There are basically two main ways in which an entire industry can participate: through voluntary cooperation or through state regulatory measures. With the "Net Zero Asset Manager Initiative" (NZAM, 2025) on the one hand and regulatory efforts, primarily in the EU, there are examples of both approaches in the business area of investment funds in particular.

9.3 Voluntary Cooperation in the NZAMI and Its Failure

The Net Zero Asset Manager Initiative stands for non-governmental initiatives; therefore, it is worth a closer view on its goals, function, and failure.

9.3.1 Failure of NZAMI

The "Net Zero Asset Manager Initiative" (NZAMI) is an important climate alliance in the fund industry. It has halted its activities for the time being following the withdrawal of BlackRock. This decision marks a turning point in the financial industry's efforts to promote a climate-neutral economy.

Launched in December 2020, NZAMI brings together international asset managers with the goal of reducing greenhouse gas emissions to zero by 2050 or sooner (NZAM, 2025). The initiative supports investors in achieving their financial goals in line with global climate targets while fulfilling their fiduciary duties (NZAM, 2025).

On January 9, 2025, BlackRock, the world's largest asset manager, announced its withdrawal from NZAMI. The reasons given were legal challenges and confusion over BlackRock's practices. This move led to NZAMI suspending its activities and initiating a review to ensure its appropriateness in the new global context (Jessen, 2025).

9.3.2 Reactions and Future Steps

NZAMI has removed all commitment statements, objectives, case studies, and the list of signatories from its website until the review is complete. This action is to ensure that the initiative remains effective and relevant. Despite the current pause, NZAMI emphasizes its role as a voluntary initiative that supports investors worldwide in the energy transition (Hoffman, 2025).

9.3.3 Challenges and Legal Aspects

Blackrock cited legal reasons for its withdrawal, including lawsuits filed by several Republican-governed U.S. states alleging that climate change efforts violate antitrust laws and drive up energy prices. These legal challenges reflect the increasing tensions between climate protection initiatives and political and economic interests (Jessen, 2025). In light of the statements made during the election campaign and the first few days and the priorities set by the second Trump administration, BlackRock's view is consistent. Quite unlike in the EU, any expectation of legal benefits for climate protection efforts in the United States is illusory and completely unrealistic.

9.3.4 Foreseeable Consequences

The temporary halt to NZAMI activities following Blackrock's withdrawal demonstrates the complexity and challenges facing climate alliances in the financial sector. The review of the initiative will be crucial to determine its future direction and effectiveness.

Blackrock's withdrawal from NZAMI has provoked mixed reactions from other asset managers. Some asset managers expressed regret at the withdrawal and emphasized the importance of the initiative in addressing climate risks and promoting a sustainable economy. A spokesperson for NZAMI said they were disappointed but respected the decision (Toledo, 2025).

Other asset managers may see BlackRock's withdrawal as a signal to reconsider their own participation in the initiative, particularly given the political pressure and legal challenges in the United States (Fredrich, 2025). There are also reports that similar climate protection initiatives such as the "Net-Zero Banking Alliance" are also losing members, indicating a broader movement against ESG investing (Toledo, 2025).

Overall, it remains to be seen how the situation will develop and whether other asset managers will reconsider their participation in NZAMI. The ongoing review of the initiative will be crucial in determining its future direction and relevance.

9.4 International State Regulatory Measures

State regulatory measures stand for a contrary approach to voluntary cooperation, they force to measures. Therefore, the most important measures will be taken into a closer view.

International trend: The trend toward greater transparency and sustainability is increasing. Companies must adapt to the fact that ESG criteria are becoming more important and take appropriate measures to meet the new requirements (Schaefer, 2024). At the same time, however, it is clear that strict requirements are more of an isolated European issue. State regulatory measures in general are more of an issue for OECD countries, in particular the USA (still), the UK, Canada, and Australia. From a global economic perspective, it should be noted in particular that the highly significant People's Republic of China is extremely cautious. Climate protection is not envisaged there until 2030.

USA: The Securities and Exchange Commission (SEC) has proposed regulations requiring companies to disclose climate-related risks and their impact on their business activities. However, these regulations have not yet been finalized (Schaefer, 2024). Against the backdrop of the second Trump administration, it seems rather unlikely that they will be pursued further, and any deepening is ruled out.

Great Britain: The Task Force on Climate-related Financial Disclosures (TCFD) Framework is becoming increasingly mandatory for large companies and financial institutions. It requires the disclosure of climate-related financial information (Schaefer, 2024). However, the TCFD Framework was stopped in 2024.

Canada: The Canadian Securities Administrators (CSA) have published guidelines on climate-related risk disclosure that encourage companies to provide comprehensive and transparent information.

Australia: The Australian Securities and Investments Commission (ASIC) requires companies to disclose climate-related risks in their annual reports. However, this is currently still on a voluntary basis.

9.5 State Regulatory Measures Using the Example of SFDR in the EU

9.5.1 EU Action Plan for Sustainable Finance

The EU traditionally saw itself as a pioneer and (at least self-proclaimed) role model when it came to climate protection and climate protection as an export good, so to speak, and sometimes even wanted to generate economic growth through climate protection. One of the first steps (in addition to strict requirements for the automotive industry) was the obligation of the financial industry.

The EU Action Plan on Sustainable Finance forms the basis for regulation of the financial industry within the EU. It was developed to strengthen the role of the financial sector in achieving a sustainable and more environmentally friendly economy. The European Commission presented this plan in March 2018 (European Commission, 2018).

The action plan is based on the recommendations of an expert group and aims to redirect financial flows toward sustainable investments. This is crucial to achieving the climate goals of the Paris Agreement, including a 40% reduction in greenhouse gas emissions by 2030 (European Commission, 2018). It is estimated that an additional investment of €180 billion per year is required to achieve these goals.

A central element of the plan is the creation of a standardized classification system, the so-called taxonomy, which defines clear criteria for sustainable investments. This should help investors to identify and support sustainable projects. In addition, the plan promotes transparency and long-term sustainability in the financial world by obliging companies to disclose their environmental, social, and governance (ESG) practices.

9.5.2 The Objectives and Background of SFDR Regulation

The EU wants to be a climate policy pioneer. As one of the first building blocks, the *Sustainable Finance Disclosure Regulation* (SFDR) was put into force there. SFDR is a key EU regulation that has been in force since March 10, 2021. It was developed as part of the EU Action Plan on Sustainable Finance to promote investment in sustainable projects and prevent greenwashing. The SFDR is primarily aimed at financial market participants and financial advisors and requires them to transparently disclose their sustainability practices and impacts. This article examines the objectives of the SFDR and the political and economic background that led to its introduction.

9.5.3 Background of SFDR Regulation

The EU action plan for sustainable finance: The SFDR is a central component of the EU Action Plan on Sustainable Finance, published in March 2018. This plan pursues the overarching goal of transforming the EU's financial system toward sustainability and promoting investment in environmentally friendly and social projects. A key issue to be addressed was the fragmentation of definitions and standards in the area of sustainable finance, which made it difficult to achieve uniform assessment and comparability.

Lack of transparency and greenwashing: Prior to the introduction of the SFDR, the market for sustainable financial products was characterized by a lack of transparency. Many providers of financial products advertised their products as sustainable without clear standards or binding disclosure obligations. This so-called greenwashing meant that investors were often unable to assess the actual level of sustainability of a product. This not only damaged investor confidence but also hampered the development of sustainable markets.

9.5.4 Objectives of the SFDR

The SFDR pursues several objectives that focus on both transparency and the management of capital flows:

Improving transparency: The main objective of the SFDR is to create transparency about the sustainability characteristics of financial products and strategies. It requires financial market participants and advisors to disclose detailed information on the consideration of sustainability risks and the impact of their investments on environmental and social factors. This transparency should enable investors to make informed decisions.

Combating greenwashing: By introducing clear disclosure obligations and standards, the SFDR aims to prevent greenwashing. Products may no longer be falsely advertised as sustainable. This protects investors from misleading information and increases confidence in the market for sustainable financial products.

Promotion of sustainable investments: The SFDR aims to steer capital flows toward sustainable economic activities. By creating transparency and promoting sustainable investments, it supports the EU in achieving its climate targets and its sustainable development agenda.

Creation of a uniform basis: Another objective of the SFDR is the harmonization of disclosure requirements within the EU. This facilitates the comparison of financial products and promotes the integration of the European financial market. A uniform basis is particularly important for cross-border investments.

Key contents and requirements of the SFDR: The SFDR obliges financial market participants and advisors to disclose sustainability information both at the company level and at the product level. The regulation distinguishes between different disclosure requirements:

Disclosures at the company level: Companies must explain how they take sustainability risks into account in their investment decisions. In addition, they must disclose whether and how they analyze the adverse effects of their investments on environmental and social factors (so-called *Principal Adverse Impacts* – PAIs).

Disclosures at product level: Financial products are divided into three categories in accordance with the SFDR:

i. **Article 6 products:** These products do not take sustainability features into account and are subject to fewer disclosure requirements.
ii. **Article 8 products:** These products promote environmental or social characteristics but do not target specific sustainable investments.
iii. **Article 9 products:** These products have explicit sustainable investment objectives and are subject to the highest disclosure requirements.

Consideration of sustainability risk: Companies must indicate how sustainability risks can affect their financial returns. This includes, for example, risks arising from climate change, regulatory changes, or social conflicts.

Use of standardized indicators: The SFDR introduces standardized indicators for measuring sustainability impacts. These are intended to ensure that the information is clear and comparable.

9.5.5 Effects of the SFDR on the Financial Market

The SFDR has far-reaching implications for the way in which financial market participants and advisors deal with sustainability. On the one hand, it is forcing companies to revise their internal processes and deal more intensively with sustainability issues. On the other hand, it has led to increased demand from investors for sustainable products, as these are now more easily recognizable.

For companies that do not take sustainability risks into account or whose products are not sustainable, the SFDR increases the pressure to adapt their strategies in order to remain competitive. At the same time, companies that have already integrated sustainable practices will benefit from increasing demand and a gain in confidence. At least that is the legislative idea. In practice, however, the SFDR leads first and foremost to new regulatory requirements and thus to costs for implementation and compliance.

Companies must disclose detailed information on their ESG practices. This applies not only to financial institutions, but also to companies that wish to obtain loans or investments from these institutions (lawcode, 2024). In addition, companies are required to collect and report extensive ESG data. This can be particularly challenging for smaller companies as they may not have the necessary resources or systems in place (Gacs, 2024).

Banks and investors are increasingly demanding ESG information from their business partners. This means that companies that cannot provide sufficient sustainability data may find it difficult to obtain financing (lawcode, 2024).

9.5.6 Challenges and Points of Criticism

Complexity and implementation costs: Compliance with the SFDR requires significant investment in data management, reporting, and internal processes. Smaller companies in particular may find it difficult to meet the requirements. Since the beginning – which seems almost unusual – clear voices have been raised at the World Economic Forum (WEF) in Davos (2025) that climate protection projects in particular lead to economically relevant costs for companies and fear resulting disadvantages, namely through bureaucracy (Davos (2025) cited in Wagener (2025)). The SFDR is a good example as it contains reporting obligations at its core.

9.5.6.1 Ambiguities in the Definition

The distinction between the categories of financial products (Articles 6, 8, and 9) and the interpretation of the sustainability criteria is often not clear in practice. This can lead to uncertainties and inconsistencies. This is one of the main areas for improvement. The great strength of the SFDR is precisely the standardization of criteria on the basis of which sustainability can be defined.

9.5.6.2 Limited Global Reach

As the SFDR only applies in the EU, companies outside the EU could remain opaque. This could distort competition between European and non-European companies. This is all the more true as it is not even remotely foreseeable that important regions or nations will follow suit to a comparable extent. Rather, since the beginning of 2025, there does not appear to be a uniform will for more climate protection, at least internationally, among leading decision-makers in business and politics. Even at the WEF, which in previous years was otherwise better known for providing impetus, including for state regulatory measures, more voices can be heard warning that it is precisely such state interventions that impair economic prosperity (Rickens, 2025).

9.5.6.3 Interim Conclusion of the Criticism of the SFDR

The SFDR will not "save the world or the climate" in the truest sense of the word. The SFDR suffers from too many problems for that (Eckhardt, 2024):

1. **Complexity and comprehensibility:** Many players in the financial sector, including advisors and investment product providers, find the SFDR too complex and difficult to understand. As a result, the rules are often not applied correctly, and investors are reluctant to make sustainable investments.
2. **Data gaps:** Another major problem is the existing data gaps. The SFDR requires extensive data to assess the sustainability of investments, but many companies struggle to obtain or process this data.

3. **Greenwashing:** Despite the good intentions of the SFDR, there are concerns that the regulation does not sufficiently tackle greenwashing. Some financial actors could continue to feign sustainable practices without actually making sustainable investments (The Market Faces the SFDR Challenge [Der Markt stellt sich der SFDR-Herausforderung], 2021).
4. **Contradictions and inconsistencies:** There are discrepancies between the SFDR and other EU regulations, such as the Green Taxonomy Regulation. These inconsistencies make it difficult for market participants to implement the regulations uniformly.
5. **Effectiveness:** Surveys and studies show that the existing EU legal framework for sustainable financing has not yet achieved the desired success. Sustainable investments have not been substantially increased, which calls into question the effectiveness of the SFDR.
6. **Equal treatment of investment products:** Critics are calling for all investment products, whether sustainable or not, to be treated equally. The current rules could lead to non-sustainable products being disadvantaged.

These points of criticism show that although the SFDR is a step toward sustainable financing, there is still considerable room for improvement. Particularly with regard to the definitions as the most important added value of the SFDR in practice.

9.6 Interim Conclusion

It is clear that there is a high degree of dependency on political will. Now that the political wind has changed, particularly in the United States, there is no longer any willingness on the part of significant sections of the (primarily United States) financial industry (as of January 2025) to participate in climate protection initiatives on a broad scale.

This leads to the conclusion that the promotion of climate protection and sustainability is not a core strategic objective that is widely shared within the financial industry.

Targeted promotion of such goals is, if all, a marginal issue for specialized players such as environmental banks or special funds. Of course, such players also generally benefit from state regulatory measures on a broad scale; however, state regulatory measures lead to a forced change of direction in business models in the financial industry toward politically desired target realization approaches that are not necessarily voluntarily desired or considered economically sensible.

The big problem in practice, however, is that even the consequences of such politically – and explicitly not economically – sensible trends are not without risk for financial market companies. The political and regulatory competitive advantages of today may be the disadvantages of tomorrow. Sustainable investment assets will find it difficult to take advantage of opportunities arising from the lifting of restrictions (as is currently the case in U.S. policy), e.g., in fossil fuel industries. It will become much more difficult to diversify and remain agile.

Restrictive legislation within the EU in particular restricts and hinders free competition without at least creating significant competitive advantages. From today's perspective (early 2025), European financial companies are more likely to be put at an international disadvantage by their "own" domestic legislators.

The evaluation of the core measures considered here shows the birth defect. These measures, especially state measures, can of course be influenced by the state, but that is no guarantee that they also serve sustainability goals or the fight against climate change. In a nutshell, the state can only make it compulsory to wear a seatbelt in a car if the seatbelt has been invented beforehand. It is therefore crucial that there are innovations that enable sustainability, for example, such as concepts for the comprehensive and, above all, economically favorable use of renewable energies. The financial market plays a decisive role in selecting which innovations can be successful on the market in the long term. By making investment decisions, it plays a decisive role in directing financial flows into sensible, in other words sustainable, innovations. In this allocation, state coercion is almost always detrimental, at best neutral.

Therefore, the legislator must also recognize that it must not play its role as a central planner, but that it is sufficient to subsidize selectively if necessary. A type of subsidy can also be regulation through, for example, disclosure or transparency obligations, which are also part of the SFDR and help investors to reduce information asymmetries. However, market laws are not subject to the legislator's ability to control them.

The difficulty is that the state-regulatory approach is essentially based on the fact that a central authority, the legislator, has to determine what behavior it expects from market participants, especially banks, in other areas such as the automotive industry. The legislator cannot act alone and always for the common good, because it is impossible for him to be fully informed and always act rationally. They fall into the rationality trap. This refers to the divergence between what is rational and reasonable for the individual (individual rationality) and what is reasonable for all individuals (collective rationality). The prerequisite for a rationality trap is that there is competition between individuals (individuals can also be states) who do not act collectively but individually. Otherwise, it would be equally impossible for climate protection measures to disadvantage companies or, conversely, to favor them in the absence of such measures.

9.7 Economic Evaluation of Climate Protection Measures

To evaluate the different approaches, a comparison of the economic effects is useful.

9.7.1 Tragic of the Commons

The fight against climate change is characterized by the tragedy of the commons.[1] The tragedy of the commons, or commons problem, describes a socio-economic dilemma in which a limited, communally used resource is depleted through individual overuse. It shows how the pursuit of maximum personal benefit by individual actors can lead to long-term damage to the entire community, as material resources are depleted or destroyed, for example through overgrazing, overfishing, or overexploitation (Acheson, 1989).

Private property and international restrictions are seen as solutions, but these remain controversial in terms of enforceability, distributive justice, and sustainable use (Becker & Ostrom, 1995). This is also at the heart of the political, legislative, and social debate on how climate change mitigation and/or sustainability can be achieved and, above all, whether to rely on state coercion in the form of state-regulatory measures or voluntary action

Goods from whose use other potential consumers cannot be excluded, but whose consumers' demands for use are rival, are referred to in economics as common goods.

If, in a world of scarce resources, completely rival goods are freely available, i.e., at a price of zero, rationing will generally occur over the waiting period. The result is a resource-consuming competition for appropriation in which everyone will try to be the first. Examples of the problematic use of natural resources for which no exclusive rights of disposal have been defined:

- Overfishing the world's oceans
- Plundering of wildlife populations and forests, especially in developing countries (overexploitation)
- Discharge of wastewater into streams and rivers
- Contamination of these through agricultural pesticides and over-fertilization
- Illegal conversion of forest into farmland (Indonesia, Latin America, Africa)
- Overexploitation of soils resulting in desertification
- Use of the atmosphere as a sink for air pollutants, resulting in air pollution.
- It acts as a motor when the demand for the common good grows strongly in comparison to the supply. A tragic escalation then occurs due to faster consumption of the common good.

(Tietzel & Mueller, 2000)

Among other things, this can be caused by locally exploding populations that need to be fed. In this case, approaches to solving the social dilemma based on the definition of rights of disposal under state control or the regulation of scarce resources, e.g., through fishing quotas or emissions trading, fail. These examples are almost identical to the generally discussed triggers of climate change.

9.7.2 General Solution Options

Three options are generally proposed for solving the problem of the commons:

- Educate and admonish: People are informed about the consequences of their actions with regard to the overuse of a common good and appealed to their sense of morality. While a moral appeal is a weak means, powerful means such as social exclusion can also be used. This aspect includes, for example, the transparency obligations of the SFDR, which aim to make it possible to recognize "unsustainable" financial products.
- Privatize: Where possible, common goods can be divided up and privatized to place the parts under private control, making overuse directly tangible.
- Binding rules: Community coercion can be exercised through requirements, prohibitions, permits, and levies. Well-known examples can be found in road traffic, broadcasting frequencies, waste and water charges, and taxes (Meadows & Wright, 2008; Meadows et al., 2019). The SFDR also falls into this category. In addition, the EU in particular is also increasingly working with bans outside the financial sector, such as bans on the production of non-electric vehicles outside fixed quotas (Kafsack, 2025).

9.7.3 Sustainability and Climate Change Mitigation through Innovation

9.7.3.1 Legislative Mandate: Disposal Rights

It is generally agreed that clear rights of disposal are a prerequisite for economic growth through investment and therefore one of the basic requirements for achieving sustainability and climate change mitigation. This is precisely where there is an obvious and readily available option for legislators. The theory of disposal rights distinguishes between the following disposal rights (Fritsch et al., 2005):

- usus: the right to use a thing and exclude the rest of the world from using it;
- usus fructus: the "right to reap the fruits"; the right to retain the income from the use of the object and the obligation to bear losses;
- ab usus: the right to change the shape and appearance of a thing;
- ius abutendi: the right to dispose of the property in whole or in part and to retain the capital gain.

(Demsetz, 1967)

Legally speaking, a legislator can shape these disposition rights by defining, guaranteeing and, above all, protecting property. An example of this is Article 14 (1) of the German Basic Law, which defines property as a legislative mandate: "*Property and the right of inheritance shall be guaranteed. Their content and limits shall be defined by the laws*".

Following Thomas Hobbes, James M. Buchanan explains the consequences of a lack of legal order: if there are no defined and enforced rights of disposal, there is little incentive to invest, as no one can be sure of reaping the benefits of these investments (Buchanan, 1984).

As a much-used example, an Indian family without rights of disposal runs the risk that another family will kill the animals it protects, so it will either not "invest" at all and hunt young animals itself, for example, or it will have to incur extremely high costs to protect its investment (guarding, fighting, etc.) (Bhattacharjee, 2014).

This means that the definition and enforcement of disposal rights is in the common interest of all, even if it is still in the individual interest not to adhere to them (i.e., not to invest and go on a raid). This is a second-order collective good problem, as it:

- collectively it is better if everyone adheres to the distribution of disposal rights, but individually, it is better not to adhere to it.
- it is in the collective interest to punish lawbreakers in order to enforce the rights of disposal, but it is in the individual's interest not to participate in the costs of punishment or enforcement.

Among the tasks that financial science assigns to the state, legislation and the allocation of rights of disposal are seen as part of the allocation function (Erlei et al., 2016). Regulatory efforts aim to achieve precisely an allocation effect by steering financial flows into climate-friendly and sustainable technologies.

9.7.3.2 Effect

The mere existence of disposal rights means that externalities, such as climate change impacts, can be solved efficiently in line with market conditions through negotiations between the polluter and the affected party.

The Coase theorem states that markets deal efficiently with externalities under the assumptions given below. It specifies the conditions under which players in a market can efficiently solve the allocation of resources through negotiations, despite market failure and the resulting existence of externalities. The solution then corresponds to a market equilibrium. This is based on purely economic considerations and does not take into account any questions of guilt or liability.

According to this theory, actors in the affected market are able to independently resolve the problems associated with externalities and allocate resources with a Pareto-efficient result. The distribution of property rights is irrelevant for the agreement on the externality (invariance hypothesis): The parties concerned will always achieve the efficient solution (Coase, 1960).

This solution is explained in most textbooks with the help of an example, which certainly represents many discussions on the consequences of climate change. The example assumes that two companies, a fishing company and a drug manufacturer, are located on a lake. In this example, the rights of disposal are held by the drug manufacturer (laissez-faire rule), so it can cause social costs. The drug manufacturer pollutes the surrounding nature and the lake through its production. As a result of the pollution, the fish population and fish diversity begin to dwindle, which represents a loss for the fishing business

The fishing company will now enter into negotiations with the drug manufacturer to offer it an incentive to avoid damage. For avoiding the first unit of damage, the fisherman offers the drug company a transfer amount that corresponds to the cost of avoiding damage. The company will avoid harm, and the fisherman will benefit from this. This negotiation is continued by both parties until the marginal damage costs are equal to the marginal avoidance costs.

The benefits of damage reduction for the fishing industry are significantly higher than the costs of avoiding pollutants. There is therefore an opportunity here to improve allocation in the sense of the Pareto criterion. Therefore, the fishing company will pay the drug manufacturer the costs of avoiding the pollutant until the marginal costs of avoiding the damage are equal to the marginal damage (Fritsch, 2018).

According to general economic theory, the accuracy of a negotiated solution is higher than that of a tax or a subsidy if the state does not have complete information. However, its application in real cases is very difficult due to transaction costs, the possibility of failed negotiations, and the problematic allocation of property rights (Fritsch, 2018).

9.7.3.3 Emissions Trading as an Economic Solution

The idea of emissions trading, which is essentially an economic instrument and an alternative to state regulatory intervention.

9.8 Functionality

Emissions trading offers a solution via disposal rights, as it creates property rights via securitization, which then become the subject of negotiation by being traded on the market

The theoretical background to emissions trading is that vested interests and conflicts of interest between groups can hinder cooperation. Incidentally, this is also evident in the political debate about the right instruments for combating climate change.

It is therefore often argued that maximizing the overall benefit through cooperation is advantageous in the long term, especially when dealing with global challenges such as climate change. This pattern of individual utility maximization, which can lead to collective ruin, is also examined by game theory, in particular the prisoner's dilemma and its variants. Among other things, it examines the question of why individuals in many cases stabilize social norms through altruistic sanctions despite high individual costs. Social psychology also points to maxim-based, i.e., not purpose-oriented, trust as a possible solution (Guo, 2020).

One suggestion is therefore that polycentric approaches in which different institutions work together at different levels (local, national, international) could be more effective. Conclusion: It is emphasized that a broadening of the moral perspective and consideration of the well-being of all groups is necessary to promote sustainable cooperation (Guo, 2020).

This can be achieved in particular by trading CO_2 certificates or by securitizing and trading emissions that are considered harmful. Emissions trading is therefore a key instrument for reducing greenhouse gases. It works according to the following principles:

- Cap-and-trade principle: An upper limit (cap) is set for total greenhouse gas emissions. This cap is divided into emission rights that companies must acquire in order to be allowed to emit greenhouse gases.
- Allocation of emission rights: Companies receive emission rights either free of charge or against payment. These rights are based on historical emission values or production capacities.
- Trading in emission rights: Companies can trade their emission rights on the market. If a company emits fewer emissions than it has been allocated, it can sell the surplus rights. Companies that emit more emissions must buy additional allowances.
- Incentives to reduce emissions: Emissions trading creates financial incentives for companies to reduce their emissions. Companies that reduce their emissions efficiently can make a profit by selling surplus rights.
- Linking and expansion: Emissions trading is increasingly being extended to other countries and regions in order to create a global carbon market. This enables companies to trade emission rights across borders and efficiently reduce greenhouse gas emissions.

9.9 The EU Emissions Trading Model

The EU Emissions Trading Scheme (EU ETS) operates in line with the above principles and is a key EU instrument for reducing greenhouse gas emissions. The EU ETS currently covers around 45% of greenhouse gas emissions in the EU and includes sectors such as energy generation, industry, and aviation (Agency, 2025).

The allocation of emission allowances in the EU ETS takes place in two main ways, by auction and by free allocation:

- The majority of emission allowances are auctioned. Companies must purchase these certificates at auctions, which ensures that the price is determined by supply and demand (European Court of Auditors, 2020).
- Some sectors that are particularly at risk of carbon leakage receive allowances free of charge. This allocation is based on a benchmarking system that takes into account the emissions intensity of the most efficient 10% of installations in a given sector (Lilico & Drury, 2023). This method is intended to ensure that companies have incentives to reduce their emissions without losing their competitiveness (Lilico & Drury, 2023).

The combination of these two methods should offer a balanced approach to achieving both economic and environmental goals. The advantage is that emissions trading can, in principle, be extended worldwide without any problems (provided there is political will).

9.10 Interim Conclusion

Emissions trading is an extremely charming instrument. With restrained political control and influence, it manages solely through the allocation of disposition rights and, in particular, requires little or no central planning instruments. In particular, it does not require complete information, which makes it impossible to determine "the right measures" in detail as scientific knowledge advances when it comes to state intervention. Legally speaking, emissions trading can certainly be reconciled with general state mandates, in particular the definition of property. Above all, trading works via existing and well-functioning systems, exchanges, and (financial) markets.

Ultimately, it can be said that it is a logical consequence of constantly dwindling resources. Scarcity leads to rising prices through competition, which in turn leads to the allocation of financial flows to cheaper technologies and thus promotes innovation.

9.10.1 Result

Irrespective of how individuals feel about the importance of climate change and the measures to combat it, whether they see an urgent need for government action or not, or whether they are willing or unwilling to make an individual contribution to combating it, it can be said that it makes objective sense for technological solutions to receive sufficient financial resources for development and further development. A contribution from the financial industry will also have to be measured against this.

This goal will not necessarily be achieved better or faster with state regulatory measures. The diametrically opposed development in the USA and the EU shows that so-called climate protection also swings with the political pendulum, and this leads to permanent uncertainty. In contrast to the opinion often circulated in politics in Central Europe, as the author has observed live from his own experience as a European, that the EU path is a global role model, a look at the USA or China – to name just two important players – shows that this opinion is wrong. State-regulatory measures based on the EU model are particularly harmful when viewed in the light of day, as they put European companies at a competitive disadvantage, and the benefits are negligible at best. However, the SFDR's requirement to provide investors with a better overview and transparency regarding the composition of investment instruments is to be expressly welcomed.

Emissions trading is a solid way to protect the climate and increase sustainability. Provided, of course, that it is operated as internationally as possible.

In the medium term, however, it can be assumed that there will always be efforts to resort to state regulatory measures. This will be a challenge for companies in the financial markets, as they will have to comply with the rules, and that means costs in any case.

Conversely, it is also true that those who profit from these state-regulatory measures cannot permanently rely on being favored or subsidized by the state. In practical terms, a business model that depends on the prevailing political will stands on stony ground.

For the field of climate protection, nothing else applies than always: a business model is good and sustainable in the strictest sense if it can be successful in the long term according to economic standards. "Being green" is certainly positive, but that alone is not enough.

Allocating capital from the evaluation of business opportunities is the core task of all financial market players and also a core competence. Climate protection is one of many building blocks in this process and, in the EU in particular, is another key regulatory requirement. But financial companies are also practiced in this area. However, it is important to take legislative and political developments and ideas on climate protection into the narrow regulatory focus.

Note

1. The literal expression tragedy of the commons is attributed, among other things, to considerations by William Forster Lloyd (1795-1852) on population development; William Forster Lloyd: Two Lectures on the Checks to Population. Oxford University Press, 1833.

References

Acheson, J. M. (1989). Management of Common-Property Resources. In S. Plattner (Ed.), *Economic Anthropology* (pp. 351–378). Stanford University Press.

Agency, E. P. (2025). *EU Emissions Trading System*. https://www.epa.ie/our-services/licensing/climate-change/eu-emissions-trading-system-/

Becker, C. D., & Ostrom, E. (1995). Human Ecology and Resource Sustainability: The Importance of Institutional Diversity. *Annual Review of Ecology and Systematics, 26*(1), 113–133. https://doi.org/10.1146/annurev.es.26.110195.000553

Bhattacharjee, S. S. (2014). *Cleaning Human Waste: "Manual Scavenging," Caste, and Discrimination in India*. Human Rights Watch.

Buchanan, J. M. (1984). *The Limits of Freedom. Between Anarchy and Leviathan [Die Grenzen der Freiheit: Zwischen Anarchie und Leviathan]*. Mohr (Siebeck).

Coase, R. H. (1960). The Problem of Social Cost. *The Journal of Law and Economics, 3*, 1–44. https://doi.org/10.1086/466560

Council of the European Union. (2025, February 21). *EU Measures Against Climate Change [Maßnahmen der EU gegen den Klimawandel]*. Consilium. https://www.consilium.europa.eu/de/policies/climate-change/

Demsetz, H. (1967). Toward a Theory of Property Rights. *The American Economic Review, 57*(2), 347–359. JSTOR.

Eckhardt, P. (2024, August 20). *Green Financial Products: Cep Calls for New Practical EU Transparency Rules*. Centrum Für Europäische Politik: Cep.Eu. https://www.cep.eu/eu-topics/details/nachhaltigkeitsbezogene-offenlegungen-im-finanzsektor.html

Endress, T., & Badir, Y. F. (Eds.). (2023). *Business and Management in Asia: Digital Innovation and Sustainability*. Springer Nature. https://doi.org/10.1007/978-981-19-6418-3

Erlei, M., Leschke, M., & Sauerland, D. (2016). *New Institutional Economics [Neue Institutionenökonomik]* (3. überarbeitete und erweiterte Auflage 2016). Schäffer-Poeschel Verlag für Wirtschaft Steuern Recht GmbH.

European Commission. (2018). *Action Plan: Financing Sustainable Growth (COM(2018) 97 final). European Union*. https://eur-lex.europa.eu/legal-content/EN/TXT/PDF/?uri=CELEX%3A52018DC0097

European Court of Auditors (2020). *The EU's Emissions Trading System: Free Allocation of Allowances Needed Better Targeting*. Publications Office. https://data.europa.eu/doi/10.2865/487419

Fredrich, G. (2025, January 11). *Blackrock Withdraws from Climate Alliance: Reasons and Consequences [Blackrock zieht sich aus Klimabündnis zurück: Gründe und Folgen]*. Nau. https://www.nau.ch/news/amerika/blackrock-zieht-sich-aus-klimabundnis-zuruck-grunde-und-folgen-66892258

Fritsch, M. (2018). *Market Failure and Economic Policy: Microeconomic Foundations of Government Action [Marktversagen und Wirtschaftspolitik: Mikroökonomische Grundlagen staatlichen Handelns]*. Verlag Franz Vahlen GmbH. https://doi.org/10.15358/9783800656448

Fritsch, M., Wein, T., & Ewers, H.-J. (2005). *Market Failure and Economic Policy: Microeconomic Foundations of Government Action [Marktversagen und Wirtschaftspolitik: Mikroökonomische Grundlagen staatlichen Handelns]* (6., überarb. und erw. Aufl). Vahlen.

Gacs, J. (2024, December 2). SFDR einfach erklärt: Was Unternehmen wissen müssen. *Green Vision Solutions*. https://greenvisionsolutions.de/sfdr/

Galipeau, D., & Endress, T. (Eds.). (2025). *A Practical Approach to Digital Technologies for Sustainability*. Taylor & Francis.

Grober, U. (2013). Original Texts—Carlowitz and the Sources of Our Concept of Sustainability [Urtexte—Carlowitz und die Quellen unseres Nachhaltigkeitsbegriffs]. *0028-0615*, *88*(2), 46–51. https://doi.org/10.17433/2.2013.50153203.46-51

Guo, Y. (2020). A Reconsideration of Inter-Group Cooperation with Defect Problem, With an Application to the Climate Change Issue. *SSRN Electronic Journal*. https://doi.org/10.2139/ssrn.3581283

Hoffman, G. (2025, January 14). *Net-Zero Asset Managers Initiative Suspends Activities After BlackRock Exit*. Independent Women's Forum. https://www.iwf.org/2025/01/14/net-zero-asset-managers-initiative-suspends-activities-after-blackrock-exit/

Jessen, J. (2025, January 14). *BlackRock Exit: Net Zero Asset Managers Suspends Activities*. https://sustainabilitymag.com/articles/blackrock-exit-net-zero-asset-managers-suspends-activities

Kafsack, H. (2025, January 14). *Threatening EU Penalties: Car Industry Under Climate Pressure [Drohende EU-Strafen: Autoindustrie im Klimakorsett]*. FAZ. https://www.faz.net/aktuell/wirtschaft/klima-nachhaltigkeit/drohende-eu-strafen-autoindustrie-im-klimakorsett-110226656.html

lawcode. (2024, March 20). *SFDR: Guide to the Sustainable Finance Disclosure Regulation*. https://www.lawcode.eu/en/blog/sustainable-finance-disclosure-regulation-sfdr/

Lilico, A., & Drury, D. (2023). *The EU Emissions Trading System: Method and Effects of Free Allowance Allocation*. https://www.europarl.europa.eu/thinktank/en/document/IPOL_IDA(2023)755098

Meadows, D. H., & Wright, D. (2008). *Thinking in Systems: A Primer*. Chelsea Green Pub.

Meadows, D. H., Wright, D., & Sustainability Institute. (2019). *The Limits of Thought [Die Grenzen des Denkens]* (K. Bossel, H. Bossel, & S. Weis-Gerhardt, Trans.). Oekom Verlag.

NZAM. (2025). *The Net Zero Asset Managers initiative – An International Group of Asset Managers Committed to Supporting the Goal of Net Zero Greenhouse Gas Emissions*. https://www.netzeroassetmanagers.org/

Pielke, R. A. (2004). What Is Climate Change? *Energy & Environment*, *15*(3), 515–520. https://doi.org/10.1260/0958305041494576

Rickens, C. (2025, January 24). *It Doesn't Matter Where the Perpetrator Had to be—The Main Thing Is That He Wasn't in the Park [Egal wo der Täter hätte sein müssen – Hauptsache nicht im Park]. Read by P. Hoffmann*. Handelsblatt Morning Briefing. https://www.handelsblatt.com/audio/podcast-morning-briefing/handelsblatt-morning-briefing-egal-wo-der-taeter-haette-sein-muessen-hauptsache-nicht-im-park/30182200.html

Rödel, M. (2013). The Invasion of Sustainability. A Linguistic Analysis of a Political and Economic Buzzword [Die Invasion der "Nachhaltigkeit": Eine linguistische Analyse eines politischen und ökonomischen Modeworts]. *Deutsche Sprache*, *2*, 115–141. https://doi.org/10.37307/j.1868-775X.2013.02.03

Schaefer, R. (2024, July 17). *BaFin—Current Topics—This Can Be Done More Easily and Effectively [BaFin—Aktuelle Themen—Das geht einfacher und wirksamer]*. https://www.bafin.de/SharedDocs/Veroeffentlichungen/DE/Fachartikel/2024/fa_bj_0717_SFDR_Review_ED_SPS.html

The Market Faces the SFDR Challenge [Der Markt stellt sich der SFDR-Herausforderung]. (2021, August 31). e-fundresearch.com. https://e-fundresearch.com/newscenter/112-axa-investment-managers/artikel/41980-der-markt-stellt-sich-der-sfdr-herausforderung

Tietzel, M., & Mueller, C. (2000). Regulatory Implications of Contract Theory [Ordnungspolitische Implikationen der Vertragstheorie]. In H. Leipold, I. Pies, & D. Cassel (Eds.), *Ordnungstheorie und Ordnungspolitik: Konzeptionen und Entwicklungsperspektiven*. Lucius und Lucius.

Toledo, M. (2025, January 9). *BlackRock Exits Net Zero Asset Managers Initiative*. Chief Investment Officer. https://www.ai-cio.com/news/blackrock-exits-net-zero-asset-managers-initiative/

Wagener, B. (2025, January 16). *Mercedes Boss Calls for Relaxation of CO_2 Targets* [Mercedes-Chef fordert Lockerung der CO_2-Ziele]. *FAZ*. https://www.faz.net/aktuell/wirtschaft/unternehmen/ola-kaellenius-mercedes-chef-fordert-lockerung-der-co-ziele-110235308.html

Werndl, C. (2016). On Defining Climate and Climate Change. *The British Journal for the Philosophy of Science*, *67*(2), 337–364. https://doi.org/10.1093/bjps/axu048

Chapter 10

The Sustainable VC Playbook: A Practical Guide for Small Fund Managers

David Galipeau

10.1 The New Paradigm in Venture Capital

The landscape of venture capital has undergone a significant transformation in the past two decades, with the environmental, social, and governance (ESG) framework emerging as a pivotal criterion for investment decisions (De Silva et al. 2024). This evolution marks the advent of a new paradigm where value creation is measured not solely by financial returns but also by the impact on society and the environment. For small investment funds, especially those with a focus on ESG-related startups, this shift presents both unique challenges and unprecedented opportunities.

Globally, the integration of ESG considerations into investment strategies has been propelled by a growing awareness of climate change, social inequality, and corporate governance issues (Endress & Badir 2023; Galipeau & Endress 2025; Lin 2022). Investors, regulators, and consumers alike are demanding more accountability and transparency from businesses. This demand has catalyzed a surge in ESG-focused investments, with global sustainable investment assets reaching trillions of dollars. However, the landscape is characterized by a disparity where large funds often have the resources to navigate this complexity, while small funds must be more strategic and agile.

DOI: 10.1201/9781003528951-10

The challenges for small funds include limited access to comprehensive ESG data, the cost of due diligence, and the need for specialized knowledge to assess ESG risks and opportunities accurately. Yet, these funds possess unique advantages: they can be nimbler in decision-making, closer to the ground to identify emerging trends, and capable of fostering deeper relationships with startups, which are crucial for early-stage investments in areas like clean tech, sustainable agriculture, and social enterprises.

In Asia, the ESG investment landscape is both diverse and rapidly evolving (Garger & Lees 2024). Countries like Japan, Singapore, and South Korea have become leaders in sustainable finance, driven by government policies, investor interest, and a burgeoning startup ecosystem focused on sustainability. However, the region also faces unique challenges such as regulatory variances, cultural nuances in business practices, and varying levels of ESG maturity across different markets.

For small investment funds in Asia, the opportunity lies in leveraging local insights and networks to tap into niche markets. The region's dynamic economic growth, coupled with urgent environmental and social issues, creates fertile ground for investments in innovative solutions. From renewable energy projects in Southeast Asia to tech-driven solutions for waste management in urban centers, the potential for impact is immense.

Moreover, the cultural emphasis on community and family in many Asian societies can align well with the social aspect of ESG, enabling investments in businesses that prioritize community welfare or family-oriented products and services. However, small funds must navigate the regulatory landscape carefully, understanding local compliance requirements while advocating for and adapting to emerging ESG standards.

10.2 Setting the Stage for Small Funds

As we delve deeper into this chapter, understanding these global and regional contexts is crucial for small fund managers. The narrative is clear: ESG is not just a trend but a fundamental shift in how investments are viewed. Small funds must adapt by integrating ESG principles not as an add-on but as a core component of their investment thesis.

This section sets the stage for a discussion on how small investment funds can strategically position themselves in this new paradigm. We will explore practical strategies for identifying promising ESG startups, managing ESG-related risks, measuring impact, and how to communicate this value to investors who are increasingly ESG-conscious. The aim is to equip fund managers with the knowledge and tools to not only survive but thrive in this evolving investment landscape, where sustainability and profitability are intertwined.

10.3 Building Your ESG Investment Strategy

In the previous section, we explored the evolving landscape of venture capital through the lens of ESG investing, highlighting both the global and Asian contexts where small investment funds operate. Understanding this backdrop is essential for crafting an effective ESG investment strategy. Here, we will delve into the nuances of building such a strategy specifically tailored for small funds, which can leverage their agility and local insights to make impactful investments in ESG-focused startups.

The first step in building your ESG investment strategy is to clearly define what ESG means for your funds. This involves setting precise criteria for what constitutes an "ESG" investment in your portfolio:

- **Environmental**: Focus on businesses that offer solutions to environmental challenges, such as reducing carbon footprints, improving waste management, or promoting renewable energy sources. In Asia, this might mean investing in solar farms in India, innovative recycling technologies in Japan, or sustainable aquaculture in Indonesia.
- **Social**: Invest in companies that enhance societal well-being through education technology, healthcare innovations, or inclusive business models that uplift underrepresented communities. The social aspect in Asia can be particularly impactful given the region's diverse demographic and cultural landscape.
- **Governance**: Prioritize startups with strong governance practices, transparency, and ethical business conduct. This is crucial in regions where governance standards might vary significantly from one country to another.

Secondly, identifying the right sectors for investment is pivotal. Small funds should leverage their ability to be sector specialists rather than generalists:

- **Niche Markets**: Look for untapped or underserved markets within ESG sectors where your fund can play a leading role. For instance, in Southeast Asia, there might be opportunities in sustainable urban planning or green logistics.
- **Local Market Needs**: Understand the unique environmental and social challenges of different Asian countries. For example, water management solutions in Thailand might differ vastly from air quality technologies needed in Beijing.
- **Growth Potential**: Analyze where ESG integration can lead to significant market disruption or where demand for sustainable solutions is growing. This could be in areas like electric mobility in Malaysia or sustainable fashion in South Korea.

For the third step, your investment strategy must include a robust due diligence process tailored to ESG:

- **Quantitative Metrics**: Develop or adopt ESG scoring systems to quantify impact alongside financial metrics. This could involve assessing carbon intensity, social impact scores, or governance transparency indices.
- **Qualitative Assessments**: Engage in deep dives into company culture, leadership commitment to ESG, and the scalability of their solution. Here, personal visits and interviews with founders and management teams are invaluable.
- **Risk Evaluation**: Understand the specific ESG risks in different markets, such as regulatory risks in China or social risks in conflict zones. Small funds can pivot more quickly to mitigate these risks compared to larger, less agile funds.

In fourth position, it is particularly important for small funds to build more intimate relationships:

- **Local Expertise**: Partner with local NGOs, think tanks, or academic institutions to gain insights into regional ESG dynamics, which can inform investment decisions.
- **Co-Investment**: Look for opportunities to co-invest with other small funds or local investors who share your ESG vision, thus pooling expertise and resources.
- **Community Involvement**: Involve local communities or beneficiaries in the due diligence process to assess the real-world impact of potential investments.

Lastly, effectively communicate your strategy:

- **Investor Education**: Educate your investors on the nuances of ESG investing, particularly how it aligns with financial returns. Use case studies of past investments or hypothetical scenarios.
- **Marketing ESG**: Market your fund not just as a financial vehicle but as a movement towards sustainability. Highlight unique investments that showcase your fund's impact.
- **Networking**: Engage in ESG-focused investment forums, both virtually and in-person, especially those with a focus on Asia, to share insights and learn from peers.

By integrating these elements into your investment strategy, small funds can not only navigate the complexities of ESG investing but can also lead by example, showing that small can indeed be mighty when it comes to driving sustainable change. This strategy should be dynamic, allowing for adaptation as you learn from each investment and as the broader ESG landscape evolves (Priya & Sharma 2024).

10.4 Designing a Due Diligence and Impact Assessment Framework

For small investment funds focusing on early-stage ESG investments, particularly in climate tech, a tailored due diligence and impact assessment framework is crucial. This framework (Figure 10.1) must balance thoroughness with practicality, providing actionable insights while managing resource constraints. Below is a comprehensive yet pragmatic approach designed for small fund managers.

10.4.1 Phase 1: Initial Screening

Objective: Identify potential investments that align with your ESG focus.

- **Sector Fit**: Ensure the startup operates within or impacts your targeted ESG sector. For climate tech, these could be innovations in renewable energy, carbon capture, or sustainable materials.
- **Preliminary Impact Assessment**: Use simple tools like the **Impact Management Project's Five Dimensions of Impact** to gauge the potential for positive environmental, social, or governance outcomes.
- **Basic Financial Health**: Quick financial checks to confirm the startup has a viable business model, even if revenue is not yet substantial.

10.4.2 Phase 2: Detailed Due Diligence

Objective: Deep dive into the company's operations, strategy, and impact potential.

- **ESG-Specific Due Diligence:**
  - **Environmental**: Assess technology viability, lifecycle analysis of products, regulatory compliance (like emissions standards), and resource efficiency. Tools like the **Global Reporting Initiative (GRI)** standards can guide this process.

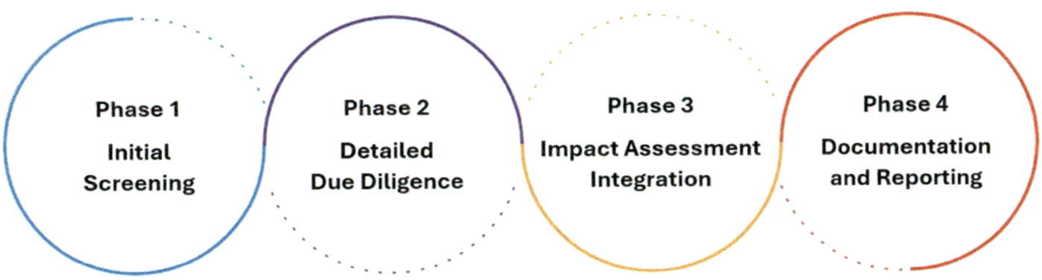

Figure 10.1 Designing a due diligence Phases 1–4.

Source: Adapted from text by author.

- **Social**: Evaluate labor practices, community engagement, and social inclusion. Use frameworks like **B Impact Assessment** to measure social performance.
- **Governance**: Review corporate governance structures, transparency in operations, and ethical practices. The **ESG Risk Ratings** from providers like Sustainalytics can be insightful.

- **Climate Tech Considerations:**
  - **Innovation and Scalability**: Evaluate the technology's novelty, patent status, and scalability potential. Engage with industry experts or academic partnerships for validation.
  - **Market Fit**: Analyze the market demand for innovation, competitive landscape, and potential for market disruption.
  - **Regulatory Pathway**: Understand the regulatory landscape, especially for technologies like carbon capture or waste-to-energy solutions, which might face different regulations across Asia.
- **Financial Due Diligence**: Traditional analysis but with an ESG lens, looking at how ESG risks might affect financial projections, funding needs for R&D, and the sustainability of the business model.

10.4.3 Phase 3: Impact Assessment Integration

Objective: Quantify and qualify the expected impact alongside financial analysis.

- **Impact Metrics Development**:
  - **Quantifiable Metrics**: Define metrics like CO2 reduction per unit produced, waste diverted from landfills, or jobs created in underserved areas. Use tools like **IRIS+** by the Global Impact Investing Network (GIIN) for standardized metrics.
  - **Qualitative Assessments**: Narratives around social change, community testimonials, or case studies of impact.
- **Impact Forecasting**: Use scenario analysis to predict future impact based on different growth scenarios. This can include models showing how scaling up operations might amplify environmental benefits or social outcomes.
- **Cost-Effective Monitoring Solutions:**
  - **Digital Tools**: Implement low-cost digital solutions for ongoing impact monitoring. Apps or platforms that integrate with company operations to automatically track metrics can be invaluable.
  - **Third-Party Verification**: When feasible, engage local universities or NGOs for independent validation of impact claims at a lower cost than international consultants.

10.4.4 Phase 4: Documentation and Reporting

Objective: Ensure all findings are systematically recorded and communicated.

- **Practical Documentation**:
  - **Standardized Templates**: Use or create templates for due diligence reports that cover ESG aspects alongside financial analysis, ensuring consistency and efficiency.
  - **Impact Scorecards**: Develop scorecards or dashboards that visually represent ESG performance and impact metrics for quick reference.
- **Report for Stakeholders:**
  - **Annual Impact Reports**: Combine financial and impact data into annual reports. Use storytelling to convey the human side of impact alongside data.
  - **Investor Updates**: Regular, concise updates focusing on both financial health and ESG achievements can maintain investor engagement without overwhelming them with information.
- **Adaptive Learning**: Document lessons learned from each investment to refine the framework over time, making it more relevant and efficient.

When implementing a due diligence framework, small funds must carefully consider several key factors to ensure effectiveness and alignment with their goals.

Resource allocation is critical, as small funds need to strategically invest their limited time and money into high-impact areas of due diligence that can significantly influence investment decisions.

Additionally, cultural sensitivity is paramount, particularly in Asia, where a deep understanding of local customs, social structures, and business practices is essential for accurate impact assessment and due diligence (Sant'Anna 2024).

Building partnerships can also enhance capabilities; small funds can co-invest with other funds or collaborate with local impact-focused organizations to share resources and expertise. Finally, staying updated with emerging ESG regulations across various Asian markets is vital to ensure the framework remains compliant and relevant in a rapidly evolving regulatory landscape.

This framework, while comprehensive, is designed to be adaptable. Small fund managers can scale the intensity of due diligence based on the stage of the investment or the specific risks and opportunities presented by each startup.

By embedding impact assessment into the due diligence process, you not only align investments with ESG goals but also enhance the decision-making process, aiming for investments that are financially sound and positively transformative.

10.5 An Innovative Financing Scenario in Singapore

In the bustling heart of Singapore, where innovation meets tradition, a small fund manager named Lin was exploring the frontiers of blended finance. Her fund, focused on sustainable urban solutions, was navigating the complex waters of impact investing in Asia. Lin understood that to maximize impact while managing risk, she needed more than traditional venture capital; she required a tapestry of funding structures woven with strategic intent.

Lin's journey began with strategic partnerships.

She knew that small funds could amplify their impact by aligning with larger organizations or local entities that share the vision for sustainability. One partnership was with a regional NGO that had deep roots in community development. Together, they co-invested in a startup specializing in affordable, eco-friendly housing materials. The NGO provided local insights and community engagement, while Lin's fund brought the necessary capital and business acumen. This synergy not only reduced risk through shared due diligence but also enhanced the startup's market penetration by leveraging the NGO's network.

The next layer Lin added to her strategy was catalytic capital.

This approach involved using initial investments to unlock additional funding from more conservative investors. She found an opportunity in a clean tech firm developing a novel water purification system. Lin's fund provided the first round of capital, which was structured as patient capital with flexible terms, allowing the company to scale without the immediate pressure of high returns. This initial investment catalyzed further interest from impact-focused angel investors and eventually from a larger climate fund, significantly boosting the company's growth trajectory. Here, the challenge was ensuring the initial terms were attractive enough to draw in subsequent investors without diluting potential impact.

Understanding the landscape of government support was crucial. Lin engaged with government initiatives in Malaysia, offering tax incentives for investments in green technologies. By navigating these mechanisms, her fund could make investments that were financially viable due to lower fiscal burdens, while still achieving high environmental impact. She invested in a solar energy project that not only benefited from these incentives but also had government contracts ensuring a steady demand. However, this came with the challenge of regulatory compliance and navigating bureaucratic processes, which could be daunting for smaller funds less equipped to manage such intricacies.

Implementing these structures was not without its trials. For instance, structuring a deal for a startup in renewable energy storage required Lin to blend grants, equity, and debt. She used a small grant from a European development agency to cover initial R&D costs, her fund's equity for growth capital, and secured a low-interest loan from a local bank interested in green initiatives. This blend reduced the company's financial risk, making it more appealing to additional investors while maintaining control over the strategic direction.

The benefits were clear: these structures allowed for higher impact per dollar invested, opened new capital sources, and helped in de-risking investments for all parties involved. However, challenges persisted. The complexity of managing diverse funding sources could strain resources, and there was always the risk of mission drift if financial pressures mounted. Moreover, aligning the interests of all parties in a blended finance structure demanded constant communication and negotiation.

Lin's narrative is a testament to the power of innovative financing for small funds in the ESG space. By skillfully weaving together partnerships, catalytic capital, and government support, she not only managed to fund impactful ventures but also learned to navigate the delicate balance between financial returns and sustainable impact. Each investment was a lesson, each success a step towards redefining how small funds can lead to the new era of finance, where every investment is an opportunity to heal the planet.

10.6 A Portfolio Management and Value Creation Scenario from Bangladesh

Small fund managers are not just financiers; they are catalysts for change, particularly in the ESG journey of their portfolio companies. From the moment of investment through to exit, these managers play a pivotal role in embedding sustainable practices that can transform businesses into leaders of environmental and social responsibility.

Upon investment, small fund managers like Raj, managing a fund in Bengaluru (Bangalore), start by integrating ESG into the company's DNA. He collaborated closely with the founders of a tech startup focusing on energy-efficient AI solutions, ensuring their business model from the outset was aligned with sustainability principles. This included setting up green policies for office operations, sustainable supply chain practices, and fostering a culture of inclusivity. Raj's early involvement meant that ESG was not an afterthought but a core strategy, helping the company not only in compliance but in attracting talent and early adopters.

Raj recognized that in markets increasingly valuing sustainability, ESG could be a significant differentiator.

He advised his portfolio companies to leverage their ESG commitments in marketing, highlighting how their products or services contribute to sustainability goals. For instance, the AI company used its energy-saving algorithms as a key selling point, distinguishing it in a crowded market. This approach not only built brand loyalty but also opened doors to new markets valuing green technology.

The value created by focusing on ESG goes beyond financial metrics. Raj implemented a strategy where each company measured and reported on its social and environmental impact, using frameworks like the B Impact Assessment. This not only helped with continuous improvement but also with storytelling to investors and customers. The AI company, for example, quantified how much energy was saved per use of their product, translating into reduced carbon emissions, which was a compelling narrative for impact-focused investors.

For small funds, managing ESG risks demands practical, resource-efficient strategies. Raj used cost-effective tools like online ESG scoring platforms for regular monitoring rather than expensive external audits. He also established simple yet effective risk management by setting clear ESG performance KPIs that were tracked quarterly. This approach allowed for early detection of issues, like potential labor rights violations in the supply chain, enabling swift corrective actions without overwhelming the company's resources.

At exit, Raj ensured that the company's ESG credentials were highlighted, attracting buyers or investors who value sustainability. He prepared detailed ESG reports that showcased the company's journey and future potential in sustainable practices, thereby potentially increasing the company's valuation due to its ESG maturity.

Through these strategies, small fund managers like Raj illustrate that sustainable practices are not just ethical choices but strategic imperatives that can drive competitive advantage, manage risks, and enhance the value of their investments from inception to exit.

10.7 Case Study: Homebrew – A Small Venture Fund That Succeeded through Focus

Homebrew believes in a Bottom-Up Economy, the idea that technology is now helping individuals and small businesses drive economic growth and innovation (Figure 10.2). For many decades, the cost, complexity, and rigidity of technology limited its power and benefits to large corporations – a Top-Down Economy. Today, we are in the midst of a transformation where technology is increasingly accessible enough, cheap enough, and flexible enough to empower individuals and small teams. Teams of 5, 50, or 500 can compete with organizations tens or hundreds of times their size or create entirely new markets with innovative products and services. The Bottom-Up Economy.

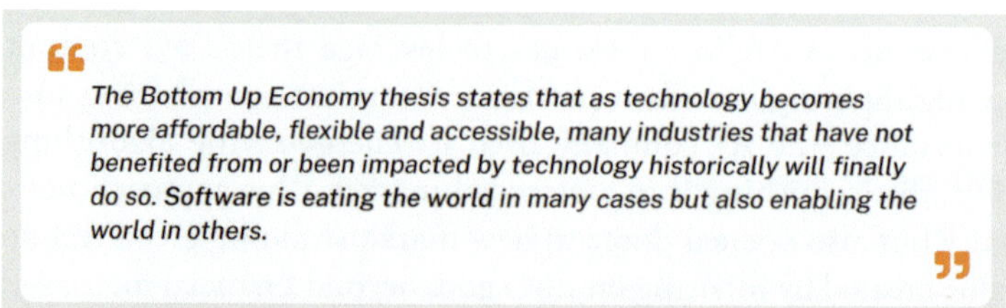

Figure 10.2 Homebrew VC investment thesis – https://www.alexanderjarvis.com/investment-thesis-homebrew/

Homebrew is a seed-stage venture fund founded in 2013 by Hunter Walk and Satya Patel, both former Google executives. The fund started with 35 million (AUM) and has grown to over 150 million (Teare 2019). Despite its small size compared to larger venture capital firms, Homebrew has built a formidable reputation and achieved success by focusing on early-stage startups and fostering deep relationships with founders.

10.7.1 Key Strategies for Success

1. Niche Focus on Seed-Stage Startups
   - Homebrew decided to focus exclusively on seed-stage investments, typically writing checks between USD500,000 and USD1 million. This allowed them to specialize in helping startups at their earliest stages, where they could provide the most value.
   - By avoiding later-stage investments, they minimized competition with larger funds and positioned themselves as experts in the seed-stage ecosystem.
2. Founder-First Philosophy
   - Homebrew adopted a "founder-first" approach, prioritizing the needs and success of the entrepreneurs they backed. They positioned themselves as "the first phone call" for founders, offering support not just with funding but also with strategy, hiring, and networking.
   - This approach helped them build trust and loyalty with founders, leading to strong referrals and repeated entrepreneurs.
3. Thematic Investing
   - Instead of spreading investments across a wide range of industries, Homebrew focused on thematic investing. They identified key trends, such as the future of work, fintech, and vertical SaaS, and concentrated their investments in these areas.
   - This thematic focus allowed them to develop deep expertise and make more informed investment decisions.
4. Hands-On Support
   - Homebrew differentiated itself by providing hands-on support to portfolio companies. The partners actively worked with founders to refine their business models, connect with potential customers, and navigate challenges.
   - For example, they helped portfolio company Chariot (a commuter shuttle service) with early customer acquisition and operational strategy before it was acquired by Ford in 2016.
5. Building a Strong Brand
   - Homebrew invested in building a strong brand within the startup ecosystem. Hunter Walk and Satya Patel were active on social media, blogs, and podcasts, sharing insights and advice for founders.
   - Their transparency and thought leadership helped them attract high-quality deal flow and establish credibility.

10.7.2 Notable Successes

Satya stated in a 2019 Crunchbase interview, "A Homebrew company is one in which there is a mission-driven founder who has a firm belief about how the world should operate and a strong set of hypotheses for how to help get there. He or she has experienced the pain of being addressed firsthand, has empathy for the customer and a deep appreciation for the target industry, disrupting it with love rather than contempt."

He further explained that the founders want to build a cap table that acts as an extension of the team, helping them increase the scale, velocity, or probability of the company's success. The company is building something that democratizes access to products, services, data, or customers for constituencies and industries that have not had access previously.

"When we come across like-minded founders operating in industries in which we feel we have expertise, relationships, or know-how, we think of those as Homebrew companies" (Teare 2019).

Homebrew's focused strategy and founder-centric approach have led to several successful investments, including:

1. Chime

   Chime is a mobile banking and finance platform. Their platform sets aside a pre-determined amount of money in savings after a transaction, and the company earns revenue from transaction fees paid by the merchant, aligning company incentives, enabling users to avoid fees, save money, and lead healthier financial lives. Chime has grown into one of the largest fintech companies in the U.S., with a valuation exceeding $25 billion at its peak. Homebrew was an early investor in Chime, benefiting significantly from its rapid growth.
2. Gusto

   Gusto is a software-as-a-service (SaaS) company specializing in Human Capital Management (HCM). It provides a comprehensive suite of HR and payroll services, including payroll processing, benefits administration, time and attendance tracking, and employee onboarding. Gusto valuation is $9.5 billion based on the Series E funding round completed in May 2022.
3. Plaid

   Plaid is a Banking-as-a-Service (BaaS) technology platform providing the tools and access needed for the development of a fully modern and digitally enabled financial system. Plaid makes it easier and safer for developers from the smallest startups to the largest financial institutions to build innovative financial services and applications. Plaid raised $425 million in Series D funding, lifting its valuation to $13.4 billion.

10.7.3 Lessons for Small Venture Funds

1. Specialize in Niche: By focusing on seed-stage startups and specific themes, Homebrew was able to stand out in a crowded market.

2. Build Strong Relationships: Their founder-first philosophy helped them build trust and loyalty, which translated into better deal flow and successful exits.
3. Provide Value Beyond Capital: Hands-on support and strategic guidance made them indispensable to their portfolio companies.
4. Leverage Personal Branding: Active engagement with the startup community helped Homebrew build a compelling reputation and attract top talent.

Homebrew's success demonstrates that small venture funds can thrive by focusing on a specific niche, building strong relationships with founders, and providing value beyond just capital. Their story is a notable example of how a small fund can compete with larger players by playing to its strengths.

10.8 Conclusion: A Roadmap for Implementing ESG Strategies in Small Funds

The journey for small fund managers in the realm of ESG investing is both challenging and rewarding. Here is a practical roadmap (Figure 10.3) to implement the strategies and frameworks discussed throughout this chapter, designed to guide you from conception to impact:

Step 1: Strategic Planning (Months 1–3)

- **Vision and Mission:** Clearly define your fund's ESG vision and mission. What specific impact are you aiming for? Align this with your investment thesis, focusing on sectors where you can have the most influence, like climate tech or sustainable agriculture in Asia.
- **Resource Assessment:** Conduct an internal audit of your current capabilities. Determine what skills you have in-house for ESG analysis, and what you will need to outsource or learn. Small funds might lack full-time ESG experts, so consider part-time consultants or partnerships.

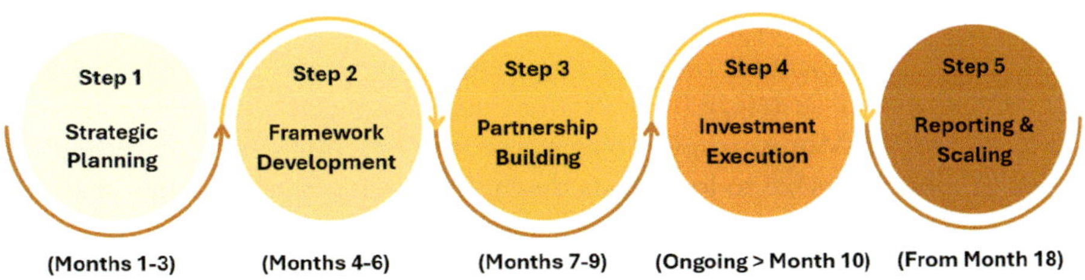

Figure 10.3 A roadmap for implementing ESG strategies in small funds.

Source: Adapted from text by author.

- **Budget Allocation:** Set aside a portion of your fund for ESG due diligence and impact monitoring. Even a small allocation can make a significant difference if used strategically.

Step 2: Framework Development (Months 4–6)

- **Custom ESG Framework:** Build or adapt an ESG due diligence framework that fits your fund's scale. Use tools like the Impact Management Project or IRIS+ for standardized impact metrics. Focus on metrics that are relevant to your sector focus.
- **Risk Management:** Develop a simple risk matrix that includes ESG risks. This should be part of your investment decision-making process, ensuring that potential environmental, social, or governance issues are addressed early.
- **Documentation:** Draft templates for due diligence reports, impact assessments, and investor updates that integrate ESG metrics. This will streamline your reporting process.

Step 3: Partnership Building (Months 7–9)

- **Local Collaborations:** Forge partnerships with local NGOs, academic institutions, or other small funds that can offer insights, co-investment opportunities, or help with impact validation at a lower cost.
- **Government and Regulatory Engagement:** Understand and engage with local government initiatives or incentives for ESG investments. This might involve attending workshops or joining business councils focused on sustainability.
- **Catalytic Capital Networks:** Look for networks or platforms that connect you with catalytic capital providers. These relationships can help unlock further investments for your portfolio companies.

Step 4: Investment Execution (Ongoing from Month 10)

- **Selective Investment:** Choose your investments based on your ESG criteria. Use your framework to screen and select companies that not only promise financial returns but also align with your impact goals.
- **Hands-On Support:** Provide portfolio companies with strategic guidance on implementing ESG practices. This might mean helping them set up their own sustainability KPIs or advising on green marketing strategies.
- **Impact Monitoring:** Implement your monitoring tools. Use technology where possible to keep costs down, like impact tracking apps or simple dashboards for ongoing assessment.

Step 5: Reporting and Scaling (From Month 18)

- **Impact Reporting:** Regularly report on both financial and impact metrics to your investors. Use storytelling to make these reports compelling, highlighting real-world changes your investments have facilitated.

– **Scaling Impact:** As you grow, look to scale your impact by either increasing the size of your fund or by replicating successful investment models in new geographies or sectors.

The initial setup phase, typically spanning the first year, is crucial for building a robust ESG strategy and framework. This foundational period sets the stage for all future activities. Once the framework is in place, the investment cycle begins, with each potential investment taking anywhere from 6 to 18 months to move from initial screening to the final decision, depending on the complexity of the opportunity. After investments are made, ongoing management becomes a priority. This involves continuous engagement with portfolio companies on ESG matters, integrating these considerations into regular quarterly reviews to ensure alignment with sustainability goals and long-term value creation.

Looking ahead, small funds should stay attuned to emerging trends that are reshaping the ESG landscape. These include the integration of AI and blockchain for more transparent and efficient ESG reporting, the rise of circular economy models, and the growing focus on biodiversity alongside climate issues. Additionally, policy shifts in Asia, such as ambitious climate targets, are creating opportunities in sectors like renewable energy and sustainable infrastructure. Consumer and investor demand is also evolving, with a clear preference for products and services that demonstrate strong ESG credentials.

This trend is expected to intensify, making ESG-focused investments not only ethically sound but also commercially viable. To position themselves for long-term success, small funds should remain agile, continuously learn from each investment, and actively contribute to the development of local ESG standards that better reflect regional nuances. This initiative-taking approach will help them stay ahead in a rapidly changing market.

In conclusion, the path for small fund managers in ESG venture capital is one of innovation, collaboration, and persistent impact measurement. By following this roadmap, you not only navigate the complexities of this landscape but also set the stage for your fund to be at the forefront of the sustainable investment revolution.

References

De Silva, Cristina, Andrea Odille Bosio, and Anna Gervasoni. 2024. "ESG and Venture Capital Research: A Bibliometric Literature Review at the Intersection of Two Fields." *Corporate Ownership and Control* 21(1):55–71. doi: 10.22495/cocv21i1art6.

Endress, Tobias, and Yuosre F. Badir, eds. 2023. *Business and Management in Asia: Digital Innovation and Sustainability*. Springer Nature.

Galipeau, David, and Tobias Endress, eds. 2025. *A Practical Approach to Digital Technologies for Sustainability*. Taylor & Francis.

Garger, Ilya, and Sean Lees. 2024. *Asia in Focus: ESG Investing and the Business and Human Rights Agenda*. United Nations Development Programme.

Lin, Lin. 2022. "Venture Capital in the Rise of Sustainable Investment." *European Business Organization Law Review* 23(1):187–216. doi: 10.1007/s40804-021-00238-8.

Priya, P., and Kavita Sharma. 2024. "Global ESG Fund Evolution-an Analysis of Sustainable Investment Growth through Comparison" edited by A. Azhar, E. Wiraguna, N. A. Sholeha, R. Siskandar, M. Rahayu, A. A. Fauzi, and M. S. Bin Mohd Azami. *E3S Web of Conferences* 577:03003. doi: 10.1051/e3sconf/202457703003.

Sant'Anna, Anderson. 2024. "Leadership Styles Across Cultures: A Comparative Study of Western and Asian Contexts Through Hofested and Deleuzian Lenses." doi: 10.13140/RG.2.2.18214.54083.

Teare, Gené. 2019. "Seed Series: Homebrew Founders Hunter Walk and Satya Patel." *Crunchbase News*. Retrieved March 2, 2025, https://news.crunchbase.com/venture/seed-series-homebrew-founders-hunter-walk-and-satya-patel/

Index

I

K

L

M

N

O

T

U

V

W

Z

For Product Safety Concerns and Information please contact our EU representative GPSR@taylorandfrancis.com Taylor & Francis Verlag GmbH, Kaufingerstraße 24, 80331 München, Germany